POLITICS, POLICY, AND PUBLIC OPTIONS

A public option is a government-provided social good that exists alongside a similar privately provided good. While the public option is typically identified with health care policy, public options have been a long-standing feature of American life in a variety of sectors, ranging from libraries to swimming pools. Public schools, for example, coexist alongside private schools. However, there is surprisingly little research on "public options" as a general category. Rather, over the last few decades, considerable scholarly and popular efforts to ensure access to important social goods have focused on market subsidies (like vouchers) or privatization – which both face increasing criticism. Uniting scholars from across disciplines, this volume delves into the theory of the public option, explores several important case studies, and shows how public options could be a corrective to the trend toward privatization and subsidies. This title is also available as Open Access on Cambridge Core.

Ganesh Sitaraman is Professor of Law and Director of the Program on Law and Government at Vanderbilt Law School. He is the author or coauthor of four books, including *The Great Democracy* and *The Crisis of the Middle-Class Constitution*, a *New York Times* Notable Book of 2017.

Anne Alstott is the Jacquin D. Bierman Professor at the Yale Law School. Professor Alstott is the author of a number of books, including *A New Deal for Old Age* (2016) and *Taxation in Six Concepts* (2015). Her articles on social welfare policy, including tax policy, have been widely published in leading law journals, including the *Harvard Law Review*, the *Yale Law Journal*, and the *Columbia Law Review*. She has written or co-written pieces for *The New York Times*, the *L.A. Times*, the *Huffington Post*, and *Slate* and has appeared on NPR.

Politics, Policy, and Public Options

Edited by

GANESH SITARAMAN

Vanderbilt Law School

ANNE ALSTOTT

Yale University Law School

CAMBRIDGE
UNIVERSITY PRESS

CAMBRIDGE
UNIVERSITY PRESS

University Printing House, Cambridge CB2 8BS, United Kingdom

One Liberty Plaza, 20th Floor, New York, NY 10006, USA

477 Williamstown Road, Port Melbourne, VIC 3207, Australia

314–321, 3rd Floor, Plot 3, Splendor Forum, Jasola District Centre, New Delhi – 110025, India

79 Anson Road, #06–04/06, Singapore 079906

Cambridge University Press is part of the University of Cambridge.

It furthers the University's mission by disseminating knowledge in the pursuit of education, learning, and research at the highest international levels of excellence.

www.cambridge.org
Information on this title: www.cambridge.org/9781108487641
DOI: 10.1017/9781108767552

First published 2021

A catalogue record for this publication is available from the British Library.

Library of Congress Cataloging-in-Publication Data
NAMES: Sitaraman, Ganesh, editor. | Alstott, Anne, 1963– editor.
TITLE: Politics, policy, and public options / edited by Ganesh Sitaraman, Vanderbilt University School of Law; Anne Alstott, Yale University Law School.
DESCRIPTION: Cambridge, United Kingdom ; New York : Cambridge University Press, 2021. | Includes bibliographical references.
IDENTIFIERS: LCCN 2021009405 (print) | LCCN 2021009406 (ebook) | ISBN 9781108487641 (hardback) | ISBN 9781108767552 (ebook)
SUBJECTS: LCSH: Social legislation – United States. | Public-private sector cooperation – Law and legislation – United States.
CLASSIFICATION: LCC KF3300 .P65 2021 (print) | LCC KF3300 (ebook) | DDC 344.7303/16–dc23
LC record available at https://lccn.loc.gov/2021009405
LC ebook record available at https://lccn.loc.gov/2021009406

ISBN 978-1-108-48764-1 Hardback

Contents

Contributors

Anne L. Alstott, Jacquin D. Bierman Professor in Taxation, Yale Law School
Mehrsa Baradaran, Professor of Law, UCI Law School
Jacob S. Hacker, Stanley Resor Professor of Political Science, Yale University
Allison K. Hoffman, Professor of Law, University of Pennsylvania Carey Law School
Henry Lishi Li, Research Fellow in Health Innovation and Policy Engagement, UCL Institute for Innovation and Public Purpose, University College London
Mariana Mazzucato, Professor in the Economics of Innovation and Public Value and Founding Director, UCL Institute for Innovation and Public Purpose, University College London
Suzanne Mettler, John L. Senior Professor of American Institutions, Cornell University
Jon D. Michaels, Professor of Law, UCLA School of Law
Kimberly J. Morgan, Professor of Political Science and International Affairs, George Washington University
Ganesh Sitaraman, Professor of Law and Director of the Program on Law and Government, Vanderbilt University Law School
Mallory E. SoRelle, Assistant Professor of Public Policy, Duke University
Shelley Welton, Associate Professor, University of South Carolina School of Law

Acknowledgments

More than other books, putting together an edited volume is a collective endeavor. We first thank the contributors for their timely and incisive contributions to this volume. The Carnegie Corporation and Hewlett Foundation provided essential funding, through an Andrew Carnegie Fellowship and support for a January 2020 roundtable on public options at Vanderbilt Law School. Quenna Stewart's assistance was critical to making the roundtable successful. At Cambridge University Press, Matt Galloway and Cameron Daddis navigated the book through the editing process with great skill. Finally, thanks to our families for suffering now through two books' worth of discussion on public options.

Introduction

Anne Alstott and Ganesh Sitaraman

A public option is a government provided social good that exists alongside a similar, privately provided good. For example, in American public policy debates over the Affordable Care Act, some scholars and policymakers advocated for a publicly provided health insurance option (like Medicare) that could coexist alongside private health insurance options; individuals would be able to choose between the public option and private options. While the public option is typically identified with health-care policy, public options have actually been a longstanding feature of American life in a variety of sectors. Public schools coexist with private schools; public swimming pools are an accessible alternative to building a pool in the backyard; public libraries provide an option to get a wide variety of books without purchasing them for one's personal library.

Surprisingly, however, scholars have not attempted to assess the category of "public options" systematically. Instead, over the last few decades, most scholarly and popular efforts to ensure access to important social goods have focused on market subsidies (like vouchers) or privatization.[1] These approaches have been applied to a variety of policy arenas – from education to roads and even to the military. Interest in privatization and market subsidies coincided with the ascension of neoliberal ideas that preferred private actors over public institutions.[2] In public debate, a narrative emerged that government curtailed freedom, stifled markets, and prevented opportunity. If public institutions acted, the argument ran, it would lead society down "the road to serfdom." This neoliberal policy approach, and at times even the rhetoric, spread across the political spectrum. Conservatives and liberals alike focused on deregulation, public–private partnerships, voucher programs, and privatization more generally.

1 On privatization see, e.g., Jon D. Michaels, *Constitutional Coup: Privatization's Threat to the American Republic* (2017); E. S. Savas, *Privatization and Public-Private Partnerships* (1999); Jody Freeman & Martha Minow, eds., *Government by Contract: Outsourcing and American Democracy* (2009). On vouchers, see, e.g., William G. Howell & Paul E. Peterson, *The Education Gap: Vouchers and Urban Schools* (Rev'd ed. 2006); C. Eugene Steuerle et al., eds., *Vouchers and the Provision of Public Services* (2000).

2 On neoliberalism, see, e.g., David Harvey, *A Brief History of Neoliberalism* (2007), Manfred B. Steger & Ravi K. Roy, *Neoliberalism: A Very Short Introduction* (2010).

In recent years, scholars and policy analysts have increasingly criticized market subsidies and privatization. Both design options have been shown, in some contexts, to have perverse effects. For example, private prisons have been criticized not only for poor conditions and recidivism rates but also for creating a political feedback loop, as the prison industry lobbies the government, to safeguard their business and grow profits.[3] Market subsidies have also fared poorly. An important body of work has shown that for-profit colleges rely heavily on profits they make from public subsidies (federal student grant and loan programs); at the same time, these institutions often provide low-quality educations to their students.[4] In addition, scholars have shown that when the government provides services through private actors, the public is less aware of the role the government plays and less supportive of public action generally.[5] More broadly, the era of market subsidies and privatization has coincided with increased economic inequality and the erosion of the capacity of and faith in public institutions.

Public provision of important social goods could be a corrective to the trend toward privatization and subsidies, and researchers can and should explore how and when it can succeed. Our book, *The Public Option*, aimed to take a first step, making the case that public options are a coherent category, with a set of benefits and limitations, and we offered a variety of examples. But we always hoped *The Public Option* would not be the last word on public options, and we invited further inquiry on a number of fronts. This volume takes up that invitation, uniting an interdisciplinary group of scholars who, together, have delved further into the theory of the public option and into several case studies of important public options.

The first four chapters adopt a wide focus, taking on cross-cutting issues relating to public options. One overarching issue for all public options is the political reception of public initiatives. In their chapter, Mallory SoRelle and Suzanne Mettler point out that the United States has a long history of public provision, but that public programs often are structured deliberately to be invisible. The result, they argue, is that "Americans erroneously attribute to the market many benefits that government has a hand in providing." On the one hand, they argue, these political dynamics could prove a stumbling block for public options, because they challenge the "myth that American life has developed historically and thrives today owing to autonomous markets, without much government aid or intervention." On the other hand, they suggest, success in creating visible public options could challenge the myth of market-based self-sufficiency: public options might help improve perceptions of government and increase democratic participation. To make that happier outcome

3 Lauren-Brooke Eisen, *Inside Private Prisons: An American Dilemma in the Age of Mass Incarceration* (2017).

4 For a discussion, see Ganesh Sitaraman & Anne Alstott, *The Public Option: How to Expand Freedom, Increase Opportunity, and Promote Equality* 20 (2019); Tressie McMillan Cottom & William A. Darity, Jr., eds., *For-Profit Universities: The Shifting Landscape of Marketized Higher Education* (2017).

5 Suzanne Mettler, *The Submerged State: How Invisible Government Policies Undermine American Democracy* (2011).

more likely, they conclude, policymakers designing a public option should expressly consider "ends that serve democracy, such as access, inclusion, fairness, and the promotion of civic education and political participation."

Perhaps one of the central objections to public provision of goods and services is that it will "crowd out" private markets. Mariana Mazzucato and Henry Lishi Li consider this argument in Chapter 2, discussing the public option within economic debates over the state's role in value creation. They argue that the public sector's contribution to economic growth and development has been severely understated, leading scholars and policymakers to neglect opportunities for innovation and inclusive growth. Rather than only addressing market failures, they show the entrepreneurial state co-shapes markets along with the private sector. Adopting this broader framework, Mazzucato and Li see greater opportunities for sharing risk and rewards across the public and private sectors. Using the pharmaceutical sector as a case study, they explore a range of options, from financing mechanisms to equity stakes to public manufacturing and production. For an entrepreneurial state that seeks inclusive growth, they conclude that public options are a critical policy tool.

A third structural problem concerns whether public options can expand equality and opportunity. In Chapter 3, Alstott and Sitaraman consider six obstacles to equitable public options. At the top of the list of barriers to equity is racism, which in overt and covert forms throughout our nation's history has undermined the equitable promise of public options. Other challenges to designing equitable public options include selection effects that can lead to public options taking on a "second class" aura if they become confined to a limited population without political power; whether a good is necessary and sufficient; the complexity involved in accessing the public option; the fracturing of provision through jurisdictional boundaries; and private outsourcing. Alstott and Sitaraman conclude that some – but by no means all – of these barriers can be addressed by good program design.

A fourth overarching issue concerns the public–private boundary. Public options, of course, blend government action with private-sector provision. In Chapter 4, Jon Michaels considers a crossover in the opposite direction: When might private actors adopt the methods of sovereign states to assume responsibility for the general welfare and remedy the failures of actual sovereigns? Michaels terms these "private options," and his chapter generalizes the idea to cover firms that "use democratic pathways and deliberative procedures" to take on responsibilities that have traditionally been assigned to government, including "voluntarily internalizing externalities, at some profit loss or legal risk; or voluntarily reducing rather than exploiting power and information asymmetries." Examples, Michaels argues, include Facebook's proposed digital currency and Google's modern company town. Looking beyond corporate actors, Michaels also identifies the collective action taken by workers seeking to alter the political stances taken by their employers. In each case, Michaels concludes, private options challenge neoliberal understandings of the marketplace, because they feature market actors pursuing ends other than profit maximization.

Chapters 5 through 9 focus on particular policy areas, offering case studies of public options that illustrate some of the challenges and opportunities more clearly. Chapters 5 and 6 begin with health care. Jacob Hacker uses recent American policy debates between supporters of a public option and Medicare for All to make the case for a robust public option. A robust public option, he argues, would initially be less costly and face less opposition than Medicare for All, making it more likely to pass. If it is designed to guarantee coverage while reducing costs, the public option would also over time "create self-reinforcing political dynamics," that would pave the way for a national system. Hacker sees this process as a "policy feedback" loop, in which policy choices today have consequences for opening up possibilities in the future.

Alison Hoffman identifies a number of challenges for a successful public option in health care. The central problem, she argues, is one of choice. A public option that is not easily differentiated from private health-care options would gain few users, as people struggle to see what benefits the program would offer. But even a superior public plan would suffer from problems of choice. Comparing deductibles, cost-sharing, and premiums require navigating a tangle of terms and conditions, in addition to making a variety of mathematical calculations. People also suffer from cognitive biases, and studies show that even well-educated people frequently err in identifying the best policy when given a choice. Moving beyond market-based bureaucracies will require thinking differently about health care, and Hoffman concludes with a set of options that might overcome the challenges she has identified.

In Chapter 7, Kimberly Morgan considers a public option for childcare and concludes that public options in early childhood education and care are the best way to "remake our current market-based system into one that lays the foundations for a more just and equitable society." The current US childcare system of market provision plus tax subsidies, she shows, has produced low-quality care for too many children, a situation that reinforces existing social inequalities. Morgan discusses several variants of a public option in childcare, including direct provision via the public schools or, alternatively, a mixed model like that used by the US military, which combines government-run childcare centers with subsidies combined with quality regulation for private providers.

Energy provision is usually considered a public utility, with regulated private providers. In Chapter 8, Shelley Welton shows that electricity generation, transmission and distribution, and procurement and delivery come in the form of a public option and that public options in these areas could be critical for transitioning to clean energy. Unlike many other public options, where the choice to use the option is made at the individual level, in the energy sector, decisions – for example, to have a publicly or privately owned grid – are made at the community level. "Community control over energy procurement," Welton writes, "provides a potent tool for effectuating [clean energy] transformation in communities that already have adequate political will." Communities that act will also serve as a yardstick by which to measure the progress of other communities – not just on price, but on the carbon content of energy.

Postal banking is a public option that, according to Mehrsa Baradaran, could remedy today's flawed and undemocratic system of private banking. In Chapter 9, Baradaran points out that the US banking system operates using federal infrastructure but that the current system has largely abandoned "lower-profit regions and customers under the guise of 'inefficiency' and market competition." Baradaran notes that the United States had a successful postal banking program in the first half of the twentieth century, and she proposes a modern update of postal banking that might include simple checking and small loans. Properly structured, she concludes, postal banking could provide consumers with an alternative to predatory check cashing services and payday lenders.

While many important themes emerge across these chapters, three are particularly worth pointing out. Most prominent is the choice among policy tools: How does the public option compare to private provision, financing mechanisms, public utility regulation, and exclusive public provision? Policymakers have many models they can utilize in pursuing the goal of universal, affordable access to a good or service. The public option is one among many tools, and sometimes it is the best choice, but not always. Policy design should be sensitive to the goals of promoting democracy, fostering social solidarity, and avoiding selection effects that can undermine the public option.

Another common theme is the importance of public salience and its relationship to policy feedback loops. Whether it is building support for the continuation of the public option, expanding the scope of the public option, or operating as a yardstick or benchmark for public goals, the degree to which public options are seen and known is critical.

Finally, virtually every author shows that public action already exists to construct the market, and that the question is therefore not whether to adopt a public or private approach, but what kind of public action is best. Because markets operate on the backdrop of laws and regulations set by the state, policymakers must make choices – and scholars can help identify the tradeoffs in making those choices. This book takes another step forward in advancing our understanding of public options – and hopefully will spark more debate and discussion on this important policy tool.

1

More Than Meets the Eye

Government Social Provision and the Politics of "Public Options"

Mallory SoRelle and Suzanne Mettler

The concept of a "public option" entered the American lexicon in 2009, during the congressional debate over what became the Affordable Care Act (ACA). It suggested what many considered a radical idea: that government itself would offer a health-care coverage plan, thereby forcing private insurance providers to compete with a lower-cost alternative. Progressive groups rallied behind the notion that a public option could bring much-needed choice into the health-care marketplace without the political challenges of adopting a single-payer system. But opponents still lambasted the entire ACA as a "government takeover" and regarded the "public option" in particular as the epitome of socialism.[1] Although that measure failed, the fact that the public option concept spurred such political controversy itself is deeply paradoxical because, in fact, public funding of social provision, as well as government intervention to support the broader market economy, has a long history in the United States – one that is far more expansive and broadly used today than many Americans realize.

Consider a thought experiment. What if, as part of the ACA, policymakers had instead offered citizens a "private option," meaning that they could decline any form of health insurance or health care that was supported by public funds? Those who object to government involvement in health care could "take the pledge" and sign a promise vowing to refrain from using public programs like Medicare, Medicaid, or veterans' health benefits. It would also require them to refuse to benefit from government subsidies that substantially lower the costs of their employer-provided health coverage; the amount that their employers pay for their health coverage would now be treated as a taxable benefit, and their taxes would increase accordingly. For anti-government purists to be satisfied with the private option for health care, those embracing it would need to swear off care in

[1] Lawrence Jacobs and Theda Skocpol, *Health Care Reform and American Politics: What Everyone Needs to Know* (Oxford: Oxford University Press, 2015).

any hospital built with the support of public funds or by any doctor whose education benefitted from federal aid; they would be committed to declining any medical treatments developed through federal grants from the National Institute for Health. In short, in order to remain true to their principles, market devotees would need to pay far more for their health care, and they would be unlikely to find providers, facilities, or treatments that measured up to those supported by public funds.

As this example highlights, the government is already heavily implicated in health insurance and health-care markets in the United States. While a public option might represent a new *form* of government intervention, it is by no means the novel incursion into an otherwise free health-care market that many portray it to be. Nor is this state of affairs unique to health care. Contemporary Americans benefit from government interventions in numerous ways across many policy domains, many of which, owing to their policy designs, are not visible. As a result, Americans erroneously attribute to the market many benefits that government has a hand in providing. Even for those benefits that obviously stem from government, people often take them – and government's role in providing them – for granted. It is not as if most of us are "self-made," having lived our lives without the aid of publicly funded goods and services; to the contrary, government plays an immense but largely unappreciated role in the everyday lives of ordinary Americans, and this is hardly new. It is "private options," not "public options," that have been the exception to the rule in the United States, but the extensive role of government has often been camouflaged by policymakers – both intentionally and unintentionally – in most policies except those targeted at the poor.

The paradox of government's expansive but frequently invisible intervention in and outright provision of a wide variety of goods and services has serious political consequences that, as we will argue, create both obstacles for those who might wish to promote public options and compelling reasons to do so. As such, while we respect the aims underlying the "public option" concept, we think it is worth turning the concept on its head by envisioning the alternative "private option" in order to expose some aspects of American politics that may bedevil reformers' success.

First, we think that the concept, as it is typically communicated, is rooted in the same market model of social life that it aims to critique. This model is out of step with the long history of government social provision in the United States, which gained momentum particularly from efforts to protect democracy, by developing good citizens and rewarding citizens who sacrificed on behalf of the nation. By adapting uncritically the concept of a public option as an exception to the private provision of goods across a variety of domains, proponents may generate unintended consequences, perpetuating the myth that American life has developed historically and thrives today owing to autonomous markets, without much government aid or intervention. Public options, by this logic, represent new incursions in an otherwise independent economic system. As we will demonstrate, this myth, which stems in part from a legacy of active but invisible government intervention, fuels anti-government attitudes and complicates efforts at policy reform.

Furthermore, we suggest that the public option concept may have trouble gaining sufficient political support to prevail precisely because of these attitudes. American voters, who typically underestimate the extent to which government is already engaged in creating, subsidizing, and regulating private provision, may have difficulty embracing the idea that government has a role to play in what they see as the sole purview of private markets. Policymakers, too, have electoral incentives to hide government's role in providing goods and services in an effort to maintain the myth of limited government.

These obstacles to the successful pursuit and adoption of new public options are not to be underestimated. But they also illuminate a crucial justification for embracing more visible public provision: Beyond the economic and social good that public options could create, increasing people's positive experiences with visible sources of government support can enhance democratic engagement and government trust. The successful implementation of public options might cause more Americans to rethink the myth of limited government, subsequently increasing their incentives to participate actively in the political life of the country.

Our analysis begins by turning to history and discussing the development of policies in terms of their relationship to the private sector. We then explain the politics these policies generate in the contemporary period, when use of government social benefits is widespread, and yet Americans often fail to see government's role in their lives. Finally, we offer our recommendations for policy renewal.

1.1 GOVERNMENT AND MARKETS ENTWINED

The concept of the "public option" may inadvertently imply that the public provision of goods and services is unusual in American life, creating a misimpression both of history and of current reality. Many assume that until at least the late nineteenth century, if not the New Deal, the United States featured an autonomously functioning market, free from government intervention.

The study of policy analysis, informed by economics, can perpetuate this mistaken interpretation of American political economy. It takes the market as the starting point and puts forward the ideal of the perfectly functioning economy in which producers maximize profits and consumers maximize utility, promoting efficiency. This approach also acknowledges, though, that predictable "market failures" occur, for example, in the case of goods or services – such as lighthouses or military defense – that private actors are unwilling to provide because there is no way to charge beneficiaries for them, or in the creation of "externalities," the side effects of economic activity that may generate consequences for nonparticipants, such as through carbon emissions that lead to global warming. In these carefully defined situations when the free-functioning market does not provide the most social utility, the logic goes, government "intervention" may be justified, requiring the provision of "public goods" or some regulation to limit externalities, for example, in response to the examples noted here.[2]

This theory of public intervention overlooks the critical role that US government institutions and polices have played from the nation's founding to the present both to make markets possible and to facilitate their growth. State governments and courts were crucial in defining rules about property and its exchange, establishing law and order to protect private property, enforcing contracts, and adjudicating disputes. The federal government promoted the development of the economy by coining money, setting market standards, regulating commerce, and stimulating the necessary system of communication, for example, by establishing the postal system early on. Government fostered the requisite transportation for market exchange, with early development of canals followed later by the regulation of railroads in the late nineteenth century and the development of the interstate highway system and air traffic control in the twentieth century. In each of these domains, government actively helped to establish the conditions under which US markets could flourish.

Beyond these investments to market infrastructure, public intervention has long been necessary to support the labor supply central to a growing market economy. The federal government began to promote the development of public schools as well as higher education by setting aside land for that purpose in the Northwest Ordinance of 1787. It declared, "Religion, morality, and knowledge, being necessary to good government and the happiness of mankind, schools and the means of education shall forever be encouraged."[3] Today, informed by the market approach to public policy, we think of education as serving the purposes of economic development, by creating human capital. Certainly, some early statesmen saw things similarly; Benjamin Franklin is remembered for embracing this approach. Yet, economic justifications were not policymakers' only considerations; the more dominant rationale for the public provision of education pertained to the promotion of citizenship, enabling self-government to thrive. Thomas Jefferson promoted education on these grounds, writing in 1820, "I know no safe depositary of the ultimate powers of the society but the people themselves; and if we think them not enlightened enough to exercise their control with a wholesome discretion, the remedy is not to take it from them, but to inform their discretion by education. This is the true corrective of abuses of constitutional power."[4]

[2] David L. Weimer and Aidan R. Vining, *Policy Analysis: Concepts and Practice*, 6th ed. (New York: Routledge, 2017).

[3] Northwest Ordinance, Section 14, Article 3, July 13, 1787, https://avalon.law.yale.edu/18th_century/nworder.asp

[4] Letter, Thomas Jefferson to William Jarvis, September 28, 1820, Founders Online https://founders.archives.gov/documents/Jefferson/98-01-02-1540

In fact, public provision of goods and services in the United States, particularly in the realm of education and social welfare, was long justified not primarily in economic terms, but rather by their role in fostering democracy. Early social provision took the form of veterans' benefits, provided to those who had taken on the role of citizen soldiers and put their lives in harm's way for the sake of the nation. This tradition began by recognizing veterans of the Revolutionary War. After the Civil War, veterans' pensions became far more generous and included benefits for veterans' survivors as well. By the early twentieth century, as Theda Skocpol has shown, a "maternalist" welfare state provided "mothers' pensions" to families in which no male breadwinner was present.[5] The rationale for these policies revolved around mothers' role in raising future citizens; it was thought that this was crucial for the nation and would be compromised if mothers had to work outside of the home.[6]

It should be noted that veterans' and mothers' pensions both operated simply as public programs with government directly offering benefits; the market did not supply a feasible alternative that would be affordable for most people. Perhaps these policies could be defined as public goods, but the rationale for them emanated not from market justifications but rather from those that prioritized the health of democracy. In the case of public support for higher education, certainly some universities and colleges already existed that were nominally "private," such as Harvard, Yale, Princeton, and several others, though even these had been established through a combination of public and private support and initiative. Once the Northwest Ordinance was in place, states seized the opportunity to create public colleges, and the number proliferated quickly. Later in the nineteenth century, the federal government promoted the development of public colleges and universities once again, after President Abraham Lincoln signed the Morrill Land Grant College Act. The second version of this law, enacted in 1890, included states of the former Confederacy and gave rise to most of the historically black colleges.[7]

Government intervention has also been leveraged in order to construct new private markets for social provision when they did not emerge "naturally," further challenging the notion that distinct private and public options exist in American social provision. One of the most notable examples of this phenomenon occurred when government stepped in to create new consumer credit markets in response to the Great Depression. The Roosevelt administration was convinced that the economy, and especially private industry, would not recover unless the problem of underconsumption could be remedied. Thus, enhancing the purchasing power of

5 Theda Skocpol, *Protecting Soldiers and Mothers: The Political Origins of Social Policy in the United States* (Cambridge, MA: Harvard University Press, 1992).

6 Ann Shola Orloff, "Gender in Early US Social Policy," *Journal of Policy History*, Vol. 3 (1991): 249–281.

7 Alice Rivlin, *The Role of the Federal Government in Financing Higher Education* (Washington, DC: Brookings Institution, 1961); Christopher Lucas, *American Higher Education: A History*, 2nd ed. (New York: Macmillan Palgrave, 2006); Claudia Goldin and Lawrence F. Katz, *The Race Between Education and Technology* (Cambridge, MA: Harvard University Press, 2004).

consumers became a central component of many New Deal policies. While efforts to put money back in the pockets of American consumers took many forms, the administration was especially focused on creating economic tools that would put the construction industry, which comprised nearly one-third of those receiving government emergency relief, back to work.[8]

Public officials sought to encourage the building of new homes and the renovation of old homes, but by 1933 the government estimated that as much as one-quarter of all home mortgages were in default, and even for homeowners lucky enough to escape the threat of foreclosure, few had the resources to finance renovation or new construction in such a precarious economy. The administration responded by offering several proposals designed to rescue mortgages and incentivize home buying and home renovation both by bolstering existing private markets and by creating new private markets from whole cloth.

The Federal Home Loan Bank Act was passed in 1932 to serve as a reserve credit system to prop up both troubled borrowers and lenders. One year later, the Home Owners' Loan Act of 1933 established the Home Owners' Loan Corporation (HOLC). HOLC introduced a new long-term, fixed-rate mortgage that made borrowing for homeownership more attainable for the average American. It also allowed defaulting borrowers to trade in their mortgage obligations for government bonds, both rescuing individual homeowners and stabilizing the lending market. In a more direct form of public support, HOLC provided limited funds to homeowners for the completion of necessary repairs.

An even more ambitious and enduring initiative, the National Housing Act (NHA), was adopted in 1934. The Act created the Federal Housing Administration (FHA) to offer federally backed mortgage insurance to approved lenders, authorized a national mortgage market to expand the availability of home loans, and created a home modernization loan program in which government subsidized banks to extend small lines of credit for home repair. It was the final plank of this program, established by Title I of the NHA, that used government incentives to establish a new consumer credit market where banks had previously been reluctant to lend. At the turn of the twentieth century, the administrative cost to issue a small personal loan was similar to that of a much larger loan. With state usury caps in place, most banks determined that the money they could earn from interest on a small loan was insufficient to cover their burdensome administration fee. As a result, reputable banks largely avoided small loan lending.

New Deal policymakers were wary of embracing a direct public loan program, so they chose instead to induce private companies to make loans to homeowners for renovation. As Marriner Eccles, then assistant secretary of the Treasury, explained to Congress during hearings for the implementation of the NHA, "There is no lack of

8 See, for example, Louis Hyman, *Debtor Nation: The History of America in Red Ink* (Princeton, NJ: Princeton University Press, 2011) and Mallory SoRelle, *Democracy Declined: The Failed Politics of Consumer Financial Protection* (Chicago: Chicago University Press, 2020).

money. It seems to me, however, that it lacks velocity."[9] Title I provided lenders with the necessary encouragement by implementing a system of government insurance on private loans for home renovation and repair for up to 20 percent of the total value of loans made by a participating lender. By 1935, about 254 million dollars in modernization loans had been issued. But perhaps the more enduring consequence of this government intervention was the new market for private small consumer loans it sparked. Through this New Deal policy, banks discovered that consumer lending could be exceedingly profitable. The next two decades witnessed the evolution of several novel forms of consumer credit, especially the credit card, that would ultimately provide a stand-in for other public social programs designed to expand consumer purchasing power.

Viewed in the context of this large and varied history of state involvement in creating, sustaining, and supplementing ostensibly private markets, the "public option" concept seems somewhat incongruous. Public roles in economic development and in social provision both have a long history in the United States. While some of these programs take the form of traditional public benefit schemes, others appear to be private in origin, masking government's critical role in their creation and continued development. Moreover, policymakers often promoted these interventions not only for economic reasons, or in some cases, not at all for such reasons, but rather because they served the aims of fostering democracy.

1.2 SOCIAL POLICY DESIGN AND GOVERNMENT VISIBILITY

From the New Deal onward, the federal government became further involved in promoting social welfare, education, and financing for American citizens, yet new policies would take a variety of forms, many of which obscured government's role as a provider of benefits. The most lauded social policy emerging from the New Deal is what we now call simply "Social Security." Enacted in 1935, this program created a payroll tax–funded system of old-age insurance (OAI) that is centrally administered by the federal government. Social Security involves the direct public provision of benefits, administered by the Social Security Administration. The state's role in the provision of these benefits is, thus, highly visible to most Americans. It bears the hallmarks of what many Americans think of as government social insurance, with redistribution that aims to achieve public purposes. The Social Security Act also laid the foundation for another pillar of the twentieth-century American welfare system: A means-tested system of public assistance programs for families with dependent children (what would become AFDC and later TANF) designed to temporarily prop up the "undeserving" poor. Unlike its more generous OAI counterpart, this means-tested public program was administered by state governments.

9 US House. Committee on Banking and Currency. 1934. National Housing Act: Hearings before the Committee on Banking and Currency. 73rd Congress, May 18–June 4, 1934.

While government's role in early forms of means-tested public assistance was highly visible, the most commonly used social policies today feature policy designs that make the role of government less apparent. These include programs like employer-provided, government-subsidized health and retirement benefits, used by 48 and 39 percent of households, respectively, and the home mortgage interest deduction, claimed by 24 percent.[10] Such policies constitute the largest "tax expenditures," programs that serve social purposes but that generally function by permitting people to pay less in taxes rather than to receive payments directly from government. None of these three was designed intentionally to serve the justifications that have become commonplace today, aiding middle-income Americans in attaining health coverage, retirement, and homeownership; each emerged through haphazard developments and grew in ways unforeseen by proponents.[11] Owing to their obscure design, Christopher Howard has called this constellation of policies the "hidden welfare state," and they form the largest components of what one of us has termed the "submerged state."[12] Jacob Hacker has shown how government's hidden role in social provision evolved to include a mass of government regulations and subsidies applied to benefits distributed by private employers.[13] Most of these policies bestow their largest benefits on the affluent; the employer-provided benefits have grown more upwardly distributive over time, as fewer jobs – particularly those that pay less – come with benefits than was the case a few decades ago.

These policies do little to make governments' role in subsidizing them evident. Beneficiaries rarely perceive government as having aided them and they are more likely to perceive the benefits to be attributable to their own efforts and private sector initiatives.[14] This is true even in the case of the Earned Income Tax Credit (EITC), which has evolved into the United States' largest form of aid to low-income people, with 19 percent of households benefitting annually in recent years.[15] Yet, 47 percent of EITC beneficiaries reported that they had never used a government social program.[16] This is striking because in the case of the EITC, many beneficiaries have no tax liability, or at least receive more through the benefits than they would have owed in taxes if it did not exist. Nonetheless, its placement in the tax code obscures its status as redistributive aid from government.

Americans' use of government social benefits from direct transfers from the federal government – Social Security, unemployment insurance, Medicare,

10 Suzanne Mettler, *The Government-Citizen Disconnect* (New York: Russell Sage Foundation, 2018: 37–38).

11 Suzanne Mettler, *The Submerged State: How Invisible Government Policies Undermine American Democracy* (Chicago: Chicago University Press, 2011: 15–20, 99–100).

12 Christopher Howard, *The Hidden Welfare State: Tax Expenditures and Social Policy in the United States* (Princeton, NJ: Princeton University Press, 1997); Mettler 2011.

13 Jacob Hacker, *The Divided Welfare State: The Battle Over Public and Private Social Benefits in the United States* (New York: Cambridge University Press, 2002).

14 Mettler 2011: 38; Mettler 2018: 99–100.

15 Mettler 2018: 37.

16 Mettler 2011: 39.

Medicaid, Supplemental Nutrition Assistance Program (SNAP, or "food stamps"), and other such policies – has increased over time. In recent years, 17 percent of the average person's income came from such benefits.[17] This does not include the "hidden" or "submerged" policies; if these are included in social spending, the United States boasts the second largest welfare state in the world after France.[18] If all of these policies are accounted for, it turns out that 96 percent of American adults report that they have used at least one federal social policy, and the average person has used five. Although specific policies target different groups, overall the pervasiveness of federal social policy usage spans differences of income, age, race and ethnicity, and partisanship, and the federal government bestows social transfers at least as liberally on "red states" as "blue states."[19]

1.3 THE POLITICAL CONSEQUENCES OF PUBLIC INVISIBILITY

These details of policy visibility are not simply an interesting footnote to the development of US public goods provision or market intervention. Decisions about policy design – particularly those that affect the visibility of government – carry major implications for how citizens think about public policies, their own and others' relationships to government, and whether to take political action or to take their demands elsewhere. Each of these consequences is of critical importance for proposals to expand public options.

Once enacted, public policies that become lasting features of the political landscape have the capacity to shape people's politics in a variety of ways.[20] These so-called policy feedback effects can take many forms, but particularly meaningful for proponents of the public option are findings about the effect of government visibility on people's political preferences and behaviors. When people experience a public policy, they are learning lessons about the relationship between citizens and the state for a particular set of issues.[21] People's experiences with policy implementation have been shown to influence their attitudes about government efficacy for a given issue. Especially relevant are findings that a lack of obvious interaction with government during the implementation of a policy can encourage citizens to underestimate the role government plays in that policy area.[22]

17 Mettler 2018: 3–4.
18 Organization for Economic Cooperation and Development 2016, figs. 1 and 4.
19 Mettler 2018, Chap. 3.
20 Theodore Lowi, "Four Systems of Policy, Politics, and Choice," *Public Administration Review*, Vol. 32 (1972): 298–310; Skocpol 1992; Paul Pierson, "When Effect Becomes Cause: Policy Feedback and Political Change," *World Politics*, Vol. 45 (1993): 595–628; Suzanne Mettler and Joe Soss, "The Consequences of Public Policy for Democratic Citizenship: Bridging Policy Studies and Mass Politics," *Perspectives on Politics*, Vol. 2 (2004): 55–73; Suzanne Mettler and Mallory SoRelle, "Policy Feedback Theory." In *Theories of the Policy Process, 4th ed*, edited by Christopher Weible and Paul A. Sabatier. (Boulder, CO: Westview Press, 2017: 103–134).
21 Mettler and Soss 2004.
22 Mettler 2011.

This has two key consequences. First, the degree of state visibility for a particular policy can affect people's perceptions of whether a problem requires a public or a private solution. When a policy obscures government's role in social provision, it will encourage people to assume that private market forces are responsible for the benefits they receive. By contrast, policies that highlight government's role will be more likely to lead people to think that government does, and should, play an active role in providing that good. As a result, government visibility can shape people's attitudes about government intervention on a given issue.

Second, and perhaps more consequentially, these perceptions can influence whether people take political action to support public programs. As Douglas Arnold argues, the electorate must be able to link policymaking to a political actor in order to engage politically on that issue.[23] So, if government's role in the provision or regulation of a particular social good is masked, it may diminish political participation on behalf of that issue. We can observe these dynamics at work across a number of policy domains.

Social Security provides a particularly interesting case to explore the effects of policy visibility on public engagement. Because Social Security is a highly visible instance of government spending, it should come as no surprise that beneficiaries and the broader public can connect the program to political actors. It is predictable, therefore, that beneficiaries represent some of the most politically active citizens,[24] and efforts to reduce or privatize Social Security have largely been met with outright public hostility and threats of electoral consequences.

Yet even in this instance, only 44 percent of beneficiaries, when asked if they had ever used a government social program, answered in the affirmative.[25] Granted, some people might associate the phrase "government social program" only with means-tested social benefits, and answer in the negative for that reason. Yet other analyses buttress the conclusion by showing that using more non-means-tested visible benefits administered directly by government – Social Security, Medicare, unemployment insurance, veterans' benefits, or the GI Bill – bears no discernable impact on an individual's likelihood of agreeing that government has helped in times of need or provided opportunities to improve one's standard of living, or that public officials care much about them.[26] This perception may flow from the fact that these policy designs involve some ambiguity: In the case of Social Security, Medicare, and unemployment benefits, Americans typically perceive themselves to have earned their benefits through their participation in the workforce, analogous to payment for private insurance. In fact, President Franklin D. Roosevelt intended the financing feature of payroll contributions to convey that beneficiaries had earned

[23] Douglas Arnold, *The Logic of Congressional Action* (New Haven: Yale University Press, 1990).

[24] Andrea Louise Campbell, "Self-Interest, Social Security, and the Distinctive Participation Patterns of Senior Citizens," *American Political Science Review*, Vol. 96 (2002): 565–574.

[25] Mettler 2011: 38.

[26] Mettler 2018: 98.

their benefits; as he put it, "We put those payroll contributions there so as to give the contributors a legal, moral, and political right to collect their pensions and their unemployment benefits. With those taxes in there, no damn politician can ever scrap my social security program."[27]

Even for means-tested social benefits, policy design can obscure the link between government assistance and the citizens who receive it, with political consequences. Recall, for example, that EITC is delivered through the tax code rather than a traditional cash transfer program. Scholars have demonstrated that having benefitted from the EITC does not make people more likely to agree that government has helped them in times of need. In fact, receiving EITC benefits negatively correlates with the likelihood that someone agrees that government has provided opportunities to improve their standard of living. Despite the fact that policymakers intend for EITC to achieve precisely that goal, the policy's design – which muddies government's role in offering assistance – seems to preempt EITC recipients from acknowledging and subsequently mobilizing in support of that intervention. Of course, feelings of government inefficacy likely also reflect that the working poor who qualify for EITC may already feel that government has failed them, leaving them in vulnerable circumstances.[28]

Another example of the consequences of policy visibility for political action plays out in the realm of financing and consumer financial protection. As previous sections described, the government has played a highly active but largely invisible role in creating and regulating consumer lending markets in the United States. The average borrower who relies on government regulations to protect them from predatory lending or who uses government-backed loans to buy a new home will rarely see the hands of the state on their financial contracts. The result of this hidden intervention is that Americans increasingly view their own financial protection as an apolitical issue, thus they are reluctant to turn to politics to demand policy reform – even when they have major grievances.[29]

For example, a recent study found that the majority of borrowers place a greater degree of blame for problems with consumer credit on financial institutions than policymakers. This affected borrowers' willingness to engage in political action to address both specific and systemic solutions to predatory lending problems. About one third of the borrowers surveyed had experienced at least one problem with credit in the past year. Of those who had problems, 80 percent took action to try and remedy the issue; however, nearly all who did (97 percent) turned to the market to do so, attempting to fix the problem with help from their lender, by finding a new lender, or by complaining to a trade association or engaging in a boycott. Only

[27] National Archives, "Congress and the New Deal: Social Security," www.archives.gov/exhibits/treasures_of_congress/text/page19_text.html

[28] Delphia Shanks-Booth and Suzanne Mettler, "The Paradox of the Earned Income Tax Credit: Appreciating Benefits But Not Their Source," *Policy Studies Journal*, Vol. 47 (2), 2019: 300–323.

[29] SoRelle 2020.

13 percent took some type of political action, like complaining to a state or federal regulatory agency, and only 3 percent exclusively took political action. Borrowers were also far more willing to contact their bank than their member of Congress or a federal regulator to support policies designed to improve consumer financial protections, despite the fact that banks have few incentives to adopt such reforms.

1.4 PUBLIC OPTIONS: POLITICAL OBSTACLES AND OPPORTUNITIES

The effects of government visibility on the politics of social goods provision have significant consequences for the pursuit of public options. In order to get constituents to support and act on behalf of these programs, people must believe that government has a role to play in specific forms of social provision. This is complicated by the two trends in policy visibility described earlier: a shift toward hidden government and a bifurcation in visibility between policies that benefit affluent versus marginalized people. With respect to the first, scholars have illuminated lawmakers' increasing fondness since the 1970s for policies that are characterized by market logic and that channel benefits and protections through market structures.[30] Jacob Hacker dubs it America's "personal responsibility crusade" and Joe Soss, Richard Fording, and Sanford Schram describe the trend as a broad neoliberal project "that turns citizens into prudent market actors who bear personal responsibility for their problems."[31] The result is that, as policymakers increasingly adopt policy designs that submerge government's role within the private market, Americans are less likely to see, to support, and subsequently to take action on behalf of public programs that expand that role. The submerged policy designs provide the illusion that Americans are "going it alone" as self-sufficient individuals who are entirely responsible for their own well-being, when, in fact, social policies embed all of us within relationships of mutual interdependence.

One notable takeaway from this observation is that proponents of public options would be well advised not to frame their proposals as "new" forms of government social provision. Suggesting that a particular public option represents a break from an existing private market, in addition to being historically inaccurate, may also reify people's belief that policymakers don't have a role to play in that specific domain, and that any program would be an onerous expansion of government into a previously free-market system. So, while it might seem intuitive to suggest to voters that a public option is simply intended to improve market competition and efficiency, a better approach might be to contextualize public options as part of a longer tradition of government assistance, demonstrating to the public that such a program

[30] Howard 1997; Jacob Hacker, *The Great Risk Shift: The New Economic Security and the Decline of the American Dream* (Oxford, UK: Oxford University Press, 2006); Joe Soss, Richard Fording, and Sanford Schram, *Disciplining the Poor: Neoliberal Paternalism and the Persistent Power of Race* (Chicago: University of Chicago Press, 2011); Mettler 2011.

[31] Hacker 2006; Soss, Fording, and Schram 2011: 51.

would not be a new and unwelcome incursion in the market, but instead a more beneficial form of existing government social provision.

The second major stumbling block in generating support for public options stems from the growing perception that government involvement is only necessary to support those who are socioeconomically marginalized. Public provision for the poor typically uses policy designs that make government's role more obvious, and beneficiaries of such policies are more supportive of increased public funding for social policies generally. Meanwhile, however, middle- and upper-income Americans – despite typically using several social policies themselves – do not gain an awareness of government's role in those policies, and they do not become more supportive of expanded social provision. Exacerbating this "government-citizen disconnect," it is the latter group who are far more likely to take political action than the former, voicing their anti-government sentiments to lawmakers even as they themselves benefit from it.[32] This bifurcation in government visibility between public interventions designed to assist those at the socioeconomic margins versus more advantaged groups offers a cautionary tale for proponents of public options designed to provide a "basic" level of assistance when the market fails to do so – for example, providing a bare bones health insurance plan for those who cannot afford more premium options. Framing public options as, effectively, another means-tested form of government intervention may reinforce these existing attitudinal and participatory divides.

Each of these consequences complicate the prospects for public options, but they also suggest a crucial benefit of successfully expanding clear public "alternatives" for social provision: improving perceptions of government and increasing democratic participation. When people are able to associate government with a particular issue or benefit, it can increase their willingness to engage politically on behalf of that program.[33] Relatedly, when people have positive experiences with government service provision, their trust in government and feelings of civic efficacy can increase.[34] The introduction of a public option could, therefore, help improve the relationship between citizens and the state. While the proposed health-care "public option" failed to gain approval as part of the ACA in 2010, the expansion of government health-care plans under the Act still offers an example of how this scenario might play out: Expanded government provision of health insurance has reshaped debate about government's role in securing health care in the years since, and support has grown for a single-payer health-care system in the United States.

Of course, this outcome is dependent upon people having positive experiences with policy disbursement. Scholars have detailed the negative consequences for

32 Mettler 2018, Chaps. 4 and 5.

33 Campbell 2002.

34 Joe Soss, "Lessons of Welfare: Policy Design, Political Learning, and Political Action," *American Political Science Review*, Vol. 93 (1999): 363–380; Suzanne Mettler, *Soldiers to Citizens: The G.I. Bill and the Making of the Greatest Generation* (New York: Oxford University Press, 2005).

political efficacy that emanate from feeling poorly treated by agents of the state[35] – effects that are more frequently incurred by marginalized communities.[36] Existing public welfare program administration exemplifies this cautionary tale. As the administrative burden increases for public benefits, people's sense of civic efficacy and their resulting political engagement decrease.[37] Thus, poorly conceived public options may do more democratic harm than good. Ensuring smooth implementation should be a priority for any proposed reforms.

Perhaps the most valuable aspect of the "public option" concept is that it could help to spur a public conversation about the role that government already plays in the lives of American citizens. Far from it being an exception to the rule, government intervention is and has long been the norm, but it is far too often unperceived and unappreciated. Policymakers should consider the impact of policy designs, not only for goals such as efficiency, but also for ends that serve democracy, such as access, inclusion, fairness, and the promotion of civic education and political participation. These latter goals each have a legacy in the United States, and the nation's future can be strengthened by finding ways to instill them once again.

[35] Soss 1999; Vesla M. Weaver and Amy E. Lerman, "Political Consequences of the Carceral State," *American Political Science Review*, Vol. 104 (2010): 817–833; Amy E. Lerman, *Good Enough for Government Work: The Public Reputation Crisis in America (And How to Fix It)* (Chicago: University of Chicago Press, 2019).

[36] Joe Soss and Vesla Weaver, "Police are our Government: Politics, Political Science, and the Policing of Race–Class Subjugated Communities," *Annual Review of Political Science*, Vol. 20 (2017): 565–591.

[37] Soss, Fording, and Schram 2011; Jamila Michener, *Fragmented Democracy: Medicaid, Federalism, and Unequal Politics* (Cambridge, UK: Cambridge University Press, 2018).

2

The Entrepreneurial State and Public Options

Socializing Risks and Rewards

Mariana Mazzucato and Henry Lishi Li

2.1 INTRODUCTION

The concept of a public option – a good or service that is government-provided, quality-assured and universally available at a reasonable and fixed price, which coexists with products from the private sector – is receiving increasing interest as a public policy tool (Sitaraman and Alstott 2019). The idea can be applied to a range of social and public services, such as health care, retirement, higher education, banking, and childcare. It can also be applied to innovation and manufacturing, especially in the pharmaceutical industry and with regard to issues that matter to citizens (access to health, clean energy, and the benefits of big data and AI). Indeed, the use of public options for sectors driven by fast innovation is developing into an exciting new area of policy.

More recently, growing interest in the public sector playing a greater role in pharmaceutical innovation and manufacturing is, in part, due to the impasse in the existing innovation system and the difficulty it has pivoting towards addressing some of the greatest public health crises of our time – from the slow-burning problem of antibiotic resistance to the fast-moving emergency of the COVID-19 pandemic. While the pharmaceutical sector receives billions in public-sector investment (e.g. in the US alone the National Institute of Health (NIH) invests over $40 billion a year – see Section 2.2), the structure of supply, patents, pricing, and access does not sufficiently enable the state to govern the benefits for the public interest. In particular, the direction of the innovation (what types of diseases are focused on) and the way the innovation system itself is governed (e.g. the way that intellectual property rights (IPR) are structured – too upstream, too wide, and too strong) hurts the public (Mazzoleni and Nelson 1998).

The main criticisms of public options concern the relationship between public and private sectors in the economy, especially the role of government in the direct provision of goods in the market – the risk of 'crowding out' the private sector (Mazzucato and Penna 2016), as well as the underlying capability and capacity of governments for implementation and delivery (Kattel and Mazzucato 2018).

Fundamentally, the criticisms center on the assumption of a clear divide between public and private sector, and the view that public-sector contribution to economic activities should remain minimal and be confined to simply fixing markets, 'regulating', and levelling the playing field (Mazzucato 2016).

This chapter frames public options as a broader policy vehicle that has an application not just for socioeconomic reasons (classic public good arguments), but also for technological change and dynamism. In doing so, it situates public options within a broader economic theory of value creation by the state (Mazzucato 2013, 2018a). We argue that the contribution to value creation by different parts of the public sectors has been theorized in problematic ways that understate the contribution of the state while overstating the contribution of other actors, with consequences for the overall distribution of rewards. In other words, while the creation of value is collective, its distribution is not. This has also meant that the full potential of the state to drive both innovation-led and inclusive growth has not been realized.

This chapter argues that a better understanding of the role that the state has and can play in the wealth-creation process is the starting point for policy solutions that can increase the rate of wealth creation, while reducing rent-seeking and ensuring a fairer distribution of that co-created wealth. Meeting the challenge of inequality requires less a redistributive state and more an *entrepreneurial state* (Mazzucato 2013; Laplane and Mazzucato 2020) or, as Rodrik has argued, shifting the focus from a 'welfare state to an innovation state' (Rodrik 2015). This is the way to create innovation-led growth that is also more inclusive growth. Seen in this light, public options are an important and proactive instrument to deliver public rewards in return for the state's risk-taking in innovation, and a tool that can foster public-sector capabilities in innovation and manufacturing in the direction of addressing societal missions.

The chapter is organized as follows. Section 2.2 reviews the economic and political thinking behind the depiction of the state as simply a market-fixer. It also looks at the role that public choice theory has had in focusing on *government failure* as an even greater problem than market failure. Section 2.3 presents an alternative view of the state as market-maker, drawing on the work of Polanyi and Keynes, as well as the neo-Schumpeterian literature that has emphasized the role of public investments in driving innovation, not just facilitating it. This section concludes with examples of public-sector wealth creation. Section 2.4 looks at the other side of the coin: government investments that have led to failures. In doing so, it considers the need to understand failure in two ways: (1) as part and parcel of the investment and innovation process; and (2) failure that arises from instances where the state is captured by vested interests, which make money simply by moving around existing wealth, not creating new wealth. In cases where the public sector is not captured and is producing new value, Section 2.5 considers how that value might be better distributed if it is understood as having arisen from a collective co-creation process where the taxpayer has also played a lead role. Based on the arguments set out in the previous sections and the examples outlined in Section 2.5, Section 2.6 examines public options as a market-shaping policy that delivers public rewards, using the pharmaceutical sector as a main example. Section 2.7 discusses the central role of public ownership in the policy instruments proposed. Section 2.8 concludes.

2.2 THE STATE AS *MARKET-FIXER*

Key to the problem is that in economic theory the state is, at best, seen as facilitating the process of wealth creation, but not being a key driver of the process itself. In microeconomics, it is seen as *fixing* markets, not creating them. In industrial-innovation economics, its role is limited to spending on public goods, such as science or infrastructure, and de-risking the activities of innovators, and does not extend to being an innovator itself. In macroeconomics, it is seen as fixing the business cycle and as a lender of last resort. It is not seen as a lead risk-taker across the business cycle or an *investor* of first resort. And if or when a public agency does dare to make strategic choices and take risks, it is often accused of crowding out the private-sector actors or of being too inept to 'pick winners'.

This limited view of the role of the state in the dynamics of wealth creation has had three problematic effects. First, it has limited policymakers' understanding of the range of tools and instruments they have for catalyzing growth, often choosing to sit on the sidelines, 'levelling' the playing field. Second, it has reduced the confidence of the public sector, making it more vulnerable to being captured by vested interests and 'rent-seeking' behaviour. Third, it has increased inequality by allowing some actors to exaggerate their role in creating wealth and extract value well beyond their contribution to its creation.

The idea that the state is, at best, a fixer of markets has its roots in neoclassical economic theory, but this view has hardened in recent years as a result of an ideological political project against the state. We review both perspectives briefly.

Based on Arrow's first fundamental theorem of welfare economics (Arrow 1962), when markets are complete, competitive, and operating in equilibrium, they are taken to be the most efficient allocators of resources. However, these conditions are rarely obtainable and five broad categories of 'market failure' that justify government 'intervention' have been identified: (1) coordination failures, including inter-temporally through the operation of the business cycle, making it difficult to coordinate expectations and preferences (Stiglitz 1974); (2) public goods such as clean air or new knowledge arising from basic research; (3) imperfect competition, whether arising from natural monopolies, network effects, or economies of scale; (4) information failures leading to adverse selection, moral hazard, or high transaction costs (Coase 1960; Stiglitz and Weiss 1981); and (5) negative externalities, such as traffic congestion or climate change (Stern 2007). Government intervention is justified when any of these conditions exist.

If government is viewed as, at best, a fixer of market failures, at worst it is seen as an impediment to growth: it is inefficient; due to its natural tendency towards corruption it is constantly vulnerable to lobbying by specific business interests (Krueger 1974; Falck, Gollier, and Woessmann 2011); and its actions risk crowding out private actors (Friedman 1979). In this caricature, governments are Hobbesian leviathans, sucking dry the dynamic energy of the market, and an ever-present threat to the creativity and dynamism of the private sector (Phelps 2013). Market failure is therefore a necessary but not sufficient condition for governments to act (Wolf 1988). There is a trade-off between two inefficient outcomes – one generated by markets and the other generated by 'government failures' from intervention. The benefits of acting must outweigh the costs that may arise from these risks of 'government failure' (Tullock, Seldon, and Brady 2002).

In this dominant view, government's main role is to set the rules of the game and to keep them working (the rule of law); fund basic public goods such as infrastructure and education; 'level the playing field' so that industry and competition can thrive (through competition rules or support to new firms in order to compete with incumbents); and devise market mechanisms to internalize external costs (e.g. pollution) or benefits (e.g. herd immunity). If and when the public sector does more than intervene in areas characterized by market failures, it is deemed to be causing different types of problems, such as: (1) crowding out the private sector; (2) government failure due to the inability of the state to 'pick winners'; and (3) government failure due to the state's inevitable vulnerability to capture by rent-seeking private interests (Buchanan 2003).

Although scepticism about the role of government dates back to the first developments of philosophy and, later, economics, the strict modern formulation of the limits to government can be traced to the rise of New Public Management theory, which grew out of Public Choice theory in the 1980s. This perspective has been used to convince governments that the way they can be less burdensome is to emulate the private sector as much as possible (Buchanan 2003). Judt (2011) has shown how the dismantling of the welfare state, a political project that began with Reagan and Thatcher in the late 1970s–early 1980s, co-evolved with this theoretical framework. And Jones (2014) shows how the neoliberal agenda was underpinned by the view of the state as an inept and constantly captured entity. These trends have led to an undermining of confidence in the positive power of public institutions and an increasing outsourcing of government functions to the private sector: it is surely easier to get business to act like business than for government to do so (Crouch 2016).

This view of government also has its roots in the way that output is measured in both macro- and microeconomics. Government typically exists in macroeconomic theory, as a redistributor of the wealth that is created by companies, and an investor in some basic public goods like infrastructure, basic research, and education. It normally exists only in macroeconomic models that look at the effect of regulation or investment at the aggregate level. And it is totally missing from the microeconomic *production function*, where value is created. In microeconomics, total output is understood in terms of the (marginal) productivity of labour, capital, and technology inputs. The production function posits the relationship between the output that a company produces and the various inputs it uses, including labour, machinery, and technology. Yet this view disregards the enormous government inputs that have created both the human capital and the technology that enter the production function, as well as the early stage high-risk financing that innovative companies require. In essence, in standard microeconomics, government is ignored, except for its role in regulating the prices of inputs and outputs, and fixing market failures of different types.

2.3 THE STATE AS *MARKET-MAKER*

The history of capitalism tells us a different story – the story of a state that has often been responsible for actively shaping and creating markets, not just fixing them. Indeed, markets themselves should be viewed as outcomes of the interactions between both public and private actors (as well as actors from the third sector and from civil society). In his seminal work, *The Great Transformation*, Karl Polanyi (1944) describes the role of the state in forcing the so-called free market into existence: 'The road to the free market was opened and kept open by an enormous increase in continuous, centrally organized and controlled interventionism' (p. 144). Polanyi's perspective debunks the notion of state actions as 'interventions'. It is rather one in which markets are deeply embedded in social and political institutions (Evans 1995), and where markets themselves are outcomes of social and political processes. Indeed, even Adam Smith's notion of the free market is amenable to this interpretation. His free market was not a naturally occurring state of nature, 'free' from government interference. For Smith the free market meant a market 'free from rent', which requires much policymaking (Smith 1776).

And yet within economic theory, there is an absence of words to refer to the ways in which the actions of public institutions (visions, investments, and regulations) contribute to value creation, not only its fixing-up or its distribution. Polanyi's analysis is not only about the way that markets form over the course of economic development. It can also be applied to understanding the most modern form of markets and in particular those driven by innovation. Some of the most important general-purpose technologies, from mass production, to aerospace, and information and communications technology trace their early investments to public-sector investments (Ruttan 2006; Block and Keller 2011). Indeed, all of the technologies which have made Apple's i-products (iPhone, iPad, etc.) 'smart' were initially funded by public-sector institutions: the Internet by the Defense Activated Research Projects Agency (DARPA); global positioning system (GPS) by the US Navy; touchscreen display by the Central Intelligence Agency (CIA); and the voice-activated personal assistant Siri by DARPA again (Mazzucato 2013).

Key to understanding the implications of these histories is that public investments in the areas named earlier were not limited to simply funding 'basic' research, a typical 'public good' in market failure theory (Nelson 1959; Arrow 1962). In the United States, for example, government agencies funded areas along the entire innovation chain: both basic *and* applied research and, in many cases, provided downstream early stage high-risk finance to companies deemed too risky by the private financial sector.

For example, in its early years, Apple received $500,000 from the Small Business Investment Corporation, a financing arm of the US government (Audretsch 2003). Likewise, Compaq and Intel received early-stage funding to set up their companies, not from venture capital but from the public Small Business Innovation Research (SBIR) programme. This programme has been particularly active in providing early-stage finance to risk-taking companies – more so than private venture capital (Keller and Block 2013). Indeed, while it is a common perception that it is private venture capital that funds start-ups, evidence shows that most high-growth innovative companies receive their early-stage high-risk finance from public sources, such as Yozma in Israel (Breznitz and Ornston 2013); venture funds in public banks (Mazzucato and Penna 2016); and the SBIR programme funds in the United States (Keller and Block 2013). Although venture capital entered the biotech industry in the late 1980s and early 1990s, all the heavy investments in this sector occurred in the 1950s, 1960s, and 1970s – and were mostly made by the state (Lazonick and Tulum 2011; Vallas, Kleinman, and Biscotti 2011). The NIH is the biggest early investor in biopharmaceuticals. Since 2000, it has invested close to $750 billion (in 2020 dollars) in the biotech-pharma knowledge base and $41.7 billion in 2020 alone.[1] NIH funding contributed to every one of the new molecular entities approved from 2010 to 2016 and previous studies have shown that it contributes to therapeutic advances that are truly innovative and impactful to human health. Between 1988 and 2005, 17.4 percent of patented new drugs approved by the US Food and Drug Administration (FDA) that underwent priority review – the most innovative drugs – had public-sector patents; 64.5 percent of priority-review new drugs and 47.8 percent of all new drugs cited either a public-sector patent or a government publication (Sampat and Lichtenberg 2011). New drugs and vaccines approved by the FDA between 1970 and 2009 led to a disproportionately large therapeutic effect through advances in cancerous and infectious diseases (Stevens et al. 2011). The NIH example here has particular relevance to the public option idea in pharmaceutical innovation, which will be discussed in Section 2.6. These 'mission-oriented' institutions (Mowery 2010; Foray, Mowery and Nelson 2012; Mazzucato 2017, 2018b) actively created new industrial and technological landscapes.

[1] Authors' calculation based on the following data sources: www.nih.gov/about-nih/what-we-do/budget; www.nih.gov/about-nih/what-we-do/nih-almanac/appropriations-section-1; www.nih.gov/about-nih/what-we-do/nih-almanac/appropriations-section-2. Inflation rates used: www.officialdata.org/us/inflation/2020.

This pattern is being repeated in renewable energy, where the US government has been behind some of the most important advances through innovation in agencies such as the Advanced Research Projects Agency–Energy (ARPA-E), the sister organisation of DARPA in the Department of Energy, as well as the recent revolution in fracking to extract shale gas (Trembath et al. 2012). Today, the Chinese government is also the largest global funder of green innovations (Mazzucato and Semieniuk 2016). In all these cases – from ICT to health and energy – it has been these early direct public investments that have prepared the ground, creating and shaping new landscapes that businesses develop only later.

Such market-shaping has also occurred through *demand pull* instruments, from government procurement policy (e.g. by purchasing a high volume of semiconductors in the early stages, the state contributes to a fall in costs), as well as bold policies to shape consumer demand, such as suburbanization, which allows the impact of the mass production revolution to become fully deployed and diffused across the economy.

Should the public sector do everything? Of course not. The point is not that the private sector is unimportant, but that in new sectors like biotechnology, nanotechnology, and the emerging green economy, private businesses have tended to invest only *after* returns were in clear sight. The animal spirits of business investors are themselves an endogenous function of public investment, roused only after public investments have laid the groundwork in the highest-risk and most capital-intensive areas. This role of public investment is recognized in terms of the 'basics', such as infrastructure (without roads, businesses would have no way of transporting goods) and protecting private property, but beyond that it is largely ignored.

2.4 GOVERNMENT FAILURES

Of course the story is not always a positive one. While the above-mentioned examples focus on public investments that have led to important successes (e.g. the Internet, GPS, shale gas, blockbuster drugs), there are also government investments that end in failure. These include investment in products like the Concorde aircraft, which ultimately failed commercially; in the discovery of new drugs (of which most attempts fail); or the provision of guaranteed loans to companies that then go bankrupt. A recent example of the latter includes the guaranteed loan of $528 million provided by the US Department of Energy to the company Solyndra for the production of solar cells. This was followed by the company's bankruptcy, when the price of silicon chips fell dramatically, leaving the taxpayer to pick up the bill (Wood 2012). Any venture capitalist will argue that attempts to innovate require exploring new and difficult paths, and that occasional failure is part of that journey. Indeed, a similar guaranteed loan ($465 million) was provided to Tesla for the development of the Model S electric car – which led to success.

This *trial-and-error* process, in which tolerance of failure is also the road to success, is accepted in the private sector, but when governments fail this is regarded as a sign of incompetence, often leading to accusations that the government is unable to 'pick winners'. As a result, public organizations are frequently told to stick to 'levelling the playing field' and to promote competition without 'distorting' the market by choosing specific technologies, sectors, or companies to invest in (Owen 2012). Yet this ignores our first point, that markets are outcomes, and they have historically been outcomes of government playing a lead role: none of the great advances of the twentieth century would have occurred without public investment.

There are, nevertheless, good reasons to worry about government failures outside this natural trial-and-error explorative process. These reasons arise from situations where 'rent-seeking' behaviour in the business community leads to government being captured by vested interests (Tullock, Seldon, and Brady 2002). Rents arise when value is extracted through special privileges (Krueger 1974) and when a company or individual grabs a large share of wealth that would have been produced without their input (Stiglitz 2012, p. 32). The idea is that profit-maximizing firms are likely to try to increase their profits through special policy-related favours and this often leads to success on their part, because politicians and policymakers are seen as naturally prone to corruption. Rent-seeking could arise from specific companies, or sectors, seeking extra funding from government through either a subsidy or a tax credit of some sort. Such concerns are valid, but these problems become more acute precisely when there is not a clear view of government value. If the state is seen as irrelevant, it will over time also become less confident and more easily corruptible by different actors who call themselves the 'wealth creators'. It is these actors who can then convince policymakers to hand out favours in order to increase wealth.

Furthermore, some rent-seeking may occur precisely as a result of problematic assumptions regarding the role of public investment. If private investment is driven by perceptions of future opportunities in a sector, and if those opportunities are highly correlated with direct public investments that create markets into which business investment later moves, then policy tools that are overly focused on indirect support to business (e.g. via tax incentives) will create far less additionality. That is, they will not make things happen that *would not have happened anyway*. They may increase profits (through a reduction of costs), but not investment. And the primary objective of the policymaker should be to increase business investment, not profits. In this sense, such policies can lead to rent-seeking outcomes, even if there were no explicit 'rent-seekers': they result in a company or individual earning income without having generated any wealth.

An example is the way in which the private equity and venture capital community successfully persuaded governments in the United States and Europe of their wealth-creating potential and of the need to reduce capital gains to make this happen. In the United States, capital gains tax fell by 50 percent in five years at the end of the 1970s as a result of pressure from the National Venture Capital Association (Lazonick and Mazzucato 2012). As the US investor Warren Buffett put it, such policies do little for investment, which is driven by expectations of growth opportunities or what Buffet calls 'sensible' investments, while increasing job destruction and inequality (Buffett 2011).

Once we admit that the state has been a market-shaper and creator, a lead investor and a risk-taker, the next question is how to make sure that policy leads not only to the socialization of risks, but also of rewards. A better realignment between risks and rewards, across public and private actors, can become a concrete way to allow smart, innovation-led growth to also become inclusive growth. We turn to this in Section 2.5.

2.5 SOCIALIZING RISKS AND REWARDS

In ignoring the entrepreneurial role of the state as lead investor and risk-taker, and focusing only on the role of the public sector as setting the background (horizontal) conditions, orthodox economic theory has also ignored the way in which the socialization of risks should be accompanied by the socialization of rewards. Indeed, the more downstream the public investments in particular technologies and firms, the higher the risk that one of those technologies or firms will fail. But this is indeed normal, as any venture capitalist would admit: for every success there are many failures. In reality, the most successful capitalist economies have had active states that made risky investments, some of them contributing to technological revolutions. The Finnish public innovation agency, SITRA, has had some great successes, but also some failures. Likewise, Israel's public venture capital fund, Yozma. In the Anglo-Saxon economies public debate has been too quick to criticize public investments when they go wrong and too slow to acknowledge the state's role in those that succeed.

However, this raises a more fundamental question: how to make sure that, like private venture capital funds, the state can reap some return from the successes (the 'upside'), in order to cover the inevitable losses (the 'downside') and finance the next round of investments. This is especially important given the path-dependent and cumulative nature of innovation. Returns arise slowly; they are negative in the beginning and gradually build up, potentially generating huge rewards after decades of investment. Indeed companies in areas like ICT, biotechnology, and nanotechnology had to accept many years of zero profits before any returns were in sight. If the collective process of innovation is not properly recognized, the result will be a narrow group of private corporations and investors reaping the full returns of projects that the state helped to initiate and finance.

So who gets the reward for innovation? Some economists argue that returns accrue to the public sector through the knowledge spillovers that are created (new knowledge that can benefit various areas of the economy) and via the taxation system due to new jobs being generated, as well as taxes being paid by companies benefitting from the investments. But the evolution of the patenting system has made it easier to take out patents on upstream research, meaning that knowledge dissemination can effectively be blocked and spillovers cannot be assumed. The cumulative nature of innovation and the dynamic returns to scale (Nelson and Winter 1982) mean that countries stand to gain significantly from being first in the development of new technologies. At the same time the global movement of capital means that the particular country or region funding initial investments in innovation is by no means guaranteed to reap all the wider economic benefits, such as those relating to employment or taxation. Indeed, corporate taxation has been falling globally, and corporate tax avoidance and evasion have been rising. Some of the technology companies that have benefitted most from public support, such as Apple and Google, have also been among those accused of using their international operations to avoid paying tax (Johnston 2014). Perhaps most importantly, while the spillovers that occur from upstream 'basic' investments, such as education and research, should not be thought of as needing to earn a *direct* return for the state, downstream investments targeted at specific companies and technologies are qualitatively different. Precisely because some investments in firms and technologies will fail; the state should treat these investments as a portfolio and enable some of the upside success to cover the downside risk.

In particular, there is a strong case for arguing that, where technological breakthroughs have occurred as a result of targeted state interventions benefitting specific companies, the state should reap some of the financial rewards over time by retaining ownership of a small proportion of the intellectual property it had a hand in creating. This is not to say that the state should ever have exclusive licence or hold a large enough proportion of the value of an innovation to deter its diffusion (and this is almost never the case). The role of government is not to run commercial enterprises; it is to spark innovation elsewhere. But by owning some of the value it has created, which over time has the potential for significant growth, funds can be generated for reinvestment into new potential innovations. By adopting a 'portfolio' approach to public investments in innovation, success from a few projects can then help cover the losses from other projects. In this way, *both* risks and rewards are socialized (Mazzucato 2016).

2.5.1 *Examples of Direct Forms of Public Rewards*

There are many examples of public organizations that have strategically considered the distribution of risks and rewards. At times, they have granted licenses to private firms willing to invest in upgrading publicly owned technologies, offering the opportunity for public and private to share risks and also rewards. For example, NASA has sometimes captured the returns from its inventions, while private partners gained on the value-added in the case of successful commercialization (Kempf, 1995). Further there are examples of state-owned venture capital activity generating royalties from public investments (e.g. in Israel – see Avnimelech 2009) or equity (e.g. in Finland via

SITRA), and the more pervasive use of equity by state development banks (e.g. in Brazil, China, and Germany – see Mazzucato and Penna 2016).

Policy instruments for tackling risk-reward issues combine supply- and demand-side mechanisms, and are geared to enabling public value creation through symbiotic public–private partnerships ('active') (Lazonick and Mazzucato 2013) and blocking value extraction ('defensive').

The different mechanisms for distributing rewards can work either directly through profit-sharing (via equity, royalties) or indirectly through conditions attached, focused more on the market-shaping role. The latter may involve conditions on the reinvestment of profits, conditions on pricing or conditions on the way that knowledge is governed. We review these later.

a) **Pricing Capping Schemes.** On the defensive side, to ensure taxpayers do not pay twice, governments might want to adopt pricing capping regulations instead of relying on market forces to spontaneously produce equitable prices. Indeed, such a possibility exists under section 203 of the Bayh-Dole Act, which established the US government's 'march-in' right over pharmaceuticals if, among other reasons, patent holders that benefitted from public funding fail to satisfy the 'health and safety needs' of consumers (Sampat and Lichtenberg 2011). Despite numerous discussions over time (Davis and Arno 2001; Korn and Heinig 2004), it has not thus far been implemented. Another instrument for ensuring competitive prices is the implementation of competition and antitrust policies, which may be far less tolerant of monopoly prices than has been the case over, say, the past forty years in the United States (Stiglitz 2017).

b) **Conditions on Reinvestments.** Another possibility is to negotiate conditions on reinvestment into the real economy, which can be achieved through regulation and/or attached to financing contracts. In fact, the inception of Bell Labs resulted from the Department of Justice's implementation of antitrust laws (Brumfiel 2008): in 1925, among the conditions imposed on AT&T in order for it to be able to retain its monopoly over the phone system, the US government required the company to reinvest a share of its profits in research. Conditions targeting the creation of specific commercial, industrial, or technological benefits in the context of defence-related procurement ('offset agreements') are also common practice in many countries. Most remarkably in Sweden, where this instrument has been explicitly part of a strategy to promote the military aircraft industry (Eliasson 2017), as well as in the United States and Brazil (Vieira and Alvares 2017), among others.

c) **Knowledge Governance.** Several measures can be articulated to advance the creation and diffusion of the key knowledge needed to tackle problems such as climate change, poverty, and so on. One is to reform the IPR system so as to harmonize it with the broader set of institutional requirements for multiple actors to access and use knowledge (Henry and Stiglitz 2010). This involves ensuring IPR is flexible enough and patents are good quality, used for productive instead of financialization purposes and narrow in scope and length (Mazzoleni and Nelson 1998; Frischmann and Lemley 2007). IPR may also be managed strategically through the exploitation of some of the flexibilities still left under the WTO-TRIPS agreement. For example, governments may choose – or threaten – to issue compulsory licenses in order to obtain access to knowledge and/or price reductions on proprietary goods. In the 2000s, this was used to promote access to medicines (e.g. in Brazil, India, Indonesia, South Africa, etc.) and genetic diagnostic tests (in France), and the purchase of antibiotics for defence purposes[2] (in the United States) (Reichman 2009). Where IPR blocks the creation and diffusion of knowledge that is key for competitors (e.g. through refusals to license or defensive patenting behaviour), competition and antitrust policies may help, as applied by European authorities (Motta 2004). These may be more effective if supplemented by alternative incentives such as 'open source' and prizes. In particular, featuring as lead investor offers more opportunities for public organizations to choose whether to hold title over resulting inventions and negotiate licensing conditions, while engendering within-industry and across-the-economy spillovers, as defence-related R&D spending in the US illustrates (Mowery 2009).

d) **Tax Reforms.** On the one hand, tackling present evasion, avoidance, loopholes, and tax incentives for unproductive entrepreneurship – like the patent box that increases profits without increasing business investments, or reduced tax rates over capital as compared to corporate gains – may enhance the government's revenues and its redistributive capacity (Lazonick and Mazzucato 2013). On the other hand, tax regulation can be designed to more actively incentivize productive entrepreneurship using measures such as low taxation for hiring labour and high for financial transactions. In addition, in seeking to capture a direct share of the profits resulting from strategic investments, the state may choose to create some form of tax-based mechanism (Enke 1967). Realistically, however, distributive tensions require governments to be creative and, wherever possible, seek tax reforms that may more commensurately reflect its role in the economy – not just 'fixing' but also 'creating' markets.

e) **Revenues beyond Taxation.** On the strategic front, to ensure that both risks and rewards are shared with supported firms, the government might claim a share of the financial gains resulting from public investments, which it can use to cover the inevitable losses and make future investments. Compared with other measures discussed earlier, direct profit-sharing can better generate directionality of innovation and enhance the flexibility of the management of the recouped revenues. The choice of a profit-sharing mechanism and its intended form of public return should

[2] See D. McNeil Jr, A nation challenged: The drug, a rush for Cipro and the global ripples, *New York Times*, 17 October 2001. Available at: www.nytimes.com/2001/10/17/world/a-nation-challenged-the-drug-a-rush-for-cipro-and-the-global-ripples.html.

be considered according to the financing instruments selected to support innovation (Laplane and Mazzucato 2020). A number of examples are summarized in Table 2.1.

This list is not meant to be exhaustive, but rather illustrates that there are multiple experiences in handling policy instruments that, implicit or explicitly, permit taking account of issues such as value extraction and enabling government to capture a share of the value it helped to generate. The latter, in particular, has been adopted by different types of agencies, at different stages of the innovation chain, but mainly downstream, involving different types of partners (e.g. firm size) and industries. However, these have not always been adjusted to the specificities of different economic, industrial, and legal settings. Without a framework that more clearly informs these policies, decisions on these matters have sometimes been made unintentionally and haphazardly, inviting both government and systemic failures.

2.6 PUBLIC OPTION AS A MARKET-SHAPING POLICY FOR DELIVERING PUBLIC REWARDS

The previous sections have described the theories behind the problematic but prevailing framing of government as a fixer of market failures, versus an alternative one that highlights the less familiar story of government as a market shaper. The latter underlines the role of government as an investor of first resort and a risk-taker in innovation. This socialization of risk-taking leads to a better way of interpreting government failures as the cost of exploration and learning, and the implication that the rewards from the resultant public-backed innovations should also be socialized. A number of policy instruments, as described earlier, can achieve this purpose.

This section will now introduce the public option as an innovation and manufacturing policy (using the pharmaceutical sector as a main example) and situate it within the broader theoretical discussion about the entrepreneurial state described earlier. In building a conceptual case for a public option pertinent to innovation and manufacturing, we argue that the public option is yet another power tool for delivering public rewards.

2.6.1 *Policy Context for a Public Option in Innovation and Manufacturing*

Building on Sitaraman and Alstott's (2019) conceptualization of the public option – which the authors apply to the examples of health care, retirement, higher education, banking, childcare, and other social and public services – policymakers, advocates, and scholars have since extended the application of the idea to the field of innovation and manufacturing, with the pharmaceutical sector being one of the most prominent examples due to its strong relevance and proximity to health policy and drug pricing policy debates.

In the United States, in late 2018, motivated by problems surrounding high drug prices and shortages of critical medicines, most prominently insulin, Senator

TABLE 2.1 *Existing policy instruments for financing innovation that allow for profit-sharing (selected examples)*

Financing instruments	Types	Key features	Returns to funding agency	Some country examples
Debt financing	Repayable grants/ advances	Repayment required, partial or total; could be granted on the basis of private co-funding	Royalties of IPR licensing or levy on sales (Windus and Schiffel 1976)	Repayment grants for start-ups from 2014 to 2016 (New Zealand), Dutch Technological Development Loan programme carried out by the Senter-agency of the Ministry of Economic Affairs from 1954 to 2001 (Kaivanto and Stoneman 2007)
Debt/equity financing	Mezzanine funding	Combination of several financing instruments that incorporate elements of debt and equity in a single investment vehicle	Interest rates plus spread	Credit line mezzanine financing (Portugal)
Equity financing	Venture capital funds and fund of funds	Funds provided by institutional investors (e.g. banks, pension funds) to be invested in firms at early-to-expansion stages Referred to as 'patient capital', due to lengthy time span for exiting (10 to 12 years)	Equity stakes	Innpulsa (Colombia), National Innovation Fund – Venture Capital Fund (Czech Republic), Corporate Venture Programme (France), Yozma Fund (Israel) (Erlich 2002; Avnimelech 2009; Lerner 2010), Scottish Co-Investment Fund (UK)
Public procurement for R&D and innovation		Demand for technologies or services that do not exist yet; or purchase of R&D services (pre-commercial procurement of R&D)	IPR of research results; agency can opt to shift ownership to contractors and establish licensing conditions	Entrepreneur Growth Strategy (Estonia), Strategy for Public Procurement (Sweden), Small Business Innovation Research (SBIR) Program (US) and SBIR-type of programmes (UK)

Source: Adaptation of OECD (2014, 2016) by Laplane and Mazzucato (2020)

Elizabeth Warren (D-Mass.) and Congresswoman Jan Schakowsky (D-Ill.) introduced the Affordable Drug Manufacturing Act. It was a public option in all but name: it would task the Department of Health and Human Services 'with the public manufacturing of generic drugs in cases where the market has failed and strengthens the generic market for the long term by jump-starting competition' (Warren 2018). Although the legislation did not progress beyond its introduction at the US Senate, the thinking behind the bill coincided with a broader, ongoing discussion about the crucial role of the state in pharmaceutical innovation in the United States and internationally, and inspired fresh thinking by lawmakers on the extent to which the state can play a more proactive part in the sector. In the United Kingdom, for example, the opposition Labour Party included the idea of a public-sector pharmaceutical company in its pharmaceutical policy, Medicines for the Many: Public Health before Private Profit, prior to the 2019 General Election. Discussions about expanding the roles of key public-sector institutions critical to biopharmaceutical innovation have along been circulating, amplified by the central role of publicly funded innovations in addressing emerging public health crises such as the Ebola outbreak (Herder, Graham, and Gold 2020) and antibiotic resistance (Singer, Kirchhelle, and Roberts 2019). Added to this, increasing interest in the importance of state-level manufacturing has been accentuated by real-world developments, most prominently the establishment of Civica Rx, a non-profit generic drug manufacturer that aims to ensure the affordable supply of essential medicines for over 120 health organizations in the United States. The public option concept provides a locus for the two strands of ideas and has set the scene for nascent policy and research efforts that examine pharmaceutical innovation and manufacturing in the context of industrial policy, and draws on empirical examples from around the world (Brown 2019).

2.6.2 *The Case for a Pharmaceutical Public Option: From Market-Fixing to Market-Shaping*

The case for a pharmaceutical public option is motivated both by theory and by practical concerns about the existing pharmaceutical sector, in which value creation by different actors are problematically attributed, as are the rewards of innovation. Through the lens of the entrepreneurial state introduced in the foregoing sections, the public option is about much more than simply fixing market failure; it is also about better enabling the state to develop transformative innovations – which it already does – and strengthening its capability to create value in the innovation system.

The public sector is a cornerstone of the pharmaceutical industry, often taking on the highest risk in the early stage of innovation. As described in Section 2.2, NIH is fundamental to biomedical science and early drug discovery, from early- through to late-stage development (Nayak, Avorn, and Kesselheim 2019). At the time of writing, the world is wrestling with the COVID-19 pandemic and in search of a coronavirus vaccine, and public investment once again forms the backbone of this crucial project. Since the 2002 SARS outbreak, NIH has spent $700 million on coronavirus R&D (Rizvi 2020). In addition, it is also a key to creating clusters that connect different actors in the innovation and manufacturing ecosystem with health system demand, thus shaping the pharmaceutical market across its entire value chain.

While the private sector is also crucial in bringing cutting edge medicines to the market, its entrenched short-termism and misalignment with public interest are equally striking (UCL Institute for Innovation and Public Purpose 2018). First, companies prioritize 'blockbusters' at the expense of commercially unappealing medicines that are hugely important to public health (Moon, Bermudez, and 't Hoen 2012). Second, the pricing of these medicines does not take into account the contribution made by other actors, including public institutions (Mazzucato and Roy 2018; Mazzucato 2018a). Third, patents are often abused, being too upstream, wide and strong (Mazzoleni and Nelson 1998), and high prices can persist even as generic competition kicks in, as a result of occasional cases of inefficient competition (Luo, Kesselheim, Greene, and Lipska 2017). Fourth, high prices are driven by, and in turn fuel, the over-financialization of parts of the industry, where share buybacks are outpacing R&D (Tulum and Lazonick 2018) These prices also lead to a drive to cut costs by outsourcing manufacturing capabilities overseas at the expense of local capacity (Pisano and Shih 2012).

Moreover, public investment has created significant private return with no effective guarantees for public return. In addition to generating knowledge spillovers, public investments have generated significant positive economic effects for the private sector. Public investment in biopharmaceutical science creates positive fiscal impact for the private sector by generating further investments ('crowding in') and substantial drug sales revenue. On the one hand, every £1 of public research expenditure is associated with an additional £0.87 to £1.07 of private sector R&D spent in the United Kingdom (Sussex et al. 2016). On the other hand, it is estimated that $10 million investment by the NIH leads to between $13.0 and $27.8 million in drug sales (Azoulay et al. 2018).

Therefore, given its fundamental role, the state should govern the drug innovation process more like a market-shaper: steering innovation, getting fair prices, ensuring that patents and competition work as intended, setting conditions for reinvestment, and safeguarding medicine supply. In other words, this is about finding a way to govern a system that is not working for members of the public, who have invested in some of the riskiest stages of drug development.

Policy instruments to capture public return described in the last section – including the examples of price capping, conditions on reinvestments, knowledge governance, tax reforms, and revenues beyond taxation – are all crucial to addressing the failings of the current system, but none of the above-mentioned can ensure public return in the form of direct provision. In this light, the pharmaceutical public option – government-provided, quality-assured medicines that are universally available at a reasonable and fixed price, which coexist with products from the private sector – can be a fresh approach to delivering public returns. Compared to these other forms of instruments, the pharmaceutical public option provides a more proactive means for the state to shape an industrial policy landscape that serves broader public interest in addition to the rights to health and access to medicines (UCL Commission for Mission-Oriented Innovation and Industrial Strategy 2019). First, having national manufacturing capabilities would be essential for protecting national security. The outsourcing of manufacturing capabilities has created vulnerability in the supply chain, which can lead to crippling shortages in quality-assured, essential medicines, especially at the times of need (US Department of Health and Human Services, Food and Drug Administration, Center for Drug Evaluation and Research, Center for Biologics Evaluation and Research 2020). Second, improving public-sector innovation and manufacturing capabilities can lead to greater national competitiveness. Building a strong, public-sector-led industrial commons would be critical in harbouring the innovation process essential to highly complex biopharmaceuticals such as biological, cell and gene therapies (Pisano and Shih 2012). Third, as argued by Sitaraman and Alstott (2019), having a yardstick pharmaceutical public option can help to establish more efficient market competition, which can be complicated or prevented by huge barriers to entry and market concentration. This can be addressed as the public option is introduced, along with transparent information on its R&D and manufacturing.

A pharmaceutical public option would require the government to be more directly involved in coordinating and executing the full range of activities in drug innovation and manufacturing. While more research is required in order to articulate the models of pharmaceutical public options and how they are best delivered in different country contexts, it is evident that the policy instrument would require government to be more directly involved in coordinating and executing the full range of activities in drug innovation and manufacturing, whatever the forms of implementation.

A degree of public ownership is necessary to allow government to retain a sufficient level of control to carry out those activities. Public ownership would equip the state with greater strategic control over long-term capital allocation and give it the resources to strengthen dynamic capability in the public sector (e.g. national laboratories and strategic agencies such as the Biomedical Advanced Research and Development Authority). Rather than micromanaging companies, public ownership needs to focus on delivering a public benefit for public investment, both in terms of achieving a public health-oriented direction of R&D, and ensuring the pricing of the resultant pharmaceuticals better reflects the public contribution and they are affordable. This is the very reason why the ex-chief economist of Goldman Sachs and former Chair of the Review on Antimicrobial

Resistance, Lord Jim O'Neill, recently called for nationalisation to help solve the crisis in antibiotics innovation (Smyth 2019). Although wholesale nationalization of the pharmaceutical industry is unlikely to neither be a realistic nor a productive approach, part-nationalization of certain pipelines that lie dormant in the private industry and are proving unresponsive to conventional market-fixing measures – antibiotics, for example – could turn out to be the only way to revive them. The next section will therefore discuss the role of public ownership in public option.

2.7 THE ROLE OF PUBLIC OWNERSHIP

The above-mentioned examples of direct forms of public returns – from the state-owning private equity to the public option – all imply some degree of public ownership. For many parts of the capitalist world, this may appear to be a significant anathema. However, the key purpose of those measures is not about the public sector taking over from the private sector – this is never part of the equation – but about building symbiotic, rather than parasitic, public–private relationships that deliver the best deals for all.

The prospect of the state owning a stake in a private corporation is not an unusual idea given that governments are already investing in the private sector. Because of that, they may as well earn a return on those investments (something even fiscal conservatives might find attractive). The state need not hold a controlling stake, but it could hold equity in the form of preferred stocks that are given priority for receiving dividends. The returns could be used to fund future innovation (Rodrik 2015). Politicians and the media have been too quick to criticize public investments when things go wrong, and too slow to reward them when things go right.

Public ownership, as an integral part of public option, is also sometimes associated with the concepts of nationalization and state-owned enterprises. In general, state-owned enterprises have been associated with various forms of wasteful inefficiencies. The accusations seem to have found confirmation in poor financial results. However, profits and losses, important as they are for the ability of a company to preserve its autonomy, are often misguiding indicators of efficiency. As argued in Section 2.4, behind government 'failures' are vast learning experiences. In addition, they can be the source of new organizational and technological capabilities, while fostering structural change in the economy at large. Several acclaimed cases of successful industrial development (e.g. Italy, South Korea, China, the Scandinavian countries, etc.) demonstrate that state-owned enterprises can become effective mechanisms for transformational policies when their activities are oriented towards industrial objectives and coordinated according to a systemic logic. In the South African economy, large state-owned companies, in the automotive sector in particular, have presided over fundamental technical capabilities accumulated through decades.

Thus, the design of a 'smart' industrial strategy, which combines a long-term general orientation towards societal missions with ordinary industrial commercial undertakings, will be of utmost importance. Also, rather than worrying so much about the 'picking winners' problem, more thinking is needed about how to realize the inherent opportunities in the systemic role of a state ownership portfolio to deliver overall returns: namely, how to reward the winning investments so they can both cover some of the eventual losses (which are inevitable in the innovation game), and also raise funds for future investments. This can be done by, first, getting the tax system to work, and, second, considering other mechanisms that allow the state to reap a direct reward in those cases when it is making specific bets on companies. If all fails, the taxpayer picks up the bill, but when it goes well, the taxpayer gets rewarded.

Going hand in hand with this consideration is the need to rethink how public investments are accounted for in the national income accounting. Investments in innovation are different to current expenditures. The latter does not add to balance-sheet assets; the former does and is potentially productive investment in the sense that it creates new value (Mazzucato and Shipman 2014). When setting limits to fiscal deficits, it is therefore necessary to distinguish public debt contracted for investment in R&D and infrastructure (value-creating investments) from public debt contracted for (public or private) consumption. In this sense, financial and accounting reforms should be regarded as a prerequisite for any successful smart and inclusive growth plan.

Finally, considering the role of government as lead risk-taker helps to debunk fundamental assumptions behind the *theory of shareholder value*, which has underpinned the exorbitant rewards earned by senior executives in recent years. Pay via stock options has been a key feature of modern capitalism, and a key driver of the inequality between the top one percent of income earners and the rest (Piketty 2014). Stock options are boosted when stock prices rise and prices often rise through 'financialised' practices such as share repurchase schemes by companies (Lazonick 2014). Focusing on boosting share prices is justified on the grounds of the theory of *shareholder value*, which holds that shareholders are the biggest risk-takers in a company, because they have no *guaranteed* rate of return (while workers earn set salaries, banks earn set interest rates, etc.). That is, they are the *residual claimants* (Jensen 1986), but this assumes that other agents do have a guaranteed rate of return. The financialization problem is part of what drives pharmaceutical companies away from R&D, as described in Section 2.6.

As we have argued throughout this chapter, precisely because what the state does is not just facilitate and de-risk the private sector, but also take major risks, there is no guarantee of success for its investments, which have historically also played a crucial role in enabling wealth creation. In the context of public option, public ownership is not only a direct and potentially effective tool for driving and orienting industrial and economic development, but also a crucial tool for safeguarding long-term value.

Without a patient long-term owner, companies could exist under a highly unsustainable governance that would favour the short-term interests of new shareholders over its various stakeholders and the economy at large. The fact that a key driver of inequality has been linked with a problematic understanding of which actors are the greatest risk-takers implies that combatting short-termism (Haldane 2016) and speculative forms of corporate governance (Kay 2012) requires not only reforming finance and corporate governance, but also rethinking the models of wealth creation upon which they are based (Lazonick and Mazzucato 2013).

2.8 CONCLUSION

The state as not only a market-fixer, but also – and especially – a market-maker and shaper, contributes to economic growth through the co-creation of value and hence a just division of rewards between public and private actors can be produced. Given the state's role as risk-taker and investor of first resort, new thinking is required for public institutions to not only share in the risks, but also the rewards. This can encourage new approaches to achieving growth that are not only 'smart' (innovation-led), but also more inclusive. In this context, public options, among other policy approaches that include elements of public ownership, provide a new venue for policy thinking to marry economic growth with societal missions.

REFERENCES

Arrow, K. (1962). Economic welfare and the allocation of resources for invention, In: Nelson, R. R., ed., *The Rate and Direction of Inventive Activity*. Princeton: Princeton University Press, pp. 609–626.

Audretsch, D. B. (2003). Standing on the shoulders of midgets: the US Small Business Innovation Research Program (SBIR). *Small Business Economics*, 20, pp. 129–135.

Avnimelech, G. (2009). *VC Policy: Yozma Program 15-years Perspective*. SSRN Scholarly Paper No. ID 2758195. Rochester, NY: Social Science Research Network. Available at: https://papers.ssrn.com/abstract=2758195.

Azoulay, P., Graff Zivin, J. S., Li, D., and Sampat, B. N. (2018). Public R&D investments and private-sector atenting: evidence from NIH funding rules. *The Review of Economic Studies*, 86(1), pp.117–152. Available at: https://academic.oup.com/restud/advance-article/doi/10.1093/restud/rdy034/5038510.

Block, F. and Keller, M. R. (2011). *Where Do Innovations Come From? Transformations in the US* Economy, 1970–2006. Working Papers in Technology Governance and Economic Dynamics No. 35, TUT Ragnar Nurkse School of Innovation and Governance.

Breznitz, D. and Ornston, D. (2013). The revolutionary power of peripheral agencies: explaining radical policy innovation in Finland and Israel. *Comparative Political Studies*, 46(10), pp. 1219–1245.

Brown, D. (2019). *Medicine for All: The Case for a Public Option in the Pharmaceutical Industry*. Available at: https://democracycollaborative.org/sites/default/files/2020-02/MedicineforAll_WEB%20%282%29.pdf.

Brumfiel, G. (2008). Bell Labs bottoms out. *Nature News*, 454(7207), pp. 927–927.

Buchanan, J. M. (2003). Public choice: the origins and development of a research program. *Champions of Freedom*, 31, pp. 13–32.
Buchanan, J. (2003). Public choice: politics without romance. [Article reprinted from Imprimis, March 2003.]. *Policy: A Journal of Public Policy and Ideas*, 19(3), pp. 13–18.
Buffet, W. E. (2011). Stop coddling the super-rich. *New York Times*. Available at: www.nytimes.com/2011/08/15/opinion/stop-coddling-the-super-rich.html (Accessed: 6 June 2016).
Coase, R. H. (1960). The problem of social cost. *Journal of Law & Economics*, 3(1), pp. 1–44.
Crouch, C. (2016). Paradoxes of privatisation and public-service outsourcing. In: Jacobs, M. and Mazzucato, M. eds., *Capitalism: Economics and Policy for Sustainable and Inclusive Growth*. Chicester, West Sussex, United Kingdom: Wiley Blackwell.
Davis, M. and Arno, P. (2001). Why don't we enforce existing drug price controls?: the unrecognized and unenforced reasonable pricing requirements imposed upon patents deriving in whole or in part from federally funded research. *Tulane Law Review*, 75(3), pp. 631–694.
Eliasson, G. (2017). *Visible Costs and Invisible Benefits: Military Procurement as Innovation Policy*. New York: Springer.
Enke, S. (1967). Government-industry development of a commercial supersonic transport. *The American Economic Review*, 57(2), pp. 71–79.
Erlich, Y. (2002). *The Yozma Program – Policy and Success Factors*. Presentation delivered at the 19th session of the Working Party on Small and Medium-Sized Enterprise and Entrepreneurship, Paris, OECD.
Evans, P. B. (1995). *Embedded Autonomy: States and Industrial Transformation*. Princeton: Princeton University Press.
Falck, O., Gollier, C., and Woessmann, L. (2011). Arguments for and against policies to promote national champions. In: O. Falck, C. Gollier and L. Woessmann, eds., *Industrial Policy for National Champions*. Cambridge, MA: MIT Press, pp. 3–9.
Foray, D., Mowery, D., and Nelson, R. R. (2012). Public R&D and social challenges: what lessons from mission R&D programs?. *Research Policy*, 41(10), pp. 1697–1902.
Friedman, B. M. (1979). Crowding out or crowding in? The economic consequences of financing government deficits. *Brookings Papers on Economic Activity*, 3, pp. 593–654.
Frischmann, B. and Lemley, M. (2007). Spillovers. *Columbia Law Review*, 107(1), pp. 257–301.
Haldane, A. (2016). 'The costs of short-termism. In: Jacobs, M. and Mazzucato, M., eds., *Capitalism: Economics and Policy for Sustainable and Inclusive Growth*. Chicester, West Sussex, United Kingdom: Wiley Blackwell.
Henry, C. and Stiglitz, J. (2010). Intellectual property, dissemination of innovation and sustainable development. *Global Policy*, 1(3), pp. 237–251.
Herder, M., Graham, J. E., and Gold, R. (2020). From discovery to delivery: public sector development of the rVSV-ZEBOV Ebola vaccine. *Journal of Law Biosciences*, Available at: https://academic.oup.com/jlb/advance-article/doi/10.1093/jlb/lsz019/5706941.
Jensen, M. (1986). Agency costs of free cash flow, corporate finance and takeovers. *American Economic Review*, 76(2), pp. 323–329.
Johnston, D. C. (2014). How Google and Apple make their taxes disappear. *Newsweek*. Available at: www.newsweek.com/2014/12/26/how-google-and-apple-make-their-taxes-disappear-291571.html (Accessed: 2 February 2016).
Jones, D. S. (2014). *Masters of the Universe: Hayek, Friedman and the Birth of Neoliberal Politics*. Princeton: Princeton University Press.
Judt, T. (2011). *Ill Fares the Land: A Treatise on our Present Discontents*. London: Penguin.

Kaivanto, K. and Stoneman, P. (2007). Public provision of sales contingent claims backed finance to SMEs: a policy alternative. *Research Policy*, 36(5), pp. 637–651.

Kay, J. (2012). *The Kay Review of UK Equity Markets and Long-term Decision Making Final Report*. Available at: https://assets.publishing.service.gov.uk/government/uploads/system/uploads/attachment_data/file/253454/bis-12–917-kay-review-of-equity-markets-final-report.pdf.

Kattel, R. and Mazzucato, M. (2018). Mission-oriented innovation policy and dynamic capabilities in the public sector. *Industrial and Corporate Change*, 27(5), pp. 787–801. Available at: https://academic.oup.com/icc/article/27/5/787/5089909

Keller, M. R. and Block, F. (2013). Explaining the transformation in the US innovation system: the impact of a small government program. *Socio-Economic Review*, 11(4), pp. 629–656.

Kempf, R. (1995). Exploitation of rights from the US space program by NASA (presented by B. Gimeno) (vol. 378, p. 27). Intellectual Property Rights and Space Activities.

Korn, D. and Heinig, S. (2004). Recoupment efforts threaten federal research. *Issues in Science and Technology*, 20(4), pp. 26–30.

Krueger, A. O. (1974). The political economy of the rent-seeking society. *American Economic Review*, 64(3), pp. 291–303.

Laplane, A. and Mazzucato, M. (2020). Socialising the risks and rewards of public investments: economic, policy and legal issues. *Research Policy* (forthcoming).

Lazonick, W. (2014). Profits without prosperity: stock buybacks manipulate the market and leave most Americans worse off. *Harvard Business Review*, September, pp. 46–55.

Lazonick, W. and Mazzucato, M. (2013). The risk-reward nexus in the innovation-inequality relationship: who takes the risks? Who gets the rewards? *Industrial and Corporate Change*, 22(4), pp. 1093–1128.

Lazonick, W. and Tulum, Ö. (2011). US biopharmaceutical finance and the sustainability of the biotech business model. *Research Policy*, 40(9), pp. 1170–1187.

Lerner, J. (2010). The future of public efforts to boost entrepreneurship and venture capital. *Small Business Economics*, 35(3), pp. 255–264.

Luo. J., Kesselheim, A. S., Greene, J., and Lipska, K. J. (2017). Strategies to improve the affordability of insulin in the USA. *Lancet Diabetes Endocrinology*, 5(3), pp. 158–159. Available at: https://pubmed.ncbi.nlm.nih.gov/28189654/.

Mazzoleni, R. and Nelson, R. (1998). The benefit and costs of strong patent protection: a contribution to the current debate. *Research Policy*, 27, pp. 273–284.

Mazzucato, M. (2013). *The Entrepreneurial State: Debunking the Public vs. Private Myth in Risk and Innovation*. London: Anthem Press.

Mazzucato, M. (2016). From market fixing to market-creating: a new framework for innovation policy. *Industry and Innovation*, 23(2), pp. 140–156.

Mazzucato, M. (2017). *Mission-Oriented Innovation Policy: Challenges and Opportunities*. UCL Institute for Innovation and Public Purpose Working Paper, 2017 (1).

Mazzucato, M. (2018a). *The Value of Everything: Making and Taking in the Global Economy*. London: Penguin-Allen Lane.

Mazzucato, M. (2018b). Mission-oriented Research and Innovation in the EU: a Problem-solving Approach to Fuel Innovation-led Growth. Directorate-General for Research and Innovation, European Commission. Available at: https://publications.europa.eu/en/publication-detail/-/publication/5b2811d1-16be-11e8-9253-01aa75ed71a1/language-en.

Mazzucato, M. and Penna, C. (2016). Beyond market failures: the market creating and shaping roles of state investment banks. *Journal of Economic Policy Reform*, 19(4), pp. 305–326. DOI: https://doi.org/10.1080/17487870.2016.1216416.

Mazzucato, M. and Roy, V. (2018). Rethinking value in health innovation: from mystifications towards prescriptions. *Journal of Economic Policy Reform*, 22(2) pp. 101–119. DOI: https://doi.org/10.1080/17487870.2018.1509712
Mazzucato, M. and Semieniuk, G. (2016). Financing renewable energy: who is financing what and why it matters. *Technological Forecasting and Structural Change*, 127, pp. 8–22. DOI: https://doi.org/10.1016/j.techfore.2017.05.021.
Mazzucato, M. and Shipman, A. (2014). Accounting for productive investment and value creation. *Industrial and Corporate Change*, 23, pp. 1059–1085.
Moon, S., Bermudez, J., and 't Hoen, E. (2012). Innovation and access to medicines for neglected populations: could a treaty address a broken pharmaceutical R&D system? *PLoS Med* 9(5), e1001218. DOI: https://doi.org/10.1371/journal.pmed.1001218.
Motta, M. (2004). *Competition Policy: Theory and Practice*. Cambridge University Press.
Mowery, D. (2009). What does economic theory tell us about mission-oriented R&D? In: Foray, D., ed., *The New Economics of Technology Policy*. Cheltenham, UK/Northampton, MA, USA: Edward Elgar Publishing, pp. 131–147.
Mowery, D. C. (2010). Military R&D and innovation. In: Hall, B. N. and Rosenberg, N., eds., *Handbook of the Economics of Innovation*, 2, pp.1219–1256.
Nayak, R. K., Avorn, J., and Kesselheim, A. S. (2019). Public sector financial support for late stage discovery of new drugs in the United States: Cohort study. *BMJ*, 367, l5766. Available at: www.bmj.com/content/367/bmj.l5766.
Nelson, R. (1959). The simple economics of basic scientific research. *Journal of Political Economy*, 67(3), pp. 297–306.
Nelson, R. R. and Winter, S. G. (1982). *An Evolutionary Theory of Economic Change*. Cambridge, MA: Belknap Press.
OECD (2014). *OECD Science, Technology and Industry Outlook 2014*. Paris: OECD.
OECD (2016). *OECD Science, Technology and Innovation Outlook 2016*. Paris: OECD.
Owen, G. (2012). Industrial policy in Europe since the Second World War: what has been learnt?. LSE ECIPE Occasional Paper 1. Brussels, Belgium: European Centre for International Political Economy. Available at: http://eprints.lse.ac.uk/41902/1/Industrial_policy_in_Europe_since_the__Second_World_War_what_has_been_learnt%28lsero%29.pdf (Accessed: 5 July 2016).
Phelps, E. S. (2013). *Mass Flourishing: How Grassroots Innovation Created Jobs, Challenge and Change*. Princeton: Princeton University Press.
Piketty, T. (2014). *Capital in the Twenty-First Century*. Cambridge, MA: Harvard University Press.
Pisano, G. P. and Shih, W. C. (2012). *Producing Prosperity: Why America Needs a Manufacturing Renaissance*. Boston, MA: Harvard Business Review Press.
Polanyi, K. (1944). *The Great Transformation: The Political and Economic Origins of Our Time*, 2001 edition. Boston: Beacon Press.
Reichman, J. (2009). Compulsory licensing of patented pharmaceutical inventions: evaluating the options. *Journal of Law, Medicine & Ethics*, 37(2), pp. 247–263.
Rizvi, Z. (2020). *Blind Spot: How the COVID-19 Outbreak Shows the Limits of Pharma's Monopoly Model*. Public Citizen. Available at: www.citizen.org/article/blind-spot/.
Rodrik, D. (2015). From welfare state to innovation state. Project Syndicate. www.project-syndicate.org/commentary/labor-saving-technology-by-dani-rodrik-2015–01 (Accessed: 9 June 2016).
Ruttan, V. (2006). *Is War Necessary for Economic Growth? Military Procurement and Technology Development*. Department of Applied Economics, University of Minnesota.
Sampat, B. and Lichtenberg, F. (2011). What are the respective roles of the public and private sectors in pharmaceutical innovation? *Health Affairs*, 30(2), pp. 332–339.

Singer, A. C., Kirchhelle, C., and Roberts, A. P. (2019). (Inter)nationalising the antibiotic research and development pipeline. *Lancet Infectious Diseases*, 20(2). Available at: www.sciencedirect.com/science/article/pii/S1473309919305523.

Sitaraman, G. and Alstott, A. L. (2019). *The Public Option: How to Expand Freedom, Increase Opportunity and Promote Equality*. Harvard University Press.

Smith (1776). *The Wealth of Nations*, 1937 edition. New York: Modern Library.

Smyth, C. (2019). Nationalise drug research to fight superbugs, urges expert. *The Times*. Available at: www.thetimes.co.uk/article/nationalise-drug-research-to-fight-superbugs-urges-expert-c7b8l3c3b.

Stern, N. (2007). *The Economics of Climate Change: The Stern Review*. Cambridge: Cambridge University Press

Stevens, A. J., Jensen, J. J., Wyller, K. Kilgore, P. C., Chatterjee, S., and Rohrbaugh, M. L. (2011). The role of public-sector research in the discovery of drugs and vaccines. *New England Journal of Medicine*, 364(6), pp. 535–541. Available at: www.nejm.org/doi/abs/10.1056/NEJMsa1008268.

Stiglitz, J. (1974). Growth with exhaustible natural resources: the competitive economy. *Review of Economic Studies*, 41(5), pp. 139–152.

Stiglitz, J. (2017). America has a monopoly problem – and it's huge. *The Nation*. Available at www.thenation.com/article/america-has-a-monopoly-problem-and-its-huge.

Stiglitz, J. E. (2012). *The Price of Inequality: How Today's Divided Society Endangers Our Future*. New York: Norton.

Stiglitz, J. and Weiss, A. (1981). Credit rationing in markets with imperfect information. *American Economic Review*, 3(71), pp. 393–410.

Sussex, J., Feng, Y., Mestre-Ferrandiz, J., Pistollato, M., Hafner, M., Burridge, P. et al. (2016). Quantifying the economic impact of government and charity funding of medical research on private research and development funding in the United Kingdom. *BMC Medicine*, 14 (1), p. 32. Available at: www.biomedcentral.com/1741–7015/14/32.

Trembath, A., Nordhaus, T., Shellenberger, M., and Jenkins, J. (2012). US government role in shale gas fracking history. Breakthrough Institute Report. Available at: https://thebreakthrough.org/articles/us-government-role-in-shale-gas-fracking-history-an-overview.

Tullock, G., Seldon, A., and Brady, G. L. (2002). *Government Failure: A Primer in Public Choice*. Washington, DC: Cato Institute.

Tulum, Ö. and Lazonick W. (2018). Financialized corporations in a national innovation system: the US pharmaceutical industry. *International Journal of Political Economy*, 47 (3–4), pp. 281–316. DOI: https://doi.org/10.1080/08911916.2018.1549842.

UCL Commission for Mission-Oriented Innovation and Industrial Strategy (MOIIS). (2019). *A Mission-oriented UK Industrial Strategy*. Available at: www.ucl.ac.uk/bartlett/public-purpose/sites/public-purpose/files/190515_iipp_report_moiis_final_artwork_digital_export.pdf.

UCL Institute for Innovation and Public Purpose. (2018). *The People's Prescription: Re-imagining Health Innovation to Deliver Public Value*. IIPP Policy Report. IIPP, Global Justice Now, Just Treatment and STOPAIDS. Available at: www.ucl.ac.uk/bartlett/public-purpose/sites/public-purpose/files/peoples_prescription_report_final_online.pdf.

US Department of Health and Human Services, Food and Drug Administration, Center for Drug Evaluation and Research, Center for Biologics Evaluation and Research. (2020). Notifying FDA of a Permanent Discontinuance or Interruption in Manufacturing Under Section 506 C of the FD & C Act Guidance for Industry Notifying FDA of a Permanent Discontinuance or Interruption in Manufacturing Under Section 506 C of the FD & C Act. Available at: www.fda.gov/media/136486/download?utm_campaign=FDA Releases Guidance for Industry on Notifying the Agency of Permanent Discontinuance

Vallas, S. P., Kleinman, D. L., and Biscotti, D. (2011). Political structures and the making of US Biotechnology. In: Block, F. and Keller, M. R. eds., *State of Innovation: The US Government's Role in Technology Development*. Boulder, CO: Paradigm, pp. 57–76.

Vieira, A. and Alvares, J. (2017). *Acordos de Compensação Tecnológica (Offset): Teoria e pratica na experiencia brasileira*. Rio de Janeiro: Lumen Juris.

Warren E. (2018). Text: S.3775 – 115th Congress (2017–2018): Affordable Drug Manufacturing Act of 2018.

Windus, M. and Schiffel, D. (1976). Recoupment of R&D expenditures: issues and practices in the USA. *Research Policy*, 5(2), pp. 180–196.

Wolf, C. (1988). *Markets or Governments: Choosing Between Imperfect Alternatives*. Cambridge, MA: MIT Press.

Wood, R. (2012). Fallen Solyndra won bankruptcy battle but faces tax war. Forbes. Available at: www.forbes.com/sites/robertwood/2012/11/06/fallen-solyndra-won-bankruptcy-battle-but-faces-tax-war (Accessed: 29 January 2013).

3

Challenges in Designing Equitable Public Options

Anne Alstott and Ganesh Sitaraman[1]

One of the aspirations of a public option is to expand equality and opportunity by offering universal access to a good or service at an affordable price.[2] But in practice, public options are not always equitable and inclusive, and people of color, the poor, the less-educated, and rural residents are often on the losing end. Policymakers who want public options to live up to the promise of expanding equality and opportunity therefore need to think seriously about the challenges that prevent public options from achieving those aims. Some of these challenges stem from the structure of the public options themselves, which can be designed in ways that advance or constrict equality and opportunity. Others will require broader reforms to politics and the allocation of power. Understanding the broader context is essential in designing public options that can advance inclusionary goals.

In this chapter, we identify six challenges in designing equitable public options. The elements on our list are not mutually exclusive; barriers to equity are often compounded, with two or more operating at the same time within the same area of public policy. Nor is our list of six exhaustive; we make no claim that these are the only challenges to designing equitable public options. But we hope that this list can be a starting point for policymakers and scholars to anticipate the factors that prevent public options from being equity-enhancing and, as a result, to develop solutions.

3.1 CHALLENGE 1: RACISM

Racist ideas, norms, and practices uphold racist policies and institutions. Any public option, like any public policy, can be racist – but they can also be designed to be deliberately anti-racist.[3]

1 Thanks to K. Sabeel Rahman and Joelle Gamble for helpful comments and suggestions.

2 Ganesh Sitaraman & Anne L. Alstott, The Public Option: How to Expand Freedom, Increase Opportunity, and Promote Equality (2019).

3 Ibram X. Kendi, How to be an Antiracist (2019).

The United States has a long history of racist public policies, including some public options. Some public options have failed to advance equity goals because of de jure racism. In the Jim Crow South, state laws prevented equal access to common carriers and public accommodations.[4] "Separate but equal" was anything but, and a variety of public options – buses, railroad cars, public schools, public water fountains – were subjected to two-tiered systems by race. After decades of segregation within public options, the Civil Rights Act of 1964 prohibited discrimination in public facilities and public schools.[5]

Housing policy in the mid-twentieth century was also defined by racist laws. Federal programs were designed to expand middle class homeownership, including by insuring mortgages and subsidizing builders. But as Richard Rothstein has documented, the Home Owners Loan Corporation, Federal Housing Administration, and Veterans Administration mapped black neighborhoods as "risky," a process called redlining, and ultimately excluded them from federal insurance programs. Homebuilders, subsidized by federal tax and highway policies, were also producing subdivisions of new homes – so long as they were not sold to black people.[6] The Fair Housing Act sought to remedy these laws and practices, but the legacy of redlining remains even today.[7]

These are just a few instances of the racism that has been toxic for both people of color and society writ-large.[8] To take one further example of the community destruction involved, consider the history of public recreation. After the civil rights laws were passed, many communities destroyed public options – like draining public swimming pools – rather than allow them to integrate. Parks, recreation centers, even zoos were shuttered because of racism, harming both white and black members of these communities.

The creation of public options for some people (often, privileged and white) has also come at the direct expense of others (typically, marginalized and nonwhite). For example, America's land grant colleges expanded opportunity for many people since their founding in the late nineteenth century. The federal government allocated public lands to states, with the proceeds of sales of those lands going to the colleges. The acquisition of these lands, however, was part of the federal government's policy of conquest of Native Americans and seizure of their lands.[9] Equality and opportunity for some was achieved at the cost of misery and subjugation for others.

4 A. K. Sandoval-Strausz, Travelers, Strangers, and Jim Crow: Law, Public Accommodations, and Civil Rights in America, 23 L. & Hist. Rev. 53 (2005).

5 See, e.g., *Katzenbach* v. *McClung*, 379 U.S. 294, 298–99 (1964) (upholding Congress's power to ban racial discrimination in restaurants).

6 Richard Rothstein, The Color of Law: A Forgotten History of How Our Government Segregated America (2017).

7 Kriston Capps & Kate Rabinowitz, How the Fair Housing Act Failed Black Homeowners, CityLab, April 11, 2018, www.citylab.com/equity/2018/04/how-the-fair-housing-act-failed-black-homeowners/557576/

8 Heather McGhee, Racism has a Cost for Everyone, TEDWomen 2019, www.ted.com/talks/heather_c_mcghee_racism_has_a_cost_for_everyone/transcript?language=en.

9 Margaret Nash, Entangled Pasts: Land-Grant Colleges and American Indian Dispossession, 59 Hist. Ed. Q. 437 (2019).

Racist policies are not always written directly into law, of course. Racist lawmakers have often drafted laws that are racially neutral on their face, even though the law's design will disproportionately harm people of color. The original design of Social Security provides one example. In order to pass the landmark baseline public option, the Roosevelt Administration had to compromise with southern segregationist Democrats in Congress. Law did not exclude people by race explicitly, but it excluded agricultural and domestic workers, many of whom were black.[10]

Other seemingly neutral policies – like stimulus spending – can also exacerbate racial inequalities. As Professor Olatunde Johnson has argued, federal spending programs with massive scale can produce and reproduce racial inequality if they are not designed to "impose explicit inclusionary norms."[11] For example, the American Recovery and Reinvestment Act of 2009 included funding for initiatives ranging from highways and low-income housing to education. Some of these programs, like K-12 education funding, deliberately seek to advance racial equity. Others, including low-income housing tax credits, do not include affirmative policies to advance inclusion. The consequence, Johnson argues, is that this flow of these funds can end up reproducing the racially unequal baselines that currently exist.

Early evidence suggests that the 2020 pandemic relief program reflects the dynamic Johnson identifies. Relief efforts that disproportionately benefit large businesses rather than smaller ones and individuals are likely to direct aid disproportionately to white-owned businesses. The Paycheck Protection Program, for instance, provided forgiveable loans to businesses but did not make inclusion a priority. The program utilized a complex and decentralized structure, requiring businesses to apply to private lenders for public loans, and did not set priorities for lending or track demographic data. An early survey suggests that minority-owned businesses received little help from the program.[12]

The physical design and layout of transit, bridges, and other infrastructure can also be indirectly designed to exclude populations, rather than enhance equity. Across the country, wealthier white neighborhoods have objected to public transit stops, with a motivation of keeping people of color away. Highways have been located to divide communities by race; bridges built so low that buses cannot pass – restricting access to areas by people who don't have private transportation. Each of these modes of "architectural exclusion," as Sarah Schindler has called them, operates in an indirect way to render public options less equitable.[13]

10 Jill Quadagno, The Color of Welfare (1996); Ira Katznelson, Fear Itself: The New Deal and the Origins of Our Time (2013).

11 Olatunde C. A. Johnson, Stimulus and Civil Rights, 111 Colum. L. Rev. 154, 160 (2011).

12 Khristopher J. Brooks, Few Minority Business Owners Got Paycheck Protection Program Loans, Survey Shows, CBS News Moneywatch, May 20, 2020.

13 Sarah Schindler, Architectural Exclusion: Discrimination and Segregation through Physical Design of the Built Environment, 124 Yale L. J. 1836 (2015).

De facto racism can also undermine public options. Public swimming pools are a good case. In the early twentieth century, public swimming pools became segregated by race – not necessarily by law, but by force. Intimidation and violence segregated pools, as Jeff Wiltse has noted in his history of this public option.[14]

De facto racism has also skewed the impact of two critical public options – public housing and public education. As we discuss in *The Public Option*, public housing has been an important source of decent and affordable housing for many Americans. But the program has been vilified in racialized terms as the locus of gangs and crime, and the location of public housing projects in minority neighborhoods has too often reinforced patterns of housing segregation.[15]

Public schools have also been a focal point for racism. Both Southern and Northern communities fought racial integration in the schools. Today, de jure racial segregation is outlawed, but de facto segregation remains a powerful force, because school districts map onto segregated neighborhoods, and political boundaries function to isolate (poorer and minority) city districts from (richer and whiter) suburbs.[16] Economist Raj Chetty and his coauthors have shown that residential segregation and other factors are correlated with economic opportunity: segregated areas have lower intergenerational mobility.[17]

In many cases, public options have failed to live up to the aspiration of expanding freedom and equality because of background social conditions. But race has also been deliberately used – explicitly or implicitly – to make public provision of goods and services more difficult to achieve and sustain. Racism has long been used as a divide-and-conquer strategy to prevent economic policies that would help working-class Americans.[18] Racist dog-whistles have served the same function, as neutral-sounding narratives like the "undeserving poor" place racially inflected pressure on public options, creating a wedge between users and nonusers and degrading the quality of public options.[19]

In a context of pervasive, overt, and legal racism, it may seem difficult to see how design can address these underlying problems. But policymakers can make design choices that make public options more equitable; policies must – and can – be designed to anticipate the racists and holdouts who will seek to defend their privilege and undermine the full potential of public options.

14 Jeff Wiltse, Contested Waters: A Social History of Swimming Pools in America (2007).

15 Sitaraman & Alstott, The Public Option, at 119–128.

16 Id. at 113–119.

17 Raj Chetty et al., Where is the Land of Opportunity? The Geography of Intergenerational Mobility in the United States, 129 Quarterly J. Econ. 1553 (2014).

18 Martin Luther King, Jr., Address at the Conclusion of the Selma to Montgomery March, March 25, 1965.

19 Ian Haney-Lopez, Dog-Whistle Politics: How Coded Racial Appeals Have Reinvented Racism and Wrecked the Middle Class (2013); Michael Katz, The Undeserving Poor: America's Enduring Confrontation with Poverty (2nd ed. 2013).

3.2 CHALLENGE 2: SECOND-CLASS PUBLIC OPTIONS?

One of the central features of public options is that they coexist with private options. Competitive public options offer effectively the same service as a private option and compete with the private option. Baseline public options provide a universal service to everyone but coexist with the private option in the sense that people may top up the basic good or service by buying more from a private provider. One of the consequences of competition is that overall social provision of the goods or services in question might end up as a two-tiered system, in which the public option is of lower quality or has a different population using it than private options. For example, in some cities, the public transportation system is used primarily by poorer residents without cars, while in other places, public transit is widely used by all social classes.

Selection effects like these can set in motion a set of dynamics that can undermine the public option in a hurry. If richer or more privileged people opt out of the public option, the result could be that the public option might not provide the same level of service or opportunity. Users of the private option might withhold their support for investing in the public option, and multiple tiers of provision can create or entrench racial and class segregation.

Policymakers must therefore anticipate selection effects that can lead to two-tier provision and think about ways around that problem. The first and most important design point is that there is a category of goods for which a competitive public option is unlikely to be the right policy choice, and the better policy is either a regulated (private) monopoly or exclusive public provision. The heartland of this category is network infrastructure, in which we want to ensure universal access at an affordable price and where financing has historically involved cross-subsidies.

The post office provides a good example. It is more expensive to send a letter from Manhattan to rural Montana than it is to send it down the street. But the price of a stamp is the same in either case. In essence, a mandate of universal service at regulated prices sets up a cross-subsidy, in which high volume and profit routes are subsidizing lower volume and profit routes. Part of the purpose of this system – which is a common feature of regulated network industries including transportation and telecommunications – is to ensure access across America's expansive geography while making the system more resilient from political attacks. These systems usually include an exclusive franchise. The post office, for example, has had a monopoly over letter delivery since its earliest years. The reason for monopoly power is simple: if private competition was allowed, the private market would capture the highest-profit routes and ignore the lower-profit routes. The result would be extremely high cost of mail service in rural areas – and likely collapse of that service. Indeed, with the shift in the 1970s and early 1980s from a regulated system based on cross-subsidies to a deregulated private marketplace for airlines, buses, and trucking, this is precisely what happened.[20]

[20] See, e.g., Ganesh Sitaraman, Morgan Ricks, and Christopher Serkin, Regulation and the Geography of Inequality, Duke L. J. (forthcoming).

A related problem of selection occurs in health insurance. The most profitable population to insure are young, healthy people because they pay premiums, but do not (on average) consume much health care. People who are older and sicker are likely to consume more health care, thereby reducing the profits for insurance companies. Ideally, in a large pool, these populations offset each other – effectively producing a cross-subsidy akin to that in letters or air-transportation. But insurance companies still have an incentive to exclude sick people, such as those with preexisting conditions, from coverage or to deny coverage to policyholders who need it. One solution would be to have a system of private insurance, in which companies are regulated akin to network industries – for rates, service, and access. The Affordable Care Act thus mandated offering insurance even in the case of preexisting conditions. Another solution is a baseline public option – like Medicare for All – which would place everyone in the same insurance pool. This would prevent private insurance from cream-skimming the healthiest people and leaving the sickest to taxpayers. A universal pool – exclusive public provision – incorporates the cross-subsidy idea that is at the heart of insurance.

In addition to cases where financing is tied to cross-subsidies, a second design consideration will be whether there is likely to be degradation in the service quality of the public option compared to the private one. And that, in turn, depends primarily on the political power of the users. Users with political power can use that power to get better funding and maintain higher quality public options. Public golf courses, for example, are used by comparatively wealthy and well-connected people. Public playgrounds and parks might be sited in wealthy areas because residents in those areas have political connections, and might not get sited in communities that have historically wielded less influence over politicians. As in other arenas, discrete groups are also often able to organize and exercise political power to benefit themselves.[21]

Part of combating these unequal power dynamics is to design public options in a way that expands political voice and builds political support for equitable public options. If usage rates of the public option are extremely high – for example, universal provision – then some degree of selection out of the public option into the private option might not matter much. High usage can create a political constituency that is committed to the public option and will advocate for its continued funding and for efforts to improve it. The elderly's ability to preserve Social Security is one good example.[22]

Whether public options have high usage rates, including a broad composition of users will partly depend on politics itself, and the structure of the program will in turn shape politics. Professor Suzanne Mettler has shown, for example, that the GI Bill affected veterans' political participation. But it did so differently among white

[21] Cf. Bruce Ackerman, Beyond Carolene Products, 98 Harv. L. Rev. 713 (1985).

[22] See, e.g., Andrea Louise Campbell, How Politics Make Citizens: Senior Political Activism and the American Welfare State (2003).

and black veterans, who experienced benefits differently. White veterans became more active in political and fraternal organizations, while black GI Bill veterans mobilized more to change political structures.[23] Political scientists have also shown that these "policy feedback loops" – policy choices that influence public engagement – can be used strategically as a political weapon to build or break support for specific policies. Conservative organizations' advocacy for anti-union legislation at the state level, for example, contributed to a decline in the strength in public sector unions, which had feedback effects on the unions' political power – and the political power of the workers they represented.[24] Policymakers should design public options in a way that accounts for feedback loops in order to prevent second-class service.

3.3 CHALLENGE 3: NECESSARY AND SUFFICIENT GOODS

Whether a public option advances equity also depends on whether access to a good or service at a reasonable price, is sufficient to achieve equity or whether, instead, it is one input (among others) toward equity. For example, clean drinking water is a sufficient good; as long as a person has access to healthy tap water, that will be sufficient to keep them hydrated. Not having access to expensive, bottled spring water is not significant, except perhaps as a matter of class stratification or signaling. For a sufficient good, the public option by itself can expand equality and access. Of course, a public option can simply fail, as in the case of the lead-tainted drinking water in Flint, Michigan. But in places where the public option provides clean water, the water itself is sufficient to ensure equity.

What is sufficient may change over time, of course, based on social needs, commercial development, and technological advances. For example, access to low-speed dial-up Internet might have been a sufficient good in the late 1990s, but in the early 2020s, high-speed broadband and wireless connectivity are essential.

In other situations, a public option may be necessary and helpful, but not sufficient. For example, even an important public good, like free K-12 public education, will not be sufficient to guarantee equity if some students cannot fully benefit from the education because of hunger or homelessness (just to take two examples). For these children, a free K-12 education is necessary but not sufficient, and the public option needs to be supplemented or even reconceived to bundle wraparound services like meals, housing assistance, and more. Or consider the GI Bill. After World War II, GI Bill benefits provided a college tuition benefit that was instrumental in building the white middle class. Although GI Bill benefits were formally available to black soldiers as well, segregation in higher education was a barrier that restricted opportunity. Financial access to higher education, without

23 Suzanne Mettler, 'The Only Good Thing was the G.I. Bill': Effects of the Education and Training Provisions on African-American Veterans' Political Participation, 19 Stud. Am. Pol. Dev. 31 (2005).

24 Alexander Hertel-Fernandez, Policy Feedback as Political Weapon: Conservative Advocacy and the Demobilization of the Public Sector Labor Movement, 16 Perspect. Polit. 364 (2018).

equal access to colleges and universities, was one of the reasons the GI Bill did not achieve the promise of being an equitable public option.

More generally, any public option may be inadequate when one-size-fits-all cannot achieve a meaningful degree of equity. All kids start with different levels of capacity, talent, home support, and opportunities. Children with disabilities, for example, may require very particular supports or accommodations in order to learn. As a result, offering access to a standardized public option for education is unlikely to be sufficient to accomplish the aim of advancing equality and opportunity. Federal special education law now offers a public option that takes the approach of targeted universalism. Different policies may be required (the targeted part) to ensure that all groups reach the public policy goals (the universal part).[25]

3.4 CHALLENGE 4: COMPLEXITY AS A BARRIER TO EQUITY

Any law or government program (or private sector product, for that matter) can be designed and administered in a way that is simple and easy to use – or extremely complicated. Simple designs and simple administration are likely to be more equitable, though it is perhaps not obvious that they would be. A complicated policy might be perfectly tailored to help every population and sub-population with precisely the service they need. But the problem is that a complicated policy is often harder for people to use. Increased paperwork, bureaucracy, and multiple steps to access a good or service may make it harder for anyone – and especially those without wealth or copious amounts of free time – to navigate program complexity and bureaucratic red tape. Simple designs and simple administration are likely to be more equitable.

Consider a few examples, starting with the Earned Income Tax Credit. Despite generally being considered a successful anti-poverty program, the EITC has complex rules including a filing requirement, an income test, a work (wages) test, and a non-intuitive definition of "child."[26] In part because of this complexity, many eligible people do not claim the EITC. For instance, in California alone, lower-income people fail to claim more than $2 billion per year in federal and state EITC payments. Non-profit organizations like CalEITC4Me have therefore sprung up to educate people on navigating tax policy in order to claim the credit.[27] Moreover, the complexity of the (federal and state) EITC programs has benefitted the private sector, as H&R Block and other commercial firms have captured the market for EITC recipients. In 2010, for instance, a majority of low-income tax filers used a paid preparer; only a tiny percentage relied on IRS help or volunteer income tax assistance programs.[28]

25 John A. Powell, Post-Racialism or Targeted Universalism?, 86 Denv. U. L. Rev. 785 (2009).
26 I.R.C. Section 32.
27 CalEITC4Me, About Us, caleitc4me.org/about-us/ (accessed May 3, 2020).
28 Tax Policy Center, Why Do Low-Income Families Use Tax Preparers? www.taxpolicycenter.org/briefing-book/why-do-low-income-families-use-tax-preparers

The irony, then, is that program complexity can undermine equitable access while enriching the private sector – and thereby creating a constituency that favors complexity. In California, Intuit (the large company that markets TurboTax) and H&R Block, among others, lobbied against and helped defeat a government initiative that would have provided free, already-prepared tax returns to Californians.[29] Intuit and other private tax preparers agreed to offer free filing for low-income taxpayers – but then proceeded to hide the free programs and upsell customers to paid options.[30]

Tax-based policies for savings (including individual retirement accounts, 401(k) programs, 529 college accounts, and health savings accounts) also illustrate how complex rules can undermine equity. One commentator puts it well, "Instead of making retirement benefits more generous, or college cheaper, or health care universal, we've created accounts upon accounts, each of which you have to have enough money to contribute to, remember to pay into, and jump through all sorts of other hoops to maintain."[31] Those who have the ability to jump through these hoops are more likely to be wealthy and more educated.

And program complexity can provide cover for other inequitable features. These tax-based savings subsidies, for instance, appear to provide an equal benefit to everyone: any taxpayer who makes a qualifying contribution can take a tax deduction. That sounds fair, unless you know (as experts and the rich do) that tax deductions are worth more to people in the highest tax brackets. The result is an upside down subsidy: a rich taxpayer in the 37 percent tax bracket receives a public subsidy of 37 cents for every dollar she or he contributes, while a lower-earning taxpayer in the 10 percent bracket receives a subsidy of only 10 cents. For these reasons, keeping public options simple should be a guiding principle for design.

3.5 CHALLENGE 5: PUBLIC OR ONLY PARTLY PUBLIC?

One of the recurring design questions for public options is how much needs to be public? For example, US health-care debates over a public option are fundamentally about public health *insurance*. That is, even the broadest public option, Medicare for All, would leave in place an insurance system that reimburses private hospitals, doctors, and nurses. By contrast, in some countries (and even through the US Veterans Administration), health care itself is publicly provided.

Similarly, public options for housing finance, like those run through FHA, leave in place a private lending and housing system, but some localities also offer public housing. Public options can also outsource some of their functions to the private

29 Alex Mayyasi and Stacey Vanek Smith, Episode 760: Tax Hero, Planet Money, NPR, March 22, 2017, www.npr.org/sections/money/2017/03/22/521132960/episode-760-tax-hero

30 Justin Elliott and Paul Kiel, The TurboTax Trap, ProPublica, October 17, 2019, www.propublica.org/article/inside-turbotax-20-year-fight-to-stop-americans-from-filing-their-taxes-for-free

31 Jack Meserve, Keep it Simple and Take Credit, Democracy J., February 3, 2017.

sector. The short-lived Pony Express, for example, operated under a contract with the postal service.[32] When designing an equitable public option, it can be critical to decide which goods or services should be considered a public option and when outsourcing to a private actor is appropriate.

The best design will depend on the particular good or service being offered. But policymakers need to take seriously that retaining a private role (or outsourcing to the private sector) can undermine the public option's ability to expand equality. The central reason is that private actors have an interest in maximizing their own profits, rather than providing their service at an affordable price. This means that privatization can compromise affordability, in particular for the people who need the public option the most.

Professor K. Sabeel Rahman has argued that these dynamics have been a feature of water utility privatization. In some cases, cities seeking to push the cost of water utilities off their books privatized provision – ultimately leading to higher prices for users. In other cases, attempts to finance improvements to the water system have pushed cities to partner with financiers, with similarly disastrous results. Bayonne, New Jersey, Rahman reports, partnered with private equity firm Kohlberg Kravis Roberts to improve its water system. The result, however, was a 28 percent hike in prices, and when many households couldn't pay these higher bills, liens tripled.[33]

The example of private tax preparers, briefly discussed in the previous section, provides another cautionary tale about private outsourcing. Policymakers have become concerned that low-income tax filers were paying large fees (often, hundreds of dollars) to private tax preparers, even though their returns were often quite simple (by expert standards). Alarmed by the possible loss of business, Intuit and other commercial tax preparers struck a deal with the IRS: The IRS would not offer a public option for free tax preparation, and in return the commercial companies themselves would offer a free product to lower-earning filers.

The privatized tax filing program, called FreeFile, might have seemed to be a win for government and consumers. The private companies already have the software needed to prepare and file tax returns, and so FreeFile saved the IRS the expense of having to reinvent the wheel. But, driven by the profit motive, commercial taxpayers have undermined FreeFile with complexity and upselling tactics. Taxpayers searching for FreeFile may find it difficult even to locate the free product; according to reports Turbotax, deliberately hid FreeFile from Google searches. In the meantime, Turbotax launched its own, purportedly free filing program that often upsells customers to a paid option, sometimes by playing on consumers' fear and uncertainty about taxes.[34]

32 US Postal Service, The Pony Express, https://about.usps.com/who-we-are/postal-history/pony-express.pdf (accessed May 3, 2020).

33 K. Sabeel Rahman, Constructing Citizenship: Exclusion and Inclusion through the Governance of Basic Necessities, 118 Colum. L. Rev. 2447, 2478 (2018).

34 Elliott and Kiel.

3.6 CHALLENGE 6: FRACTURED PROVISION

Another challenge for designing equitable public options is the US system of federalism, which can often lead to fractured provision of public options – with detrimental consequences for equity.

A glaring example is the funding and quality of public education. Public schools are funded largely through local property taxes, leading to a system of urban development, housing policy, and zoning that have been tied to racial exclusion. White flight to the suburbs after desegregation orders for schools, coupled with zoning laws that prohibited density, ensured de facto segregation – now enforced through facially neutral zoning laws and housing costs rather than overtly racist Jim Crow laws. The fracturing of school financing and operations means a lack of equity within and across states.

Fractured provision of public options also takes place at the national level, with equally problematic consequences. After the Supreme Court allowed states to choose whether to expand Medicaid under the Affordable Care Act,[35] many states refused to expand that health insurance program. The result was that millions of lower-income people were denied access to health insurance. Fractured provision of Medicaid can also create policy feedback loops that further shape that program and even others. As Professor Jamila Michener has argued, different experiences with Medicaid state-by-state can lead participants to draw different conclusions about the value of political participation.[36]

Unemployment insurance provides another example of how federalism can undermine equity. The program is a joint program of the federal government and the states, but the states have vast authority to set the terms of unemployment benefits. Some states, like Florida, have spent years deliberately dismantling the unemployment system. When the COVID-19 pandemic hit and unemployment skyrocketed, Floridians who lost their jobs were significantly disadvantaged, compared to those in other states.[37]

Indeed, the strategy of devolution to the states has frequently undermined equitable efforts. Since 1996, the major (non-tax) welfare program for families, Temporary Assistance for Needy Families (TANF), has taken the form of a block grant to states, with states granted enormous leeway to set the terms of eligibility. Over time, states have set such onerous conditions and such meager benefits that TANF has all but fallen into disuse. In the 1980s, the predecessor welfare program (AFDC, or Aid to Families with Dependent Children) had a participation rate of about 80 percent, meaning that 80 percent of eligible families claimed and received

[35] *Nat'l Fed. Ind. Bus.* v. *Sebelius*, 567 U.S. 519 (2012).

[36] Jamila Michener, Fragmented Democracy: Medicaid, Federalism, and Unequal Politics (2018).

[37] Patricia Mazzei & Sabrina Tavernise, Florida is a Terrible Place to be an Unemployed Person, N.Y. Times, April 23, 2020.

benefits. As of 2016, the figure for TANF is under 30 percent.[38] Fractured provision – through states and local governments – can thus undermine the ability of a public option to enhance equity, even when the purpose of the program is to do just that.

The problem of fractured provision does not mean that all public options have to be operated at the federal level. But federal and state policymakers cannot assume that federalism or local control will always be beneficial; they need to consider whether fracturing public options will have negative consequences for equity and inclusion.

3.7 CONCLUSION: DESIGNING INCLUSIVE PUBLIC OPTIONS

The six challenges we have outlined may seem daunting: How can public options succeed in promoting equity when there are so many ways that they can fail? But the history of public options also contains hopeful lessons about the power of inclusive design.

Perhaps the clearest lesson is to design public options for universal access, not only to ensure equity itself but also to build a coalition that will sustain the public option. Social Security, for instance, began as a tiny program that paid low benefits and excluded many black workers. But over time, the mission and coverage of the program expanded, and today it covers 97 percent of US workers.[39] The advent and growth of Social Security created a novel but durable coalition of older people, which uses its considerable political power to monitor and protect Social Security benefits.

The Americans with Disabilities Act provides another example of inclusive policy dynamics. Among its other features, the Act required buildings, transportation, and other architectural features to be accessible. One of the consequences was the widespread adoption of elevators and ramps throughout public buildings and services. The subway system in New York, for example, now has ramps and elevators. This kind of inclusive design of the public option turns out to benefit more than those in wheelchairs. Parents with strollers, elderly people who walk but are worried about falling, people carrying luggage, all benefit from the inclusive design of this public transportation option.[40] And, together, they represent a larger constituency that can protest when these features are permitted to decay.

A second common strategy for addressing racism in public options has been legal enforcement through the courts. But as Professor Olatunde Johnson has argued, both private and public enforcement have severe limitations.[41] Johnson shows that both "neutral" judicial decisions that shape access to the courts and decisions on the

38 Linda Giannarelli, What Was the TANF Participate Rate in 2016?, Urban Institute, July 2019, www.urban.org/sites/default/files/publication/100521/what_was_the_tanf_participation_rate_in_2016_2.pdf

39 Social Security, Never Beneficiaries, Aged 60-89, 2015, www.ssa.gov/policy/docs/population-profiles/never-beneficiaries.html (last visited Jan. 1, 2021)

40 Joseph Shapiro, In Helping those with Disabilities, the ADA Improves Access for All, NPR, July 24, 2015.

41 Olatunde C. A. Johnson, Beyond the Private Attorney General: Equality Directives in American Law, 87 N.Y.U. L. Rev. 1339 (2012).

substantive standards for evaluating racist laws can make private lawsuits more difficult for plaintiffs to bring and to win. Administrative agencies also often fall short in public enforcement.

But judicial enforcement is not the only way for public agencies to advance equity. A complementary approach, Johnson argues, involves "equality directives," regulatory regimes that require agencies to push actors to pursue equality goals. For example, Title VIII of the Fair Housing Act and VI of the Civil Rights Act require federal agencies to advance anti-discrimination goals in housing and public spending.[42] These laws, she argues, use "administrative, programmatic, and regulatory power to promote civil rights."[43] Of course, whether these powers will themselves be enforced depends on the degree to which the administration in power has anti-racist commitments.

Moving beyond design choices, administrative power, and judicial enforcement, Professor K. Sabeel Rahman argues that equitable program design also requires oversight and accountability, and that bodies designed with those goals in mind should be more representative and participatory.[44] He describes these strategies as critical for "inclusionary administration of public goods," not only because they ensure that public programs achieve their equity goals but also because they build inclusion into the process itself. Incorporating participation and representation values into the design of oversight mechanisms helps make sure that a wide range of people – especially including those closest to the program – can shape its future.

Getting inclusive design right is not easy. No single public option can, for instance, magically erase the racist policies that have undermined equity in education, employment, and housing. But it would be unduly pessimistic to suppose that public options are doomed to be inequitable. With due attention to policy design, public options can contribute to expanding equity and opportunity.

42 Fair Housing Act, 42 U.S.C. § 3608(d); Civil Rights Act, 42 U.S.C. § 2000d.

43 Johnson, Beyond the Private Attorney General, at 1368.

44 Rahman, Constructing Citizenship, at 2486.

4

What about Private Options?

Jon D. Michaels

There is today considerable enthusiasm for public options, notably in the health-care and banking sectors. A compromise between entirely private commercial provisions and wholly bureaucratic, tax-and-transfer government provisions, public options are designed to offer citizen-consumers greater choice and protection. In blending (rather than choosing between) market ordering and state welfare, government must *cross over*. Government officials must step out of their sovereign lane, forgoing legislative and regulatory tools in favor of commercial ones.

This is no small step. For the better part of a hundred years, government officials have done most of their work within the confines of the sovereign lane. That is to say, they have passed laws, promulgated rules, and imposed taxes to discipline markets and empower consumers, workers, and townspeople affected by various businesses and business transactions. Now, with public options, they are seeking to achieve substantially similar ends but through market participation: buying, selling, trading, and leasing, just like any commercial actor.

For example, public options in the health-care sector stand in for old-school regulation of private providers and old-school redistribution to better support those struggling to pay for private insurance and medical services.[1] Public options in banking work substantially the same way. The government casts aside sovereign tools of democratic lawmaking, tools that may be used to require (or nudge) banks to accept customers deemed poor or risky. Instead, government officials set up and run public banks, offering a range of commercial services to "unbanked" and "under-banked" cohorts.[2]

1 *See* Ganesh Sitaraman & Anne L. Alstott, The Public Option: How to Expand Freedom, Increase Opportunity, and Promote Equality 202–21 (2019); Jacob S. Hacker, *Health Care for America*, Econ. Pol'y Inst.(January 11, 2007), https://perma.cc/8B2A-MKL3.

2 *See* Jordan Weissman, *Kirsten Gillibrand Unveils Her Ambitious Plan to Turn the Post Office into a Bank*, Slate (April 25, 2018), https://perma.cc/VA2N-DH9B; *see also* Sitaraman & Alstott, *supra* note 1, at 169–78; Mehrsa Baradaran, *It's Time for Postal Banking*, 127 Harv. L. Rev. Forum 165, 165 (2014), https://perma.cc/L7H4-FALD; Seth Victor, *Postal Banking and Government Profitability: When Should Government Have to Make Money?*, 19 Conn. Pub. Int. L.J. 15 (2019).

Public options represent a crossing over in one direction: from the sovereign to commercial. There is, to be sure, plenty of thoughtful work on public options, in this volume and elsewhere.[3] For that reason, this essay turns its attention to the converse phenomenon – the emergence, or rather reemergence of *private options*.

Private options may seem like a gussied-up label for a familiar concept. That's partly true. Everyday examples of private self-help or private ordering certainly constitute alternatives to government provision. But here context really matters. Just as public options involve governments using commercial – not sovereign – pathways to remedy market failures, private options involve firms (or groups of employees) adopting sovereign – not commercial – postures to remedy government failures.

Private, sovereign-like interventions refer to one or more of the following: (1) Firms (or subsets of firm stakeholders) use democratic pathways and deliberative procedures in furtherance of some public policy. In effect, they follow the laws of democracy rather than the laws of capitalism – namely, buying, selling, and trading pursuant to the demands and dictates of supply and demand. (2) Firms (or subsets of firm stakeholders) take on substantive responsibilities that modern liberal democracies have, by and large, consistently assigned to government actors.[4] (3) Firms (or, once more, subsets of firm stakeholders) provide principally for the general welfare and they proceed in ways that suggest they may be, among other things, voluntarily internalizing externalities, at some profit loss or legal risk; or voluntarily reducing rather than exploiting power and information asymmetries.

These either democratically deliberative or paternalistically public-regarding activities may (but need not) stand in some, perhaps quite stark, tension with profit-maximization – the central and almost always overriding imperative of twenty- and early twenty-first century corporate law and political economy.[5] That is to say, when it comes to private options, the eschewal of profits is neither a necessary nor sufficient condition.

Private options of a quasi-sovereign variety include such things as Facebook's proposed digital currency[6] and its self-styled supreme court tasked with rendering

3 *See, e.g.*, Sitaraman & Alstott, *supra* note 1.

4 Note that what I'm describing earlier – namely, firms taking on responsibilities traditionally handled by government actors – ought not be confused or conflated with government outsourcing. Government outsourcing, a pervasive practice, is not the same as deregulation or abdication. When government deregulates or abdicates responsibility, it may well be up to the private sector to fill the newly created void. By contrast, when the government outsources, it is still carrying out the assigned duties, albeit with the (often substantial) help of an alternative workforce. *See* Jon D. Michaels, *We the Shareholders: Government Market Participation in the Postliberal U.S. Political Economy*, 120 Colum. L. Rev. 465, 525–28 (2020).

5 *See, e.g.*, Michael C. Jensen, *Value Maximization, Stakeholder Theory and the Corporate Objective Function*, 12 Bus. Ethics. Q. 235 (2002); Henry Hansmann & Reinier Kraakman, *The End of History for Corporate Law*, 89 Geo. L. J. 439, 439 (2000).

6 *See, e.g.*, Mike Isaac & Nathaniel Popper, *Facebook Plans Global Financial System Based on Cryptocurrency*, N.Y. Times (June 18, 2019), https://perma.cc/66LQ-L3DW.

adjudicatory decisions as to user and advertiser content.[7] They also include Apple and Google's planned stewardship over what is in many respects the twenty-first century reboot of an old-school company town.[8] We may even look beyond the C-suite and consider workforces as fashioning their own private options, quite possibly as commercial analogs to the body politic. Specifically, worker strikes and protests over their companies' participation in politically questionable government programs may likewise constitute private options. These workers are not taking steps to augment their own wages and benefits. To the contrary, they are risking their own financial security to stand in for the American electorate when that electorate is, for reasons of a structural government failure, unable to influence, say, US immigration or defense policy.[9]

This essay drills down on private options, starting what I hope becomes a broader conversation about private options, their defining characteristics, the timing of their (re)emergence, and their role within the larger ecosystem of government and market institutions and actors. Section 4.1 begins by discussing how public and private options represent major challenges to modern legal liberalism. Whereas modern legal liberalism has been marked by the separation of state and private power – and specialization within each sector– today we see not only a blurring of public and private identities but also a commingling of sovereign and commercial responsibilities. Section 4.2 incorporates the concept of *government failure*, noting reasons why and circumstances when the state is unable to govern legitimately or effectively, if at all. Section 4.3 then explains why firms may be especially well positioned today to take on various quasi-sovereign projects, (for better or worse) filling gaps left by stymied state officials unable or unwilling to overcome one or more government failures. Section 4.4 offers illustrations of private options, each corresponding to specific government failures. Section 4.5 concludes by teeing up some of the normative and legal considerations that demand our attention going forward.[10]

4.1 FROM LEGAL LIBERALISM TO PUBLIC CAPITALISM

Public and private options constitute new and challenging efforts to blur, erase, or transcend one of the most resonant and relevant dividing lines of twentieth-century American law and political economy. It was, after all, the advent of modern legal liberalism that brought with it, first, the separation of state and private power, understood principally in terms of state efforts to protect and respect private ordering

7 *See* Tony Romm, *Facebook Unveils Charter for Its 'Supreme Court,' Where Users Can Go to Contest the Company's Decisions*, WASH. POST (September 17, 2019), https://perma.cc/X2AT-TXD5.

8 *See* Ashlee Vance, *Google and Mountain View Recast Company-Town Model*, N.Y. TIMES (February 18, 2010), https://perma.cc/E9SW-U3G4.

9 *See infra* Section IV.D.

10 Indeed, constraints of space and scope prevent me from delving more deeply into what it means for companies to wield private yet quasi-sovereign power. For present purposes, I merely note the need for greater scrutiny of the sort I intend to apply in subsequent projects.

in commercial, civic, religious, and social affairs; second, the specialization and compartmentalization of state and private power, such that each sector advanced different agendas, used different procedures and tools, was held accountable by different legal and moral standards, and was answerable to different constituencies; and, third, competition between state and private actors to determine whether a given policy domain ought to be subject to greater or lesser government-imposed redistribution and regulation.[11]

At the risk of oversimplification, in the modern American political economy federal, state, and local governments lessened their often routine and haphazard commercial forms of engagement, privatizing some functions and converting others into more decidedly noncommercial programs – that is, bureaucratic, coercive, and generally redistributive.[12] And firms, which in premodern times were known to be (and expected to be) somewhat if not manifestly paternalistic and public-regarding,[13] started focusing exclusively on profit-maximization, thus leaving little space or opportunity to engage in anything akin to quasi-sovereign projects.[14]

Public options constitute an alternative, a third-way mashup of modern legal liberalism's binary choice between state sovereign (regulation and redistribution) programs and private commercial offerings. Instead of choosing either state regulation or private ordering, policymakers split the difference. That is to say, government advances its sundry aims and commitments using commercial, rather than sovereign, tools and pathways. The same is substantially true for firms as they reach into the state's trusty toolbox to appropriate some sovereign tools. Elsewhere I call this bidirectional, twenty-first century postliberal mashup *public capitalism*.[15]

Under public capitalism, public and private identities matter less than sovereign and commercial postures. This is because both state and private actors are each taking on sovereign and commercial projects, each utilizing sovereign and commercial

11 For a fuller description, see Michaels, *We the Shareholders*, *supra* note 4, at 472–75.

12 *See, e.g.*, Joseph L. Weiner, *The New Deal and the Corporation*, 19 U. Chi. L. Rev. 724, 727–30 (1952); James Q. Whitman, *Of Corporatism, Fascism, and the First New Deal*, 39 Am. J. Comp. L. 747 (1991).

13 Citizens United v. FEC, 558 U.S. 310, 427 (2010) (Stevens, J., dissenting) ("Corporations were [originally] created, supervised, and conceptualized as quasi-public entities, 'designed to serve a social function for the state.'") (internal citation omitted); Kent Greenfield, *Ultra Vires Lives! A Stakeholder Analysis of Corporate Illegality (with Notes on How Corporate Law Could Reinforce International Law Norms)*, 87 Va. L. Rev. 1279, 1303 (2001) ("The nineteenth century conception of the [corporation], as a historical matter, included a much stronger nod toward the public purpose of the firm than does the modern view.").

14 *See* Hansmann & Kraakman, *supra* note 5; Jensen, *supra* note 5. Note, however, that firms have long been permitted to devote a "reasonable amount of resources to public welfare, humanitarian, educational, and philanthropic purposes." Principles of Corporate Governance, American Law Inst. § 2.01 (October 2019); *see also* Jonathan R. Macey, *A Close Read of an Excellent Commentary on* Dodge v. Ford, 3 Va. L. & Bus. Rev. 177, 178–79 (2008)(characterizing the quoted language as a "minor exception[] to the shareholder wealth maximization norm" that ensures "corporations be given sufficient latitude to act like responsible community members").

15 Michaels, *We the Shareholders*, *supra* note 4, at 503–22.

pathways, and each toggling between the two sets of projects and pathways as circumstances and opportunities so dictate.

Showing the robustness of this public capitalism moment in one direction is relatively easy. Public options and many other forms of government market participation are clearly on the rise.[16] But we haven't, as yet, paid as close attention to movement in the other direction – wherein private (and heretofore entirely commercial) actors take on sovereign roles and duties, principally to address one or more government shortcomings or outright failures.

4.2 GOVERNMENT FAILURES

Generally speaking, government interventions via regulation and redistribution are (and have long been) justified as responses to one or more so-called market failures, such as unequal bargaining power, unequal information, externalities, and public goods.[17] We know and talk a lot about market failures. But as much as we study – and complain about – government, rarely are we called upon to ponder, let alone enumerate, an analogous set of government failures that, among other things, may help us better apprehend and analyze private options. With that in mind, consider the following categories of government failure.

Constitutional failures. The US Constitution does not provide government officials with all the tools they may need to advance policies supported by even rather sizable political majorities. Some of this is by design, as evidenced by the constitutional drafters' preferences for limited government. And some of this may be attributable to the inevitable shortsightedness of the framers who set forth a governing blueprint at a very different cultural, political, technological, economic, and geostrategic moment. Reasonable minds might disagree about how best to regulate hate speech and gun ownership. But the Constitution – or at least Supreme Court jurisprudence – renders many of those debates academic. Similar to when we're confronted with market failures that firms are unable or unwilling to address on their own, we as a community may countenance various constitutional failures, try to address them directly (through, say, constitutional amendments or judicial appointments), or look to nongovernmental actors to devise compensatory or ameliorative countermeasures.

Policy Failures. Sounding in a slightly different register are government policy failures. One may be hard pressed to find a rational basis for disputing the need to take at least modest steps to address climate change, to assure the existence of affordable housing, and to improve our public infrastructure. Yet very few, if any, legislative initiatives are forthcoming. Part of the explanation may connect to other government failures – namely, jurisdictional failures, constitutional (that is, powers-of-Congress) failures,

16 *See, e.g.*, *id.*, at 490–500.

17 *See, e.g.*, Stephen Breyer, Regulation and Its Reform 15–34 (1982).

and democratic failures. But perhaps just as likely, the reason we don't address climate change, the affordable housing crisis, or our dangerously outdated physical infrastructure is that we have a selfish, present-minded polity. That is to say, there may be instances when there are no other government failures impeding efforts to reduce carbon emissions, increase the housing stock, and upgrade crumbling bridges and roads. In those instances, what we have are otherwise unencumbered majorities simply unwilling to invest in their communities, presumably because the costs will be borne by present-day voters while the benefits accrue substantially, if not exclusively, to future generations. When and where we are confronted with policy failures of this sort, there may be a need for alternative collective enterprises, outside of the state, to step up and safeguard our shared future.

Jurisdictional failures. This government failure is perhaps the closest analog to the externalities concern commonly encountered in the marketplace. Notwithstanding its numerous historic and enduring virtues, the Westphalian system organized around powerful nation-states limits our ability to address any number of contemporary public policy challenges that transcend national borders. Environmental policy stands out, given the diffuse causes and effects of climate change. But financial, counterterrorism, public health, trade, migration, and labor policies are likewise of transnational significance. For national governments to effectively regulate beyond their borders, they need either to take Herculean steps to construct transnational regulatory regimes or to internalize the costs that, say, domestic pollution has on the world at large – and regulate accordingly. In either case, nation-states must act contrary to their own immediate self-interest and do so knowing they may not succeed. Hence, as with constitutional failures, there may be reason to look to nongovernmental actors, including multinational firms, as possibly better positioned to address transnational externalities.

Democratic failures. To speak of a democratic failure presupposes one has in mind a certain normative understanding of healthy politics. But assuming, as I do, that there is some consensus around democratic politics that includes a baseline commitment to one-person, one-vote,[18] then it is safe to say that the United States has an impoverished, structurally unequal system for collective self-governance. Among other things, the US Senate ranks among the least democratic legislative bodies in the world.[19] And then there is our presidential election system, mediated (and distorted) by federalism and the Electoral College.[20] Recall the last two Republican presidents – George W. Bush and Donald Trump – each won the White House while losing the popular vote, the latter

18 *See, e.g.*, Stephen Ansolabehere & James M. Snyder, Jr., The End of Inequality: One Person, One Vote and the Transformation of American Politics (2008).

19 Alfred C. Stepan, *Federalism and Democracy: Beyond the U.S. Model*, 10 J. Dem. 19 (1999); Todd N. Tucker, *Fixing the Senate: Equitable and Full Representation for the 21st Century*, Roosevelt Inst., at 6 (March 2019), https://perma.cc/838K-WHXD. Given demographic and mobility trends, the Senate is apt to become even more undemocratic with each passing year. *Id* at 8.

20 *See, e.g.*, Sanford Levinson, Our Undemocratic Constitution 87–97 (2006).

by nearly 3,000,000 votes in 2016. In light of these patterns of democratic failure, often reinforced by constitutionally protected campaign finance practices that privilege plutocracy, by gerrymandering schemes, and by voter suppression efforts,[21] one might expect, and even desire, the engendering of alternative venues for self-governance – locales where it is conceivable that a different, more democratic version of politics may play out.

4.3 FIRMS AS QUASI-SOVEREIGNS

Government is the go-to venue for addressing market failures. Can, and should, the market return the favor by helping to overcome or compensate for various government failures? Given how singularly focused firms (and groups of employees) have been on profit maximization throughout the modern era, it may seem far-fetched to assume the market will do much more than exploit most government failures. A typical commercial response to the government's failure to regulate guns (because of the Court's Second Amendment jurisprudence) would be to undertake various self-help measures. Firms might, predictably, increase security at worksites, thereby more fully insulating employees, executives, and customers from the potential dangers associated with this particular government failure – but do little to safeguard the rest of the community. Some especially entrepreneurial firms might develop and sell new security services or goods, such as bulletproof vests and backpacks.[22] But that's as far as many firms will be apt to go. After all, firms have limited resources and may be loath to expend funds in furtherance of public-regarding, nonremunerative outcomes that would also be of considerable benefit to rival businesses and their customers. That is, after all, why they pay taxes.

Yet notwithstanding understandable, intuitive grounds for skepticism, there are several reasons why market actors might be well positioned, today at least, to counteract or compensate for government failures – and to do so in an ostensibly public-regarding fashion, as if they were quasi-sovereigns themselves. Due to a convergence of novel conditions and circumstances, firms have the financial wherewithal, the clout, the maneuverability, and quite possibly the will (if not always the best of intentions) to stand in for the government. And, the public, for its part, may be sufficiently disillusioned with the promises and practices of legal liberalism to be receptive to private interventions of a quasi-sovereign sort.

In this subsection, I first address corporate capacity for, and interest in, taking on quasi-sovereign projects. I then turn to consider why, at this particular moment, the public may be amenable to firms taking on these projects.

[21] *Rucho* v. *Common Cause*, 139 S. Ct. 2484, 2509 (2019) (*Kagan*, J., dissenting); *Citizens United*, 558 U.S. at 427 (*Stevens*, J., dissenting); Gilda R. Daniels, Uncounted: The Crisis of Voter Suppression in America (2020); Lawrence Lessig, Republic, Lost: How Money Corrupts Congress—And a Plan to Stop It (2011); Nicholas Stephanopoulos, *The Anti-Carolene Court*, 2020 Sup. Ct. Rev. (forthcoming), https://papers.ssrn.com/sol3/papers.cfm?abstract_id=3483321.

[22] Sadly, such products exist. *See, e.g.*, David Yaffe-Bellany, *Bulletproof Backpacks in Demand for Back-to-School Shopping*, N.Y. Times (August 6, 2019), https://perma.cc/Z3G4-DU8Q.

4.3.1 *Corporate Capacity*

Bigness. A handful of firms today are so large and influential that they wield significant power over markets, consumers, and even governments. The size and dominance of these companies are leading some to characterize the instant moment as a second Gilded Age.[23] The first such age coincided with the rise of industrial capitalism in the late-nineteenth century, the concentration of market power, the leveraging of that market power for political gain, and the engendering of great wealth and income inequality.[24]

We're seeing similar patterns at play today, with the chief differences being, first, that instead of industrial capitalism we're in a moment of high-tech capitalism; and, second, that the reemergence of a gilded political economy is especially problematic given the range of regulatory and redistributive laws and regulations instituted in response to the first Gilded Age. Yet here we are. Currently, the richest 400 Americans combine to own more of the nation's wealth than do the 150 million Americans constituting the bottom 60 percent. Since the 1980s, the richest 400 have tripled their share of the nation's wealth, generating levels of inequality and wealth concentration "last seen during the Roaring Twenties."[25] (To put things in even starker perspective, three men – Bill Gates, Jeff Bezos, and Warren Buffett – combine to possess more wealth than the bottom 50 percent of the US population.[26]) Even within the rarefied world of the Standard & Poor's 500, we see tremendous inequality. In 2015, the top 28 firms generated more profits than did the other 472.[27] And, more recently, in 2019, Apple and Microsoft alone accounted for 15 percent of the S&P's aggregate gains, with Amazon, Facebook, and Alphabet/Google rounding out the top five firms.[28]

Firms dominating the instant Gilded Age constrain customer choice, inflate prices, and cause us to worry about morally hazardous behavior and systemic shocks, at least to the extent these entities are understood to be too big to fail. The "too big to fail" label took on special salience a decade ago in the wake of the global financial crisis. At that time, "too big to fail" referred principally to financial services firms.[29] But we'd be hard pressed today to say that we're any less reliant on the likes of

[23] Jack M. Balkin, *The First Amendment in the Second Gilded Age*, 66 Buff. L. Rev. 979 (2018) ("We are now well into America's Second Gilded Age.").

[24] Richard White, The Republic for which It Stands: The United States during Reconstruction and the Gilded Age, 1865–1896 (2017).

[25] Christopher Ingraham, *Wealth concentration returning to 'levels last seen during the Roaring Twenties,' according to new research*, Wash. Post (February 8, 2019), https://perma.cc/YH58-UDG7 (quoting UC-Berkeley economist Gabriel Zucman).

[26] Sophie Smith, *Bill Gates, Jeff Bezos and Warren Buffett Own More Wealth than the Poorest Half of the US*, Telegraph (UK) (November 9, 2017), https://perma.cc/BYS6-TB85.

[27] Matt Krantz, *6% of Companies Make 50% of U.S. Profit*, USA TODAY (March 2, 2016), https://perma.cc/C463-DL6H.

[28] Yun Li, *The Five Biggest Stocks are Dwarfing the Rest of the Stock Market at an "Unprecedented" Level*, CNBC (January 13, 2020), https://perma.cc/QXY7-89NK.

[29] Andrew Ross Sorkin, Too Big to Fail: The Inside Story of How Wall Street and Washington Fought to Save the Financial System–and Themselves (2009).

Google, Facebook, Apple, and Amazon, given those firms' role in facilitating our (and everyone else's) social, cultural, economic, and political exchanges. Simply put, disruptions in high-tech services would prove catastrophic.[30]

What I just described is the conventional doom-and-gloom story. But there are less carefully attended to and more complicated consequences of oligarchical firms reaping supernormal profits. For better or worse, these firms have the market share and financial cushion to stray a bit outside of their traditional lane of commercial engagement – a lane whose boundaries have been enforced by the prevailing and largely unquestioned legal norms and professional mores of twentieth-century corporate governance and industrial competition.

Before the emergence of modern liberal political economies, firms weren't so cabined both by a robust regulatory state and by legally empowered shareholders. Indeed, early American corporate charters placed special emphasis on the public-regarding purposes of corporations,[31] a seemingly reasonable imposition on firms receiving the special legal benefits (and limited liabilities) of corporate personhood. Back then, we witnessed big, powerful firms acting with quasi-sovereign intent and taking on quasi-sovereign projects, including the governing of de facto company towns.[32]

In the modern era, many of these premodern colossi lost market share as a result of changing economic patterns, were broken up by antitrust authorities, or were penned into their commercial, profit-maximizing lane by courts, regulatory agencies, and shareholders. Modern legal and professional duties and obligations narrowed the scope of firms' ambitions – and limited their ability to commit resources to quasi-statist projects. Now, however, the size and market dominance of leading tech firms take us back to those days before we had a fully modernized political economy. It thus may stand to reason that today's giant firms have greater power and flexibility to reengage in quasi-sovereign projects, including ones that address government failures.

CEO-Owners. Another key feature of quite a few of today's mega firms is a special leadership dynamic, again at least in many respects unlike what we've experienced since the tail-end of the first Gilded Age. The leaders of today – like the old-school steel, coal, oil, and banking magnates – are not professional corporate managers with

30 *See* RANA FOROOHAR, DON'T BE EVIL: HOW BIG TECH BETRAYED ITS FOUNDING PRINCIPLES – AND ALL OF US (2019); James Titcomb, *Tech Giants Have Become the New "Too Big to Fail,"* TELEGRAPH (UK) (November 25, 2019), https://perma.cc/5PMH-8LMW.

31 *See supra* note 13 and accompanying text.

32 *See* QUENTIN R. SKRABEC, JR., BENEVOLENT BARONS: AMERICAN WORKER-CENTERED INDUSTRIALISTS, 1850–1910, at 53–56 (2011) (describing Lowell mill town as a company town that aimed to meet employees' housing, educational, cultural, and spiritual needs – and did so in a way that purported to promote healthy and wholesome living); see also LINDA CARLSON, COMPANY TOWNS OF THE PACIFIC NORTHWEST 36–40 (2017); Richard M. Candee, *New Towns of the Early New England Textile Industry*, 1 PERSP. IN VERNACULAR ARCH. 31, 31–36 (1982); Rickey Hendricks, *Medical Practice Embattled: Kaiser Permanente, the American Medical Association, and Henry J. Kaiser on the West Coast, 1945–1955*, 60 PAC. HIST. REV. 439, 440 (1991); Diana Davids Hinton, *Creating Company Culture: Oil Company Camps in the Southwest, 1920–1960*, 11 SW. HIST. Q. 369, 375 (2008).

limited equity. Even the most charismatic and influential among that modern corporate-manager cohort – think Lee Iacocca, Jack Welch, or Michael Eisner– could do little that strayed beyond the profit-maximization directive. So while there was the occasional Sam Walton, Oprah Winfrey, or Ted Turner, who created, controlled, and ran vast companies, most corporate heads in modern times have been glorified employees and acted as such. Today's Zuckerberg, Bezos, Musk, Brin, and Page are throwbacks to the age when larger-than-life corporate heads were also the principal founder-owners. They accordingly possess greater legal freedom, institutional authority, and cultural capital to push projects potentially orthogonal to the pursuit of profits. And each of these latter-day founder-owners has expressed interest in, and demonstrated some commitment to, doing precisely that.[33]

Corporate Social Responsibility (CSR). Businesses today are well aware of the growing importance and heightened political salience of CSR. Throughout the modern era of legal liberalism, the legally and culturally instantiated profit-maximization imperative left little opportunity for advancing the interests of anyone other than shareholders. But over the past decade or so, American corporations have become more attentive, in word[34] if not (yet?) in deed[35] to the interests of customers, employees, business partners, and community members alike. For instance, the Business Roundtable, a prominent umbrella organization comprising the CEOs of leading American corporations, recently took a dramatic step to redefine the corporation. The Roundtable committed to de-emphasizing profits and, in keeping with that commitment, announced that "Americans deserve an economy that allows each person to succeed through hard work and creativity and to lead a life of meaning and dignity."[36] This recognition that firms need to, once again, attend to broader sets of stakeholders may be nothing more than disingenuous virtue-signaling.[37] But if there is any substance to the Roundtable's "redefin[ing] the purpose of a corporation," then we may well see some of America's most powerful firms taking it upon themselves to address one or more government failures.[38]

33 Conor Dougherty, *Facebook Pledges $1 Billion to Ease Housing Crisis Inflamed by Big Tech*, N.Y. TIMES (October 22, 2019), https://perma.cc/3SZE-TMS4; David McCabe and Karen Weise, *Amazon Accelerates Efforts to Fight Climate Change*, N.Y. TIMES (September 19, 2019), https://perma.cc/8MLQ-V6PW.

34 Rebecca M. Henderson, *More and More CEOs Are Taking Their Social Responsibility Seriously*, HARV. BUS. REV. (February 12, 2018), https://perma.cc/LWV8-SSLC.

35 See Lucian A. Bebchuk & Roberto Tallarita, *The Illusory Promise of Stakeholder Governance* (March 5, 2020), https://papers.ssrn.com/sol3/papers.cfm?abstract_id=3544978.

36 Jena McGregor, *Group of Top CEOs Says Maximizing Shareholder Profits No Longer Can Be the Primary Goal of Corporations*, WASH. POST (August 19, 2019), https://perma.cc/5UQ2-B9JQ; *Business Roundtable, Statement on the Purpose of a Corporation* (August 19, 2019), https://perma.cc/552D-BGP9.

37 Bebchuk & Tallarita, *supra* note 35.

38 *See, e.g.*, *Energy Management: Balancing Climate, Cost, and Choice*, Deloitte Resources 2019 Study, at 17, https://perma.cc/6S4F-YHWN; Hugh MacArthur, et al., *Investing with Impact: Today's ESG Mandate in Private Equity*, Bain & Co. 2020 Global Private Equity Report, https://perma.cc/T5PU-F759.

Patriotic Philanthropy. Stymied in large part by an American electorate hostile to taxes, government officials are increasingly soliciting corporate patrons to sponsor any number of state programs or initiatives. They thus seek financial support for municipal education, national parks, public health research, and even government-initiated litigation.[39] This patriotic philanthropy, as it has come to be called, allows corporations to donate to specific government causes while claiming a tax deduction for the charitable giving.[40] Given some of the donor-attached strings – witness Mark Zuckerberg's control over curriculum and personnel attendant to his $100 million donation to the Newark, New Jersey schools[41] – it is no longer such a big step for firms to take on big quasi-sovereign projects directly, bypassing government agencies as the proverbial (and, by many an entrepreneur's lights, woefully bureaucratized) middlemen.

4.3.2 *Public Receptivity*

Pervasive Blending of Public and Private. Though the public and private have never been hermetically sealed from one another, one of the attributes (if not unqualified accomplishments) of modern legal liberalism was the development of a sizable, robust, and professional public bureaucracy that could carry out practically all of the work of the state in a manner divorced from the push and pull of the marketplace.[42] Yet despite this capacity, the government has, for the past several decades, strived to downplay the specialness of the state sector and to narrow the gap between the public and private spheres.[43] To that end, government officials have deputized private actors to police neighborhoods, lead combat missions, analyze counterterrorism data, patrol borders, conduct environmental and occupational safety inspections, and adjudicate welfare-eligibility disputes.[44] This late twentieth and early twenty-first century blurring of the public–private boundary (and corresponding effort to run government like a business[45]) seemingly makes it easier today to accept various crossover interventions, both public options[46] and corporate-led projects of a quasi-sovereign variety.

Disillusionment with Modern Legal Liberalism. There is, currently, considerable frustration and distrust with both the state *qua* sovereign and firms *qua* commercial

39 *See* Michaels, *We the Shareholders*, *supra* note 4, at 498–99.

40 *See* Margaret H. Lemos & Guy Uriel-Charles, *Patriotic Philanthropy? Financing the State with Gifts to Government*, 106 CAL. L. REV. 1129 (2018).

41 DALE RUSSAKOFF, THE PRIZE: WHO'S IN CHARGE OF AMERICA'S SCHOOLS (2015).

42 *See* JON D. MICHAELS, CONSTITUTIONAL COUP: PRIVATIZATION'S THREAT TO THE AMERICAN REPUBLIC 39–50 (2017).

43 *See* Jon D. Michaels, *Running Government as a Business . . . Then and Now*, 128 HARV. L. REV. 1152, 1159–67 (2015).

44 *See* Jon D. Michaels *Privatization's Pretensions*, 77 U. CHI. L. REV. 717 (2010); Jon D. Michaels, *Deputizing Homeland Security*, 88 TEX. L. REV. 1435 (2010).

45 *See* Michaels, *Running Government*, *supra* note 43.

46 Michaels, *We the Shareholders*, *supra* note 4, at 506–13.

profit-maximizers.[47] When one is no longer in the thralls of the state (as, say, champions of the New Deal and Great Society might have been), or in the thralls of the market (as, say, champions of the 1960s Chicago School, Reaganomics, or even the Clinton/Gore "third way" might have been), it becomes easier to abandon the specialization, separation, and stylized competition we associate with legal liberalism. Beholden to neither archetype, disillusioned citizen-consumers would seemingly be more amenable to, even welcoming of, innovative crossover practices, both government market participation and firms acting as quasi-sovereigns.[48]

Transactional, Unbundled, One-Off Exchanges. For a variety of reasons, we're much more likely today to think of our various social and commercial relationships transactionally. Consider the popularity of Tinder – as compared to traditional courtship-driven dating; and Task Rabbit – as compared to forging relationships built on friendship and reciprocity with handy neighbors. Consider too many TV viewers' preference for various curated streaming services over all-inclusive cable packages. Lastly, note consumers' fondness for singular AirBnB flats, perfect for this particular trip (but perhaps never again), over cookie-cutter Marriotts and Hiltons. In these important spaces, our relationships have become more transactional, more unbundled, and more one-off and ad hoc (as opposed to long term and consistent).[49]

The same may also be true when it comes to our relationship with the state. Already, as a result both of the public's anti-tax sentiments and the government's efforts to give off a businesslike vibe, we may be increasingly thinking about our interactions with the state as if we're customers of discrete services, rather than citizens of the sum total of government benefits and obligations. These transactional, unbundled forms of engagement suggest less of a holistic, all-in relationship with any one entity and more of an individuated, modular relationship with any number of potential service providers. Thus it may be easy for us to query whether the US Postal Service is insufficiently commercially oriented, something President Trump brings up when arguing that the Postal Service should be charging the likes of Amazon a whole lot more. And it may be quite natural today to press Facebook and Twitter to act more custodially, and do more content regulation notwithstanding a potential loss of profits. In other words, the more we see the world as a series of one-off transactions, the more willing we may be to ask commercial firms to act, in any particular instance, more or less profit-maximizing and ask government units, similarly in any particular instance, to act more or less commercially. This too paves the way for encouraging and ultimately endorsing government agencies providing public options and firms stepping into the shoes of a sovereign.

47 *See, e.g.*, Uri Friedman, *Trust is Collapsing in American*, ATLANTIC (January 21, 2018), https://perma.cc/WXC3-BCRM; Matthew Harrington, *Survey: People's Trust Has Declined in Business, Media, Government, and NGOs*, HARV. BUS. REV. (January 16, 2017), https://perma.cc/TUT5-7L93; Matt Stevens, *Falling Trust in Government Makes It Harder to Solve Problems, Americans Say*, N.Y. TIMES (July 22, 2019), https://perma.cc/FFT9-HPHX.

48 *See* Michaels, *We the Shareholders*, supra note 4, at 513–15.

49 *Id.* at 518–19.

4.4 PRIVATE OPTIONS

Consider the following plucked-from-the-headlines examples of what I'm classifying as private options and note how they line up with the various government failures identified in Section 4.2. In this section, I describe a quartet of private options, pair them with specific genres of government failure, and explain how these private options present opportunities and challenges different from those we associate with either conventional sovereign government services or conventional commercial firm offerings. Left to the side, for present purposes, are discussions of the efficacy, constitutionality, and legitimacy of these (or any other) private options. Though I believe concern, if not alarm, is warranted, inquiries along those lines are beyond the scope of this introductory essay and must, instead, be taken up in subsequent projects.

4.4.1 *Governing Public Fora (Constitutional Failures)*

Social media sites are increasingly viewed as public or quasi-public fora.[50] This ought not to be surprising given the fact that Facebook, Twitter, and, God help us, Instagram, host important political and civic announcements, conversations, and debates.[51] They're where news is announced, made, discussed, reframed, endorsed, distorted (or falsified), and further disseminated.[52] These digital venues are, to be sure, a marked change from the physical spaces – city halls, high school auditoriums, and town squares – where prior generations gathered to educate one another, persuade one another, and participate in our various democratic and civic projects.

Today's digital public fora are real and empowering in ways that would astonish those who came of age fifty or a hundred years ago. But they're also incredibly fraught spaces full of scam artists, bigots, and the like. Hucksters and haters obviously predate the digital age. But old-timey grifters and saboteurs couldn't reach as far, penetrate as deeply, or operate as deceptively when they had to do their damage at the retail level, and without the benefit of near or total anonymity. As a result of the promises and dangers of the digital public fora – *not to mention the First Amendment's limitations on government-imposed speech regulations* – the giant tech firms that administer these spaces face consumer and political pressure

50 For some important judicial treatments, see Packingham v. North Carolina, 137 S. Ct. 1730, 1735 (2017); Knight First Am. Inst. v. Trump, 928 F. 3d 226 (2d Cir. 2019), *Davison* v. *Randall*, 912 F. 3d 666, 680–81 (4th Cir. 2019).

51 *See, e.g.*, Jeremy Shapiro, *Trump Has Redefined Political Communication for the Whole World—and Soon Everyone Could Speak Like Him*, Bus. Insider (October 20, 2018), https://perma.cc/R9H9-L4KZ; Antonio Garcia Martinez, *How Alexandria Ocasio-Cortez Shapes a New Political Reality*, Wired (January 9, 2019), https://perma.cc/AL2V-T5CC.

52 Elisa Shearer, *Social Media Outpaces Print Newspapers in the U.S. as a News Source*, Pew Research Ctr. (December 10, 2018), https://perma.cc/UK4Z-YUAX.

to function as stewards, if not outright regulators.[53] Acting as regulators might entail aggressively filtering out fraudulent, hurtful, and even gratuitously graphic or obscene content.

Some of the tech firms are beginning to step into the constitutional void. They're developing procedures that they insist will filter, refine, and enrich content. Facebook, for example, is convening what it calls a supreme court to judge content. Members of this "court" reportedly will be walled off from the firm's executives – and vice versa – to insure against financial considerations distorting the adjudicative process. Twitter, for its part, has banned all paid political content, "including appeals for votes, solicitations of financial support, and advocacy for or against" a wide range of matters relating to elections and public policy; it has also blocked PACs, SuperPACs, and 501(c)(4)s from advertising on its platform.[54] Brad Parscale, President Trump's reelection campaign manager, criticized Twitter's decision, arguing that "Twitter just walked away from hundreds of millions of dollars of potential revenue, a very dumb decision for their stockholders."[55] In response, Twitter's CEO simply underscored his discomfort with the role money plays in influencing political outcomes and expressed his belief that "political message reach should be earned, not bought."[56]

One may certainly quibble with the procedures Facebook's court employs, and question whether the court can ever be truly independent from the Menlo Park bean counters. One may, likewise, criticize Twitter's policy and question how consistently and effectively it'll be applied in practice. But given Facebook and Twitter's importance to public discourse, it is difficult to deny that these media giants are acting as quasi-sovereigns, regulating access to effectively public fora, deciding what is and isn't objectionable, protecting (we hope) the integrity of elections, and helping restore confidence and encourage more participation in the democratic process (and doing so in part by making clear they're acting orthogonally to, if not squarely against, their commercial interests).[57]

When big tech firms regulate their platforms, the intent and effect is very different from, say, a bowling alley policing its clientele's speech or conduct. The owners of *300 Bowl* have a lot of governing to do. They need to ensure everyone's health and safety, not a small feat given their high-volume shoe rental business and the potentially tumultuous admixture of free-flowing brews and fast-throwing twelve-pound balls. And they may decide that they have to regulate what may be said at, say, Open-Mic Fridays in the bowlers' lounge. How *300 Bowl* governs itself matters, but

53 Kate Klonick, *The New Governors: The People, Rules, and Processes Governing Online Speech*, 131 Harv. L. Rev. 1598 (2017).

54 Twitter, https://perma.cc/N6JX-KULN (last visited March 25, 2020).

55 Kendall Karson & Matt Zarnell, *Twitter Outlines Sweeping Details of Ban on Political Ads*, ABC News (November 15, 2019), https://perma.cc/9TAD-WPY6. For what it is worth, it seems as if Twitter nets far less revenue from political ads than does Facebook and Google. *See id.*

56 *Id.*

57 *Cf.* Nixon v. Shrink Missouri Government PAC, 528 U.S. 377, 401 (2000) (Breyer, J., concurring).

in a way qualitatively different from how Facebook regulates its social media platform. We'd have to squint really hard to gauge the marginal effect *300 Bowl*'s open-mic policy has on our democracy or broader political economy. When it comes to Facebook or Twitter, the converse is decidedly true. Content regulation by the behemoths of social media affects the legitimacy of elections, the stability of our economy, and the sanctity of our civil rights and civil liberties. In all these respects, Twitter and Facebook might well be more impactful than many full-fledged sovereign states, quite a few of which find themselves at the mercy of social media platforms.[58]

Thus, though there is not a sharp analytical distinction between a local bowling alley and a social media juggernaut each having governance rules about speech and debate, there are plenty of reasons to treat the two entities completely differently. Among them, first and foremost is a simple matter of scale. When it comes to tech giants, we cannot speak in terms of discrete groups of specially affected employees and customers. These firms have a global impact. Second is a question of third-party effects. If you never set foot in *300 Bowl*, their house rules aren't going to affect your rights, liberty, or quality of life. And if you enjoy bowling but dislike *300 Bowl*'s rules, you can go for a short drive and find an alley more to your liking. By contrast, if you never log on to Facebook or Twitter, your life, livelihood, and even "IRL" conversations are nonetheless affected by what happens on those sites, simply because so many other people are dialed in and often socially, politically, and economically dependent on those sites. That is to say, going off the grid, or onto a different platform, is likely highly limiting, in a way switching bowling alleys would never be. Third is a question of the supremacy of law. *300 Bowl*'s house rules are entirely subordinate to local, state, and federal law. Questions of the primacy of public law vis-à-vis tech giants are more difficult to answer. Depending on how they incorporate, where they operate, and where they locate their servers, some tech firms may be able to evade any number of jurisdiction-sensitive laws.[59]

4.4.2 *Providing Social Services (Policy Failures)*

It is hardly a secret that there are major housing, transportation, and overall affordability crises in some of the nation's largest and most prominent cities and metropolitan areas, including those, such as Seattle and Silicon Valley, home to highly profitable and rapidly expanding tech businesses.

During the twentieth-century heyday of legal liberalism, periods of economic growth and contraction were managed principally through sovereign government interventions. State and local governments zoned aggressively, built additional infrastructure, and provided various tax or regulatory incentives to encourage or

58 *See* Anupam Chander, *Facebookistan*, 90 N.C. L. Rev. 1807 (2012); Kristen E. Eichensehr, *Digital Switzerlands*, 167 Pa. L. Rev. 665 (2019).

59 *See* Eichensehr, *supra* note 58.

deter commercial expansion. That doesn't mean government officials always succeeded – but they generally tried (and were expected to try). Of late, however, public stewardship has been sorely lacking, no doubt a function of our political culture becoming fanatically anti-tax and more brazenly selfish – including but not limited to rising NIMBY activism.

So, in light of various government policy failures – meaning, again, the state's inability to address housing, transportation, or health-care shortfalls – some of the giant tech firms have undertaken self-help measures. Taking care of their own, they offset some of their employees' expenses and inconveniences. But housing stipends, transportation services, on-site medical, childcare, and gym facilities, and free or heavily subsidized meals are not substitutes for sovereign welfarist measures. They're in fact additional or alternative forms of compensation – and thus very much in keeping with a business-first commercial mindset. Indeed, if anything, many of these in-kind employee benefits actually exacerbate community crises. Employer-sponsored subsidies inflate the prices of local goods, housing, and services. What's more, because executives and employees of Google, Amazon, and Facebook have many of their needs and wants privately provided for, they are no longer motivated as citizens to clamor for greater public spending. Truth be told, unless they are especially other-regarding, these tech employees awash in in-kind benefits have reason to oppose additional public expenditures.

Now, however, tech giants face ever greater internal and external pressure to fix the damage their presence and policies have either caused or magnified – in part because government won't do so, at least not forcefully, through sovereign regulatory or tax-and-transfer programs. Absent wholesale government redistribution, wildly profitable and powerful firms may feel compelled to do far more than just subsidize their employees. To date, a few firms are beginning to respond. Three of the big tech companies – Apple, Microsoft, and Google – have committed to spending a combined $4 billion to address the housing crises in the Bay Area and Seattle.[60] Relatedly, Apple, Amazon, and Facebook are advancing incredibly ambitious and expensive planning initiatives, complete with mixed housing developments, retail offerings, brand-new municipal infrastructure, greenways, and parks that strike quite a few observers as points of entry for big tech firms to establish neo-company towns (over which the firms exercise substantial regulatory authority).[61]

60 Bill Chappell, *Apple Pledges $2.5 Billion To Combat California's Housing Crisis*, NPR (November 4, 2019), https://perma.cc/VL75-JKFE; Daisuke Wakabayashi & Conor Dougherty, *Google Pledges to Invest $1 Billion to Ease Bay Area Housing Crisis*, N.Y. Times (June 18, 2019), https://perma.cc/TWC7-AKZC; Karen Weise, *Microsoft Pledges $500 Million for Affordable Housing in Seattle Area*, N.Y. Times (January 16, 2019), https://perma.cc/MU23-29B4.

61 David Streitfeld, *Welcome to Zucktown. Where Everything Is Just Zucky*, N. Y. Times (March 21, 2018), https://perma.cc/HUP3-R9XM; Leanna Garfield, *Facebook and Amazon Are So Big They're Creating Their Own Company Towns – Here's the 200-year Evolution*, Bus. Insider (March 26, 2018), https://perma.cc/424R-8NGC. It's perhaps hard to dispute that classification when Google's "Mountain View and San Jose projects build on existing plans the cities had been working on for quite some time."

To be clear, the differences between employee-targeted firm interventions and community-wide firm interventions are important. First, the employee-targeted interventions reify the sovereign/commercial distinction and likely engender greater socioeconomic inequality for the reasons stated earlier; the communitywide interventions, by contrast, blur the sovereign and commercial and have the potential to achieve greater communal inclusiveness – albeit on terms set by the firm.

Note too the differences between a private, quasi-sovereign Amazon or Google company town and, say, a city like Seattle or a county like Santa Clara that is willing and able to compel profitable firms, their owners, and their executives to pay their fair share of taxes into the public fisc.[62] The *neo-company town* approach lowers firms' taxable income by reinvesting what would otherwise be taxable profits into quasi-public works projects – projects the firms direct and, once completed, largely manage. The *conventional municipal town* approach vests control over community welfare squarely in government institutions, underscoring the sovereign primacy of those public institutions and reinforcing the sovereign/commercial divide. Thus, in acting as a steward of a company town, the firm marginalizes the government by leaving public officials with fewer resources, opportunities, and reasons to make sovereign interventions. Community members will, for better or worse, have even greater need to look to leading firms for guidance, assistance, benevolence, or redress.[63]

4.4.3 *Issuing Currency (Jurisdictional Failures)*

There are all sorts of inefficiencies baked into our global monetary system. Exchange rates between sovereign currencies fluctuate unpredictably, transaction costs are nonzero, and aggressive arbitraging by firms, investors, and speculators tends to disadvantage smaller, non-repeat players.[64] What's more, competing sets of national banking regulations further complicate easy trading from one nation-state to another. As we become a more globalized, seamless economy through which

Ingrid Burrington, *Who Gets to Live in Silicon Valley?*, Atlantic (June 25, 2018), https://perma.cc/2FQY-JMUV.

62 In drawing a comparison of this sort, some numbers from the Seattle area may be helpful. The entire Seattle Housing Authority's 2019 proposed annual budget was less than $300 million, and the City of Seattle's 2019 proposed Office of Housing budget was less than $70 million. *Calendar Year 2019 SHA Proposed Annual Budget: Summary*, Seattle Housing Authority (2018), https://perma.cc/YRN2-GANU ; *City Budget Office: Online Budget, Housing*, City of Seattle (2019), https://perma.cc/7ZBG-HQAY. The King County Housing Authority, which serves the communities surrounding Seattle, expends another $300 million. *See Overview*, King County (Wash.) Housing Authority (last visited March 3, 2020), https://perma.cc/Q7F8-WWG9. By contrast, Microsoft alone has pledged $500 million. *See* Weise, *supra* note 60.

63 *See* Burrington, *supra* note 61.

64 *See, e.g.*, Claus D. Zimmermann, *The Concept of Monetary Sovereignty Revisited*, 24 Eur. J. Int'l L. 797 (2013) (describing historical and enduring associations of state sovereignty with rights and duties associated with national currencies).

labor, goods, and services flow freely across national borders, the sundry costs of bridging sovereign currencies may well undercut the expected, let alone full, benefits of free trade, weaken North-to-South lending initiatives, and dilute the impact of North-to-South remittances.[65]

These inefficiencies bespeak a jurisdictional failure. Of course, nations – and national governments – still matter. They still matter even though commerce crosses national boundaries with a speed, frequency, and insouciance that startle many a central banker. The European Union (EU) is obviously one major political undertaking that, among other things, helps minimize the jurisdictional mismatch between nation-states and economic communities. But even within Europe there are limitations – notably, between the EU and the rest of Europe, the United States, and Japan.

Private firms may quite naturally seek to overcome this particular, if inescapable, government failure. True to form, the first major effort in the twenty-first century to short-circuit nations' sovereign monopoly on currency has been a decidedly commercial one. Bitcoin presents itself as a commercial alternative to national currencies and exchanges. But Bitcoin has no trappings of sovereignty. There is no centralized governance, no body of overseers, managers, or guarantors. Instead, the *crypto*currency operates flatly, via permissionless blockchain that functions autonomously in a manner seemingly consistent with Adam Smith's "invisible hand." Bitcoin, moreover, is a speculative currency, not a transactional one that, again, depends on stewards to maintain stability.

But now a second-wave – this time, sovereign-seeming – private intervention is in the offing. To overcome the jurisdictional failure associated with national currencies, Facebook and a variety of partners are set to roll out a currency they call Libra. Libra is billed as a readily transferable form of digital exchange, purportedly superior to national currencies precisely because of its transnational fungibility.[66] To this extent, Libra sounds a fair bit like Bitcoin. But Libra is provoking different, more worried responses. The French Finance Minister expressed concern that currency-issuing tech giants are "turning into private states – states over which citizens have no control and where democracy has no place."[67] The minister's concerns seem more than justified. After all, Libra promises to be a centrally governed reserve currency.

65 Such concerns obviously predate the contemporary globalization era. *See, e.g.*, J.S. Mill, 2 Principles of Political Economy 155 (1848) (remarking that "almost all independent countries choose to assert their nationality by having, to their own inconvenience and that of their neighbors, a peculiar currency of their own").

66 *Libra White Paper*, https://perma.cc/WSE8-9FJC; Olga Kharif, *Why (Almost) Everybody Hates Facebook's Digital Coin*, Wash. Post (October 7, 2019), https://perma.cc/WC6D-4297; Carrie Mihalcik, *Facebook's Libra May Look to Multiple Digital Coins Based on National Currencies*, C|net (October 21, 2019), https://perma.cc/T22E-79Q9; Andrew Morse, *Here's What You Need to Know about Facebook's Controversial Libra Cryptocurrency*, C|net (October 24, 2019), https://perma.cc/4PJP-XS6D.

67 Leigh Thomas, *G7 Finance Ministers Look to Rein in Tech Giants at French Meeting*, Reuters (July 17, 2019), https://perma.cc/QCJ9-CT2B.

Facebook and its partners will fund the exchange, regulate how it is put into circulation, resolve disputes over how Libra is traded or redeemed, and stabilize its value in times of systemic shock.[68] Libra also is bound to be a giant player from the outset, if for no other reason than it will readily sync up with Facebook's vast network of nearly two billion users and business partners scattered across more than one hundred nations.[69] Thus not only is Libra poised to be on roughly equal footing with some of the world's major currencies – meaning that Facebook can, if it chooses, engage in serious macroeconomic statecraft – it is also well situated to displace some less-developed countries' currencies (as well as the sovereign reserve currencies those and other countries currently rely on).

4.4.4 *Workplace Governance (Democratic Failures)*

It isn't just corporate directors and managers who are adopting quasi-sovereign guises and standing in for state officials hamstrung by one or more government failures. It is also workers effectuating seemingly democratic projects within the corridors of their place of employment.

Consider some recent examples involving employees of Google and Wayfair, among others. In the case of Google, company engineers pushed corporate decision-makers to stop doing business with US Customs and Border Protection, Immigration and Customs Enforcement, and the Office of Refugee Resettlement, at least so long as those departments advanced what the protesting employees deemed cruel and possibly unlawful initiatives. Among other things, the engineers alleged the feds were perpetrating "human rights abuses;" they criticized their firm's efforts to "support agencies engaged in caging and torturing vulnerable people;" and they insisted Google was "trading its integrity for a bit of profit."[70] (Microsoft and Amazon employees mounted similar intra-firm campaigns.[71]) On another occasion, Google employees successfully pressured management to walk away from another federal contract, fearing in this particular case that the AI technology it was furnishing would be used in combat situations.[72]

Way across the country, employees of Wayfair first signed a petition and then staged a highly publicized walkout in opposition to the Boston-based firm's arrangement to sell bedding to private detention centers housing migrant children separated from the rest of their families. The petition stated that Wayfair should take "no part

68 *See* Libra White Paper, *supra* note 66; Kharif, *supra* note 66; Mihalcik, *supra* note 66; Morse, *supra* note 66.

69 Kharif, *supra* note 66.

70 Cat Zakrzewski, *The Technology 202: Googlers Demand Company Renounce Working with Trump Immigration Agencies*, Wash. Post (August 15, 2009), https://perma.cc/6W55-KV5E. For the actual protest letter, see No GCP for CBP, *Google must stand against human rights abuses: #NoGCPforCBP*, Medium (August 14, 2019), https://perma.cc/H74F-YU7E.

71 *See* Zakrzewski, *supra* note 70.

72 *See id.*

in enabling, supporting, or profiting from" what the employees classified as malicious and unethical family separation policies and practices.[73]

What's going on here? Recall that modern legal liberalism enabled separation of the public from the private and specialization within each sphere. The public sphere democratized, incorporating and elevating the voices and projects of an inclusive polity. At the same time, the private sphere grew singularly focused on the maximization of shareholder profits. Social welfare was to be advanced through legislation, regulation, and, if necessary, adjudication. And the economy was to be strengthened through market competition and the laws of corporate governance.

Recall too that today's public levers are increasingly unresponsive. The great democratic revolution of the twentieth century is being rolled back, a result of hyper-libertarian campaign finance rulings, a lapsing commitment to voting rights (as voter suppression efforts target those on the racial or socioeconomic margins), and demographic dispersal patterns that invest some, often-unrepresentative constituencies with disproportionate voting power. In short, rising plutocracy coupled with the exacerbation of anti-democratic dynamics hardwired into the Constitution have made it harder for political majorities to influence public policy.

One way to deal with this current democratic failure is to overhaul the Constitution, passing amendments to overturn such cases as *Citizens United*. But that approach strikes many as daunting, if not hopeless. So instead of trying to make the seemingly corrupted public sphere more democratically responsive and thus public-regarding, some may seek an alternative approach. That approach may involve *corrupting* the private sphere by converting the corporate workplace into a democratic forum (at least when the real thing – that is, the conventional democratic forum – seems broken). Thus concerned citizens may not be able to use their voting power to stop the Trump administration's family separation policies. But maybe concerned workers – upon whom the government relies – can.[74]

Note the symmetry between employee-centered public policy initiatives and government market participation. In the latter cases, citizens see themselves in a business relationship with the government. And, here, in the former case, we have employees seeing themselves as part of a polity, relating to the firm first and foremost as concerned citizens, and raising policy objections orthogonal to, if not directly at odds with, their own financial well-being.

Employee-centered public policy initiatives of this sort appear to be in keeping with something that Kent Greenfield has been advancing for some years. Greenfield suggests that if a community cannot readily change a plutocratic political system, perhaps they ought to change corporate law. The employee protests at Google and Wayfair are attempts to get corporations to intervene in the political functioning of the state – not through voter drives or fundraising initiatives but rather by

73 Kate Taylor, *Wayfair Furniture Employees Walked Out Over Sales to Migrant Facilities*, N.Y. Times (June 25, 2019), https://perma.cc/A7MD-8GX9.

74 *See id. Cf.* Zakrzewski, *supra* note 70.

withholding goods and services in a way that either embarrasses or disadvantages the government and perhaps forces the government to rethink their projects.

Employee protests, much like consumer boycott campaigns, may or may not work. Success seemingly depends on the political salience of the issue, the relative market power protesting employees possess, and the firm's market share.[75] That's why Greenfield champions a set of changes far broader and less ad hoc than groups of workers acting the part of concerned citizens and hoping for the best. Specifically, he suggests corporate law be amended to define wealth maximization more broadly, prioritizing the maximization of value (*and not necessarily monetary value*) to all stakeholders, not just shareholders. Greenfield further advocates requiring corporations to include workers and other stakeholders on their boards, so that firms are better positioned to consider overall community welfare and, again, not just shareholder welfare. Last, he proposes compelling firms to extend their duty of care to workers and community members, too, such that firms have to take seriously ethical and practical objections to indisputably profitable business decisions.[76]

Many have painted reforms of this sort as aspirational rather than attainable – perhaps just as quixotic as a constitutional amendment overturning *Citizens United*. But just a few years after Greenfield proffered these arguments, the Business Roundtable announced its newer, broader, and more inclusive understanding of corporations and their purpose.[77] If Roundtable members commit to this revolutionary paradigm shift, firms may well stand in for government, particularly when state institutions are structurally unresponsive to the demands and needs of political majorities.[78]

4.5 CONCLUSION

We find ourselves in a moment when sovereign and commercial roles are in flux, as evidenced by, among other things, public and private options. With respect to

75 *See* Kent Greenfield, *The Stakeholder Society*, DEMOCRACY (Fall 2012), https://perma.cc/Z93S-SVA9. Palantir presents a countervailing case study. Palantir, more so than Google, Microsoft, or Wayfair, is dependent on the US government for steady work – and thus Palantir executives may be less inclined to back their employees when those employees object to certain government contracts. See Douglas MacMillan & Elizabeth Dworkin, *The War Inside Palantir: Data-mining Firm's Ties to ICE Under Attack by Employees*, WASH. POST (August 22, 2019), https://perma.cc/AQ2T-YK8J.

76 *See* Greenfield, *supra* note 75.

77 *See supra* note 36 and accompanying text.

78 One might even consider the Trump Justice Department's efforts to use labor and employment law, seemingly to weaken the political independence of immigration judges, who have proven to be at least somewhat at odds with the political leadership's strident positions on immigration enforcement. Ordinarily, we might expect legislation or regulation to be the primary means by which the roles and responsibilities of government officials are defined and altered. But the Justice Department is also using market pressures – specifically, by trying to have the immigration judges' union decertified – to effectuate the desired change in public policy. *See, e.g.*, Matt Zapotosky, *Justice Department Moves to Potentially Decertify Immigration Judges' Union*, WASH. POST (August 9, 2019), https://perma.cc/4BQD-77GT.

private options, the focus of this essay, it is clear that government failures are far-ranging, consequential, and unlikely to be addressed directly – that is, remedied through constitutional reforms or political awakenings. It is also clear that, for a variety of reasons, powerful firms and groups of employees have the agility, clout, resources, ambition, and possibly civic mindedness to swoop in and (try to) save the day.

Opportunities to create additional or alternative democratic spaces are, to be sure, exciting. But we must be cautious, even watchful. Exercises of private power – however much divorced from the logic and lure of profit-maximization – are, after all, still exercises of private power. Indeed, it strikes me that some, if not all, of the private options discussed in this essay raise serious concerns. What normative criteria would allow us to, say, embrace Facebook's currency or Apple's company town? And even if many of us applaud Silicon Valley engineers' resistance to the Trump administration's family separation policy, how would we feel if those same engineers, flexing their libertarian muscles, held up software essential to implementing duly enacted Medicare for All legislation?

But perhaps greater nuance is required. Perhaps, that is, our standards are too high, at least so long as our democratic institutions are subverted, debased, and distorted by such things as plutocracy, obscurantism, and incompetence.

Thus, as tempting as it might be to reject private options out of hand, we must recognize the litany of government failures that create governance gaps – gaps that firms and firm employees are endeavoring to fill. And appreciating that we may be in a world of only second-bests – where we are forced to choose between greedy, unrepresentative firms and captured, clunky government institutions – we may need to temper our expectations and consider whether to (a) embrace public capitalism *and work like crazy to democratize market actors and institutions*; (b) recommit to legal liberalism *and work just as hard to revitalize government actors and institutions*; or (c) let things play out, regulate on the margins, and hope the existence of sovereign-commercial competition – a hallmark of public capitalism – brings out the best in everyone.

Obviously, much work, normative, legal, and empirical, remains to be done. This essay represents just an initial foray, one that – I hope – spurs further research, debate, and refinement.

5

The Original – And Still the Best?

The Health Insurance Public Option and the Politics of Social Reform

Jacob S. Hacker

In late 2009, in an event space beneath the US Capitol plaza, a small celebration centered on a big decision. The Majority Leader of the US Senate, Nevada Democrat Harry Reid, announced he would support the inclusion of a public option in the health-care bill that would soon be considered on the Senate floor. As one of the policy experts who had pushed for the public option, I was in the audience – gratified that Reid had decided to fight for the goal yet unsure of what would come next. Earlier in the year, the House had passed its own health legislation, which included a Medicare-like public option. But from the moment it had become a major element of Democratic campaign proposals during the 2008 presidential race, the public option had been controversial – viewed as a step too far not only by Republicans and the medical industry, but also by many middle-of-the-road Democrats. Now, in signaling he would back it, Reid was also suggesting he could convince skeptical Senate Democrats to go along.

He couldn't. Within a few weeks, the public option was dead. Reid needed every one of the Senate's sixty Democrats to overcome a Republican filibuster, and Connecticut's Joe Lieberman, a moderate friendly to the insurance industry, insisted the provision be dropped. The Affordable Care Act (ACA) passed the next year, but the landmark law signed by President Obama did not contain the public option he had advocated for during his successful presidential campaign. Even in the many areas where few commercial insurers operated, the choice for those not eligible for Medicaid was private insurance or no insurance at all. A prominent Democratic idea seemed destined for the dustbin of history.

Ten years later, however, the public option was out of the dustbin – and back in the crosshairs. Yet this time, the attacks were mostly coming from the left of the Democratic Party. Among moderate Democrats, the public option was no longer dismissed as a liberal fantasy; it was seen as the sensible starting point for building on the ACA. Indeed, all of the middle-of-the-road candidates vying for the party's 2020 presidential nomination – from billionaire ex-Republican Michael Bloomberg to eventual winner (of the primary and presidential election) Joe Biden – said they would back a public option.[1] The more progressive candidates, by contrast, said they would go well beyond the public option and fight for a universal Medicare program, aka "Medicare for All." According to the leading voice of the left, Bernie Sanders, only Medicare for All could fix the problems in American health care; the public option, Sanders argued, would "essentially … maintain what I consider to be a dysfunctional and cruel health care system."[2]

This chapter examines the rise, fall, and rebirth of the public option. My goal is not to retread familiar history, but to draw out the underlying political logic of the public option and consider whether that logic still applies a decade after the passage of the ACA. During the debate over the ACA, the public option was viewed by its opponents as a back door to universal Medicare. Now, however, many on the left believe they can open the front door. Is there still a case for the public option? Would it work – that is, substantially restrain prices and provide economic security to all Americans? And what kinds of dynamics *would* it unleash? Would it lead inevitably to Medicare for All? Would it be marginalized by its private competitors? Or would it achieve a stable equilibrium, and if so of what sort?

To tackle these questions, I draw on a burgeoning body of research on what political scientists term "policy feedback," the processes by which large-scale public policies reshape public opinion, interest-group alignments, the capacities of government, and other fundamental features of the political world.[3,4] The health-care public option was the most prominent major proposal since the 1970s for what Sitaraman and Alstott call a "competitive public option" – a public plan that would compete with private ones on a level-playing field. Those who supported it believed government insurance would be more efficient and equitable. Yet they also had a theory – sometimes explicit, usually implicit – about how this competitive public option would evolve over time and reshape American politics.[5] The aim of this chapter is to draw out this theory, subject it to scrutiny, and tease out its implications.

1 Tricia Neuman, Karen Pollitz, Jennifer Tolbert, Robin Rudowitz, and Wyatt Koma, "10 Key Questions on Public Option Proposals," *Kaiser Family Foundation*, December 18, 2019, www.kff.org/health-reform/issue-brief/10-key-questions-on-public-option-proposals/.

2 Bart Jansen, "Joe Biden, Bernie Sanders Spar Over Long Records on Trade, Entitlements, Guns and Iran as Primaries Push On," *USA Today*, March 10, 2020, www.usatoday.com/story/news/politics/elections/2020/03/10/joe-biden-bernie-sanders-spar-over-trade-entitlements-guns-and-iraq/4965512002/.

3 Jacob S. Hacker and Paul Pierson eds., "New Policies, New Politics? Policy Feedback, Power-Building, and American Governance," Special issue, *The Annals of the American Academy of Political and Social Science* 685, no. 1 (September 2019), https://journals.sagepub.com/toc/anna/685/1.

4 Jacob S. Hacker, "Medicare Expansion as a Path as well as a Destination: Achieving Universal Insurance through a New Politics of Medicare," *The Annals of the American Academy of Political and Social Science* 685, no. 1 (2019): 135–153, https://doi.org/10.1177/0002716219871017.

5 Ganesh Sitaraman and Anne L. Alstott, *The Public Option: How to Expand Freedom, Increase Opportunity, and Promote Equality* (Cambridge, MA: Harvard University Press, 2019), 24–43, 78–80, and 202–222.

The main conclusion I reach is that the public option still has formidable advantages over Medicare for All. Although no one should underestimate how hard it will be to enact, it is certain to pose less threat to well-insured Americans than Medicare for All, to require less up-front public spending (and hence new taxation), and to face more divided opposition from the medical industry. A corollary, however, is that the specific design of the public option will have a major effect not only on the likelihood of its enactment but also on its future entrenchment and expansion. A pared-back public option of the sort that might have passed in 2010 is no longer up to the challenge. Instead, proposals with the most promise – I call them the "Public Option 2.0" – all put in place strong measures to guarantee universal coverage and expand the reach of public cost controls over time. Such a system, I argue, could move the nation a fair way toward Medicare for All. Designed properly, it could also create self-reinforcing political dynamics, drawing Americans together in pursuit of affordable health care for all, rather than tearing them apart.

5.1 A BRIEF HISTORY OF THE PUBLIC OPTION

The public option burst into the health-care debate during the 2008 presidential campaign. Yet the idea has a long lineage – one that well predates the proposals I wrote starting in the early 2000s that helped push the idea into the spotlight.[6,7,8,9] Most notably, Medicare itself has evolved into something of a public option, albeit one limited to the elderly and disabled. That's because Medicare beneficiaries have long been able to choose between regulated private plans that contract with Medicare and the traditional public plan. This feature of Medicare is very similar to the framework for a public option I developed. Under this system, now labeled "Medicare Advantage," the public option is the default and beneficiaries must affirmatively choose private plans available in their region. In turn, these plans are heavily regulated and, in theory at least, paid amounts that reflect the expected cost of treating beneficiaries to discourage them from trying to select healthier patients. Today, roughly a third of beneficiaries are enrolled in private plans through Medicare Advantage.[10] The remaining two-thirds

6 Jacob S. Hacker, "Medicare Plus: Increasing Healthcare Coverage by Expanding Medicare," in *Covering America: Real Remedies for the Uninsured*, eds. Jack A. Meyer and Elliot K. Wicks (Washington, DC: Economic and Social Research Institute, 2001), 73–100, www.jacobhacker.com/assets/9a_medicare-plus.pdf.

7 Jacob S. Hacker, "Health Care for America: A Proposal for Guaranteed, Affordable Health Care for all Americans Building on Medicare and Employment-Based Insurance." *Economic Policy Institute*, Briefing Paper No. 180, January 11, 2007, www.jacobhacker.com/assets/9_health_care_for_america.pdf.

8 Jacob S. Hacker, "Medicare Part E (for 'Everyone')," November 14, 2017, www.jacobhacker.com/assets/hacker–medicare-part-e–11-14-2017.pdf.

9 Jacob S. Hacker, "The Road to Medicare for Everyone," *The American Prospect*, January 3, 2018, https://prospect.org/health/road-medicare-everyone/.

10 Gretchen Jacobson, Anthony Damico, and Tricia Neuman, "A Dozen Facts About Medicare Advantage," *Kaiser Family Foundation*, November 13, 2018, www.kff.org/medicare/issue-brief/a-dozen-facts-about-medicare-advantage/.

are in traditional Medicare, though most also have supplemental private insurance that reduces Medicare's out-of-pocket costs.[11]

Though Medicare's system was my basic model, I argued for a number of significant departures from its template. One was a requirement that benefits packages for the public option and private plans be more or less the same. In Medicare Advantage, private plans are attractive to Medicare enrollees in major part because they cover a wider range of benefits and, unlike Medicare, offer integrated prescription drug coverage. (Those covered by traditional Medicare must buy a stand-alone private plan under Medicare Part D.) This tilts the playing field in favor of the private plans. In addition, the requirement that beneficiaries get their drug coverage from private plans eliminates the ability of Medicare to bargain for lower drug prices – a major potential source of cost savings that the pharmaceutical industry has so far successfully resisted.

Another precondition for a successful public option that I emphasized was a much better system for paying private plans. The current approach is flawed in three major respects. First, it offers an explicit subsidy to private plans, which should be eliminated. Second, it does not adequately adjust for the actual cost of treating enrolled beneficiaries; better "risk adjustment," both prospective and retrospective, would better discourage the selective enrollment of healthier patients and disenrollment of less healthy ones. Finally, payments to plans are not set through true competitive bidding. Plans should instead be required to bid to provide standardized benefits, and payments to plans should be based on a weighted average of plan bids within its geographic area, as opposed to the current approach.[12,13]

These proposed changes were so important because, by 2008, the public option was not seen as an alternative to the basic policy framework that inspired much of the ACA – a framework in which uninsured Americans would be able to choose among subsidized and regulated private plans. Instead, it was seen as a crucial addition to that framework. In the House legislation, for example, larger employers were required to insure their workers or pay a mandated contribution; those without workplace coverage were given access to Medicaid (if they had lower incomes) or to a new insurance purchasing pool run by their states; and this pool would make available both private plans and a national public option modeled after Medicare.[14]

11 Juliette Cubanski, Anthony Damico, Tricia Neuman, and Gretchen Jacobson, "Sources of Supplemental Coverage Among Medicare Beneficiaries in 2016," *Kaiser Family Foundation*, November 28, 2018, www.kff.org/medicare/issue-brief/sources-of-supplemental-coverage-among-medicare-beneficiaries-in-2016/.

12 Jacob S. Hacker, "Healthy Competition: How to Structure Public Health Insurance Plan Choice to Ensure Risk-Sharing, Cost Control, and Quality Improvement," *Institute for America's Future and the Berkeley Center on Health, Economic and Family Security*, Policy Brief, Berkeley, CA, April 2009, www.jacobhacker.com/assets/6_hacker_healthy_competition.pdf.

13 Steven M. Lieberman et al., "The Case for Reforming Competitive Bidding in Medicare Advantage," *Brookings Institute*, May 10, 2018, www.brookings.edu/blog/usc-brookings-schaeffer-on-health-policy/2018/05/10/the-case-for-reforming-competitive-bidding-in-medicare-advantage/.

14 Affordable Health Care for America Act, H.R. 3962, 111th Cong. (2009).

Thus, the public option would be available alongside regulated private plans to anyone who lacked coverage through Medicaid or an employer.

The case I made for this sort of public option can be summed up in what I called the "three B's" of public plan choice: a Medicare-like plan would be a *backup* in places where insurance competition was weak, a *benchmark* for competing private plans, and a cost-control *backstop*, bringing the consolidated purchasing power of the federal government to bear in a larger share of the market.[15] The last "b" was particularly crucial. Medicare's per capita spending has grown much more slowly than per capita expenditures for private insurance on a comparable set of services, and this cost-control advantage has grown over time.[16] Moreover, I envisioned a major effort to improve Medicare price and volume regulations and integrated payment methods over time. Thus, the public option wasn't simply designed to make coverage available. It was designed to be a major cost-control measure whose scope would grow over time as the public option expanded and became more closely integrated with Medicare itself (with the two systems ultimately merging, at least in the proposals I developed).

I did not offer a fourth b-word, but many critics did, arguing that the plan was also a *backdoor* route to Medicare for All. Some who supported the public option made this argument, too.[17] My view, however, was more conditional: although the role of the public plan would surely expand, its scope would depend far more on what happened with private employment-based insurance than on how well it fared in competition with private plans. Under the House legislation, for instance, most employers were expected to continue providing their own coverage, and the public option would only be available for those purchasing regulated and subsidized insurance outside the workplace. Unless that changed, even the most successful public option would cover tens of millions of Americans, not hundreds.

In light of this, it may be tempting to look back at the reform circus of 2009 and 2010 and see the public option as a sideshow. But while it certainly wasn't in the main ring, it was an important part of the production. First, it was one of the most genuinely popular aspects of Democratic reform proposals. Polls showed not just that Americans liked it, but that they found a mandate to have coverage more acceptable if those required to be insured had the option of enrolling in a plan like Medicare.[18] Second, it engaged progressive activists and politicians who were

15 Jacob S. Hacker, "The Case for Public Plan Choice in National Health Reform," *Berkeley Law* and *Institute for America's Future*, December 2008, http://citeseerx.ist.psu.edu/viewdoc/download?doi=10.1.1.522.2310&rep=rep1&type=pdf.

16 Juliette Cubanski, Tricia Neuman, and Meredith Freed, "The Facts on Medicare Spending and Financing," *Kaiser Family Foundation*, Issue Brief, August 2019, http://files.kff.org/attachment/Issue-Brief-Facts-on-Medicaid-Spending-and-Financing

17 Kevin Sack, "Health Care Up to Public, Edwards Says," *New York Times*, January 25, 2008, www.nytimes.com/2008/01/25/us/politics/25edwards.html.

18 Mike Lux, "The Public Option Fight Gets Engaged in Public for the First Time Next Week," *Huffington Post*, November 25, 2009, www.huffpost.com/entry/the-public-option-fight-g_b_299970.

skeptical of the exclusive reliance on private insurance. Though the public option did not survive, a strong case can be made that it encouraged coalition-building that pushed out the boundaries of the possible, facilitating a law that was broader than it might have been otherwise.[19,20]

Because it did not survive, however, we cannot know how it might have evolved had it made it into law. On the one hand, the public option that passed through the House was relatively weak – for example, it could not require that physicians who took Medicare participate in it, and it did not have authority to use Medicare's rates. On the other hand, it would have created a focal point for expanded coverage and still offered considerable advantages over private plans, particularly in the many areas of the country where private insurers were scarce and providers highly consolidated. Moreover, US social policies have often started small and grown bigger over time, and there was good reason to think that a public option would expand and become more robust, at least if it were able to survive the initial political backlash.

Since the passage of the ACA, both the pricing advantage of Medicare and the weakness of the state-based insurance pools (now known as "marketplaces") have become more and more apparent. So too, alas, has the ferocity of that initial backlash. In part because of the ceaseless Republican attacks on the law, far fewer Americans have enrolled through the marketplaces than expected, many of these state insurance pools feature a limited number of plan choices, and the nonprofit "cooperatives" championed by moderate Democrats as an alternative to the public option have largely gone bust.[21,22,23] In sum, there's little doubt that the public option would have provided a valuable source of coverage in the many areas of the country where private insurance competition is weak to nonexistent.

5.2 THE PUBLIC OPTION IN TODAY'S DEBATE

Still, it is now clear that the place of the public option in any future reform will depend on mechanisms of enrollment as much as on how the public option itself is designed. Simply adding a public option to the existing state marketplaces will not

19 Richard Kirsch, *Fighting for Our Health: The Epic Battle to Make Health Care a Right in the United States* (Albany, NY: Rockefeller Institute Press, 2011).

20 Lawrence Jacobs and Theda Skocpol, *Health Care Reform and American Politics: What Everyone Needs to Know* (New York, NY: Oxford University Press, 2015).

21 Jayne O'Donnell, "Signs of Trouble – and Progress – as Obamacare 2019 Open Enrollment Nears," *USA Today*, August 19, 2019, www.usatoday.com/story/news/health/2019/08/19/obamacare-2019-open-enrollment-nears-signs-trouble-progress/1996342001/.

22 Rachel Fehr, Rabah Kamal, and Cynthia Cox, "Insurer Participation on ACA Marketplaces, 2014–2020," *Kaiser Family Foundation*, November 21, 2019, www.kff.org/private-insurance/issue-brief/insurer-participation-on-aca-marketplaces-2014-2020/.

23 Sabrina Corlette, Sean Miskell, Julia Lerche, and Justin Giovannelli, "Why Are Many CO-OPs Failing? How New Nonprofit Health Plans Have Responded to Market Competition," *The Commonwealth Fund*, December 10, 2015, www.commonwealthfund.org/publications/fund-reports/2015/dec/why-are-many-co-ops-failing-how-new-nonprofit-health-plans-have.

make a large difference unless the marketplaces reach a much larger share of Americans. The public option's scope will obviously affect whether and how quickly the United States reaches universal coverage. Again, however, it may well be even more fundamental to the capacity of the federal government to use its purchasing power to restrain spending over time. Small public option, small effects.

Indeed, the current public option plans with the most promise and prominence – the Medicare for America Act sponsored by Representatives Rosa DeLauro and Jan Schakowsky (on which I worked) and the Center for American Progress's "Medicare Extra for All" – largely bypass the marketplaces, allowing employers to directly buy into the public option or pay a contribution in lieu of providing coverage that funds the same public coverage. They also emphasize the need for automatic enrollment procedures (mainly through the workplace) and expanded federal subsidies to reach the roughly 30 million Americans who continue to lack coverage. Finally, these proposals do something that the House bill did not: they allow people to opt out of their existing employment-based coverage and enroll in the public option directly. All these features distinguish The Public Option 2.0 from its predecessors. They also raise important questions about policy design that have yet to be sufficiently tackled.

The rebirth of the public option also raises a more fundamental issue: Has its time come and gone? The case for the public option in 2009 and 2010 was primarily a political one. For one, it was far more likely to be enacted than a full-scale Medicare for All. For another, like other major social programs that coexisted with private alternatives, such as Social Security, it could have provided a foundation for the further expansion of national public coverage over time. Let us call these two distinct political virtues (or vices, depending on your point of view) *feasibility* and *expandability*. The public option could pass, and it could grow.

Feasibility and expandability are obviously in tension. Insurers, pharmaceutical companies, and other health-care lobbies fought the public option so fiercely not because of what it was in the House bill – a relatively modest expansion of government's insurance role – but because of what it could become: a sizable competitor and price-bargainer with popular and political support. They recognized what reformers sometimes forget: policies change politics. Policies do not just deliver benefits, they create institutions that can be focal points for political mobilization, and they can change the resources and goals of political actors, from voters to interest groups to public officials themselves.

As noted, a large and growing body of political science research explores these policy feedback effects and provides a relatively sophisticated set of insights for thinking about them. These concepts and findings go beyond the traditional focus on the initial passage of laws to examine what makes them more or less likely to become politically entrenched and expand over time. This established literature – and recent work building on it to examine contemporary policy issues in our increasingly polarized political environment – provides timely guidance as experts, advocates, and officials debate the best ways of building on the ACA, and in particular whether to embrace the public option or the bigger ambition of Medicare for All.

On the one side, backers of Medicare for All argue that the public option is half a loaf that does not need to be accepted when the whole loaf now lies within reach. Many also argue that anything that Democrats propose that involves a substantial expansion of public coverage will encounter fierce industry and Republican resistance, meaning a public option offers little political-feasibility advantage over Medicare for All. Finally, some Medicare for All advocates dispute that the public option would actually work, much less expand toward universal Medicare. In short, skeptics contest both the feasibility and the expandability of the public option.[24]

On the other side, those who back the public option have refined their case by emphasizing the centrality of enrollment and strengthening their proposed public plan relative to what was seriously considered in 2009 and 2010. Public Option 2.0 proposals also put greater emphasis on the cost-control capacity of the federal government, which has become more and more apparent over time.[25] Some have also made a forthright argument for the public option as a stepping stone to Medicare for All – an argument generally made sotto voce, if at all, a decade ago.[26] Finally, most argue that Medicare for All, while a worthy goal, lies beyond immediate reach because of its high public price tag and the fierce resistance it would provoke. For those who make this last argument, feasibility still looms large.

The coming sections consider these competing arguments. The next looks at the basic political trade-offs involved in public option proposals and contrasts them with those raised by Medicare for All. The following two sections consider, in turn, the likely policy effects of the public option and the potential *political* dynamics it might unleash – that is, the kinds of policy feedback effects it is likely to create. Here I unpack some of the differences between existing public option proposals, drawing on the revealing contrasts among the plans offered under the banner by some of the Democratic candidates who were prominent in the 2020 presidential race. What form the public option takes, it turns out, matters enormously not only for its workability, but also its likely political effects.

5.3 RECONSIDERING THE POLITICS OF THE PUBLIC OPTION

In *The Public Option*, Sitaraman and Alstott define a public option as a policy guaranteeing access to a valued good at a controlled price alongside competing

24 Adam Gaffney, "The Case against the Public Option," *Jacobin Magazine*, July 19, 2017, www.jacobinmag.com/2017/07/trumpcare-obamacare-repeal-public-option-single-payer.

25 Zack Cooper, Stuart V Craig, Martin Gaynor, and John Van Reenen, "The Price Ain't Right? Hospital Prices and Health Spending on the Privately Insured," *The Quarterly Journal of Economics* 134, no. 1 (2019): 51–107, https://doi.org/10.1093/qje/qjy020.

26 Elizabeth Warren, "My First Term Plan for Reducing Health Care Costs in America and Transitioning to Medicare for All," *Medium*, November 15, 2019, https://elizabethwarren.com/plans/m4a-transition?source=soc-WB-ew-tw-rollout-20191115.

private alternatives.[27] They distinguish between "baseline" public options, in which private provision can top off the publicly offered good and "competitive" public options, in which private provision competes in the same general market. In health care, a baseline-style public option would take the form of less-than-complete public coverage, which people would supplement with private insurance. Although this is a common approach in other rich democracies, the form of public option under discussion here is one in which the public option and private plans are competing to offer similarly comprehensive coverage.[28]

Medicare for All is *not* a public option – certainly not a competitive one, nor even a baseline version. All of the leading Medicare for All proposals are extremely comprehensive and thus would leave limited scope for private insurance. Virtually all of them, moreover, get rid of Medicare Advantage and thus would not allow people to choose regulated private plans as current Medicare beneficiaries do.

Competitive public options could, in theory, take many forms. In practice, existing proposals all largely follow a model that focuses on Medicare – the model I outlined earlier. There are compelling reasons for this focus: Medicare is not only familiar and popular; as noted, it's also become more effective at containing prices over time, as consolidated provider groups have put growing upward pressure on private spending. Accordingly, advocates of the public option argue either for immediately expanding Medicare or for creating a "Medicare-like" plan that would merge with Medicare in the future. It is this general approach that I will contrast and compare with Medicare for All as I consider the feasibility and expandability of leading proposals.

For all the value of Sitaraman and Alstott's book, its guidance here is more limited. With a few exceptions, theirs is an equilibrium analysis, in which they examine public options that have come to occupy a central place in US public policy and propose public options that they believe could come to occupy that place. These analyses and recommendations are vital. But critical to the pros and cons of the public option is the prospect of *disequilibrium*. After all, competition is a dynamic, often unstable process in which some competitors prosper and others do not. Indeed, the idea of the public option as a benchmark (Sitaraman and Alstott use the term "yardstick") implies that public options should thrive or wither based on their comparative performance. It should come as no surprise, then, that both advocates and opponents of the health-care public option have strong and differing views about how it will fare in the competitive fray.

These competing forecasts highlight the biggest political trade-off posed by the public option. Compared with Medicare for All, it is less of a political lift, for reasons we shall explore. But it also leaves uncertain what the ultimate role of the public

27 Ganesh Sitaraman and Anne L. Alstott, *The Public Option: How to Expand Freedom, Increase Opportunity, and Promote Equality* (Cambridge, MA: Harvard University Press, 2019), 27.

28 Roosa Tikkanen, "Variation on a Theme: A Look at Universal Health Coverage in Eight Countries," *To the Point* (blog), *The Commonwealth Fund*, March 22, 2019, https://doi.org/10.26099/x056-8s85.

option will be. At the same time, it leaves in place many of the existing interests that might be wholly or substantially displaced by Medicare for All. Among the feedback effects that policies can have, perhaps the most powerful is the elimination or sidelining of major organized interests. Airline deregulation, for example, quickly decimated the incumbent carriers, reducing any organized pressure on politicians to reconstruct the dismantled regulatory regime.[29] Medicare for All, if fully implemented, would have a similar effect on private insurers. A health-care public option, by contrast, would keep private insurers around, albeit within a more regulated market, and thus also preserve a major lobbying force that will work to limit the public option's reach.

One way to think about this set of trade-offs is as a *constitutional* process. As the scholarship on constitution-building has shown, incumbent elites generally need some assurance that their interests will be at least partially protected, and the prospects for such bargains hinge on uncertainty about which factions will be ultimately most likely to win in more open contestation.[30,31] In the same way, the public option is likely to gain support if it offers some protections for existing private interests, especially commercial insurers and health-care providers, as well as genuine uncertainty about the extent to which the public option will grow over time. To achieve these conditions, however, requires designing the public option in ways that make it less likely to achieve the kinds of transformative changes envisioned by Medicare for All, at least at the outset.

But the transformative effect of Medicare for All is a weakness as well as a strength. Medicare for All poses an existential threat to the insurance industry; the public option does not. Some defenders of Medicare for All dispute that this really matters politically, since critics will call whatever progressives try to do a "government takeover." But this understates the political liabilities of Medicare for All. Not only is the health-care industry certain to be fiercely opposed; Medicare for All also faces two other substantial hurdles.

The first is the difficulty of raising the necessary funds through new taxation – the magnitude of which would exceed any prior tax increase in American history as a share of GDP. The second is the reality that many Americans otherwise sympathetic to an expanded Medicare program (including beneficiaries themselves) can be scared into thinking that they will be worse off under Medicare for All, because it will displace or diminish the quality of their coverage. These liabilities – intense industry opposition, tax resistance, the fears of the currently well-insured – mean Medicare for All will require substantial progressive majorities, capable not only of

29 Eric M. Patashnik, *Reforms at Risk: What Happens After Major Policy Changes are Enacted* (Princeton, NJ: Pinceton University Press, 2008), 110–135.

30 James A. Robinson and Daron Acemoglu, *Economic Origins of Dictatorship and Democracy* (Cambridge, UK: Cambridge University Press, 2006).

31 Carles Boix, *Democracy and Redistribution* (Cambridge, UK: Cambridge University Press, 2003), DOI:10.1017/CBO9780511804960.

passing a controversial law over fierce resistance, but also holding onto it through subsequent elections in the face of the inevitable backlash that such large-scale changes will provoke.

When these concerns are raised, advocates of Medicare for All generally offer two main responses. The first is that Medicare for All is based on a different political logic than the public option; by promising a dramatically better system and rallying Americans behind transformative change, it can overcome the hurdles on which more conventional reform approaches founder. The second is that Medicare for All plans typically embody a transition process that creates intermediate policies – including, in the leading proposals, a public option – that can smooth the path to full-scale Medicare for All.

The first argument is highly contestable. Public views on Medicare for All are polarized and malleable. Depending on the poll, modest majorities of Americans express support for the general goal, but support drops off quickly when the potential drawbacks, including higher taxes and the replacement of existing private coverage, are mentioned even innocuously.[32,33] In any case, recent scholarship on public policy is not kind to the view that strong public support for a policy goal – in the absence of highly conductive partisan and interest-group configurations – is sufficient for major policy change. This is especially true in policy areas where the affluent and major organized interests hold different positions than do middle class and poor Americans, and health and social policies feature particularly large divides of this sort.[34,35]

The second response – that many advocates of Medicare for All envision a relatively lengthy, multistep transition – needs to be unpacked to be fairly evaluated. Some Medicare for All proposals (most notably, Senator Sanders's) do contain a legislated transition period. But these intermediate steps, lasting just four years in the Sanders plan, are unlikely to make it any easier to pass Medicare for All. That's because these proposals envision their wholesale replacement with a universal Medicare program with generous benefits and no private plans. Opponents of Medicare for All are not going to be more supportive simply because of a slightly delayed implementation of the entire program, nor do the intermediate steps seem designed to create political momentum for full implementation, given their relatively short expected life.

32 Ashley Kirzinger, Cailey Muñana, and Mollyan Brodie, "KFF Health Tracking Poll – January 2019: The Public on Next Steps for the ACA and Proposals to Expand Coverage," *Kaiser Family Foundation*, January 23, 2019, Fig. 6, www.kff.org/health-reform/poll-finding/kff-health-tracking-poll-january-2019/.

33 Washington Post and ABC News, "Washington Post-ABC News poll, June 28–July 1, 2019," July 11, 2019, www.washingtonpost.com/context/washington-post-abc-news-poll-june-28-july-1-2019/23419a67-9e70-42e3-a96d-65d92555e29b/?itid=lk_inline_manual_2.

34 Jacob S. Hacker and Paul Pierson, "Policy Feedback in an Age of Polarization," *The Annals of the American Academy of Political and Social Science* 685, no. 1 (2019): 8–28, https://doi.org/10.1177/0002716219871222.

35 Martin Gilens, *Affluence and Influence: Economic Inequality and Political Power in America* (Princeton, NJ: Princeton University Press, 2012).

In short, the transition period in Medicare for All plans is a "staged" implementation of the full program. That should be contrasted with what I've called "sequencing," in which early legislative steps are designed to ease the transition to a larger public program by creating essential policy infrastructure and supportive political dynamics.[36] Senator Elizabeth Warren, for example, backed away from the Sanders plan and offered a sequenced approach instead, in which she envisions a number of large-scale changes, including the creation of a highly robust public option, that she argues would pave the way for additional legislation creating Medicare for All.[37] This approach does indeed make the passage of her plan more likely. But, of course, it is also open to the criticism that it may not be able to achieve Medicare for All despite these big initial steps. In this respect, Senator Warren's campaign proposal can be seen as an ambitious public option plan designed to create pressure for full-scale Medicare for All, which may or may not achieve that goal depending on post-enactment political and policy dynamics.

To sum up, the health-care public option faces less formidable political hurdles than does Medicare for All, but this comes at the cost of leaving in place key organized interests that could compromise the policy in the future. Medicare for All offers the opposite balance sheet: high barriers to passage and initial establishment, but greater prospect of immediately transforming the political context in ways conducive to its entrenchment. The typical transition provisions in Medicare for All plans change this ledger modestly if at all. They reduce the scope of initial change and thus are likely to ease implementation. Yet, opponents will recognize that these are only intermediate provisions. In fact, the transition periods may give opponents greater ability to scuttle the law before it is fully implemented.

The big policy divide, then, is between proposals that explicitly establish a Medicare for All system and public-option proposals that expand Medicare but leave open whether Medicare for All will be established in the future. In judging the latter proposals, both on their own and in comparison with Medicare for All, the two crucial questions are, first, how well would they work at achieving the policy goal of universal affordable health care; and, second, how would they evolve in the future? The next two sections take up these questions in turn.

5.4 THE (CONTINUING) CASE FOR THE PUBLIC OPTION

When I first proposed the public option, I cast it as a means of expanding Medicare that accommodated the "path-dependent" development of American health insurance. Unique among rich democracies, the United States came to rely on private health plans sponsored by employers to insure the majority of Americans, with its two main public programs, Medicare and Medicaid, designed to reach populations ill-served by the employment-based system: the elderly and

[36] *See note 4.*
[37] *See note 26.*

the poor.[38] Over the past generation, this system has gradually but inexorably eroded, with private health insurance less and less available in the workplace. Still, roughly half the US population continues to receive insurance through employment-based plans, and while those plans too often leave workers facing high costs, Americans remain relatively satisfied with them.

The public option accommodates America's unusual system in two distinct ways. First, it allows those without workplace insurance to choose between public and private plans, reproducing the basic structure of Medicare Advantage. (In some proposals, current Medicaid beneficiaries are folded into this framework of plan choice; in others, they remain insured through state Medicaid programs.) Second, public option proposals generally have some mechanism for ensuring that employers either cover their workers or contribute to the cost of coverage, in which case their employees would have the same choice of public and private plans as other Americans lacking workplace insurance. These provisions leave a substantial role for private health insurance in general and for employment-based private insurance in particular. They also leave a substantial amount of financing in the private sector. In doing so, they not only reduce the disruption to existing arrangements, but also the up-front tax costs of expanded coverage, while leaving open exactly how the system will evolve in the future.

Nonetheless, the new federal spending required for public option plans is not trivial. During the 2020 campaign, the more moderate candidates offered public option proposals that would require on the order of a trillion dollars in new ten-year federal spending.[39] These new federal costs pale, however, next to those implied by Medicare for All. According to independent estimates, Sanders's plan would require around $30 *trillion* in new federal spending over a decade.[40]

To be sure, this new spending would substitute for insurance premiums and other private payments. (Generally, experts find that total national health spending will remain similar to current forecasts in the initial years – despite universal comprehensive coverage – and then decline relative to forecasted spending over time, as the greater cost-control capacity of the federal government kicks in.[41]) Still, $30 trillion is more than half as large as the entire amount that the federal government is projected

[38] Jacob S. Hacker, *The Divided Welfare State: The Battle Over Public and Private Social Benefits in the United States* (Cambridge, UK: Cambridge University Press, 2002).

[39] Linda J. Blumberg, John Holahan, Matthew Buettgens et al., "From Incremental to Comprehensive Health Insurance Reform: How Various Reform Options Compare on Coverage Costs," *Health Policy Center* (Report), *Urban Institute*, October 2019, www.urban.org/sites/default/files/2019/10/15/from_incremental_to_comprehensive_health_insurance_reform-how_various_reform_options_compare_on_coverage_and_costs.pdf.

[40] Linda J. Blumberg, John Holahan, and Michael Simpson, "Don't Confuse Changes in Federal Health Spending with National Health Spending," *Urban Wire: Health and Health Policy* (Blog), *Urban Institute*, October 16, 2019, www.urban.org/urban-wire/dont-confuse-changes-federal-health-spending-national-health-spending.

[41] Glenn Kessler, "Sanders's Apples-and-Oranges Comparison on Medicare-for-All Costs," *Fact Checker* (Blog), *The Washington Post*, September 19, 2019, www.washingtonpost.com/politics/2019/09/18/sanderss-apples-and-oranges-comparison-medicare-for-all-costs/.

to spend in the next decade ($52 trillion, according to the Congressional Budget Office[42]), and would require very large tax increases or spending cuts.

Of course, the price tag of the public option will depend on the size of the public plan, as well as whether it attracts disproportionately unhealthy patients. The latter concern, I have noted, is reinforced by the experience of Medicare Advantage, where private plans have historically benefitted from favorable risk selection (and still do so today, though the ACA substantially reduced "excess" payments to private plans[43]). Critics of the public option on the left rightly worry that, in the absence of an improved system for paying private plans, the public option could end up saddled with higher-risk patients.

Public Option 2.0 proposals, however, have much broader benefits than the current Medicare program, including an integrated prescription drug plan with the power to directly bargain for lower pharmaceutical prices. (Recall that a major reason why so many Medicare beneficiaries enroll in private plans is that they are able to offer broader benefits that encompass prescription drugs.) Moreover, the robust public option envisioned by these plans would have some big inherent advantages: a virtually universal provider network, greater capacity to bargain for lower prices, and the familiarity and popularity of Medicare. With a properly level field, one would expect private plans to play a role in regions of the country where highly integrated private plans are common and among consumers who highly valued the private plan "label." But the public option would likely be the dominant player in much of the nongroup market.

The key variable that will determine the size of the public option, however, is not the relative balance of public and private plans outside the employment-based insurance sector, but how big that sector will be. This, in turn, depends on many factors, the most important of which is the relative cost to employers of providing insurance directly. Employers offer insurance because it is valued by workers; it is one part of the compensation they use to attract and motivate employees (for this reason, they do not really pay for it; workers do through lower wages and/or less generous non-health benefits). However, employers can provide insurance at a lower cost than individuals pay on their own, both because employment-based insurance is tax-subsidized and because they can pool risk and take advantage of economies of scale. The question for employers, then, is when the recruitment and motivating advantage of employment-based insurance is sufficient to justify sponsoring coverage.

As already mentioned, Public Option 2.0 proposals shape that calculus by providing a public route to obtaining coverage, by imposing a cost on employers that do not provide coverage themselves, and by the terms on which they require such provision,

42 Ronald Brownstein, "The Sixty Trillion Dollar Man," *The Atlantic*, February 26, 2020, www.theatlantic.com/politics/archive/2020/02/sanderss-pricey-tax-and-spending-plans/607105/.

43 Yash M. Patel and Stuart Gutterman, "The Evolution of Private Plans in Medicare," *The Commonwealth Fund*, December 8, 2017, www.commonwealthfund.org/publications/issue-briefs/2017/dec/evolution-private-plans-medicare.

including the generosity of required coverage and whether workers can opt out of it and enroll in the public option. Under the ACA, large employers are required to provide coverage or pay a penalty (if their workers receive subsidized insurance through the marketplaces). Public Option 2.0 proposals would turn this "play-or-penalty" approach into a true "play-or-pay" one, in which employers that chose not to insure their workers would be required to contribute to the cost of their coverage. Without getting into the specifics of these contribution requirements, it's obvious that the lower this mandated contribution, the more likely it will be that employers choose to pay rather than play – and hence the larger the scope for the competitive public option.

Finally, the role played by the public option will depend on whether workers can enroll in the public option even if their employers offer coverage. President Joe Biden portrayed his campaign's public option proposal as completing the unfinished business of the ACA. However, the Biden proposal departs substantially from the public option considered in 2009, because it would be open to all workers, not just those whose employers failed to provide qualified private coverage. In other words, Biden's proposal would allow workers to opt out of employment-based plans even if they met the minimum standards set by the ACA.

Because the Biden public option is not particularly generous (it caps premiums, for example, at 8.5 percent of income), it is not clear that many workers would avail themselves of it.[44] Yet, in the face of the COVID-19 pandemic, Biden expressed support for a more ambition public option, which would involve a much larger exodus out of public coverage. Indeed, critics of the public option on the right – and, yes, some advocates as well – forecast exactly the opposite outcome as do critics on the left: a rapid move to Medicare for All. Whether these fears (or hopes) are realistic is our next question.

5.5 FORECASTING THE FEEDBACK EFFECTS OF THE PUBLIC OPTION

In predicting the future role of the public option, its policy effects may ultimately be less important than its *political* effects. Research on policy feedback has identified three main channels through which policies, once enacted, reshape political possibilities. First, they shape public opinion and thereby future electoral dynamics. Second, they shape the universe of interest groups and the goals those groups pursue and coalitions they form. Third, in doing so, as well as by creating new administrative structures, they change the incentives and capacities of policymakers themselves.[45] The public option would likely have major effects at all three levels.

[44] *See note* 39.
[45] *See note* 34.

Americans tend to support social programs once they are in place, however controversial the policies were at the outset, and often that support crosses the partisan divide present at the program's creation. Social Security and Medicare are almost universally popular, and even more controversial programs, like Medicaid, have broader public support than the fierce partisan struggles over them suggest. Once in place, programs become familiar and provide tangible benefits. They also become a powerful basis for mobilization when politicians threaten those tangible benefits.

To play this role, however, programs need to be visible and understandable, clearly linked to public authority, and structured in ways that make benefits visible and costs comparatively hidden.[46] The public option meets this test. It has a ready analogue in an existing program that's highly popular, its financing would come through a mix of sources, including relatively hidden employer contributions, and it would offer a highly valued benefit. Once in place, Americans are likely to become more protective of it and more supportive of its expansion.

A crucial question is whether a public option can create a greater community of interest among Americans now divided by their differential access to good insurance (differences that of course closely track deep divides of class and race). If the public option is accompanied by an upgrading of both Medicare and private workplace plans, and if the public option is gradually integrated with Medicare, there is good reason to believe it could foster a broader sense of shared fate among those it covers.[47]

A crucial issue here will be the future trajectory of Medicaid. Some Public Option 2.0 plans fold nonelderly Medicaid beneficiaries into the public option; others create strong incentives for states to enroll their nonelderly Medicaid populations in the public plan; still others retain Medicaid as a separate state-based program. Ultimately, covering poorer Americans through the same system as more affluent Americans is critical to overcoming the formidable barriers to social solidarity that are created by our current fragmented system.

How much such solidarity can overcome our nation's deep political divisions is open to debate. The polarization of American politics means that many fewer voters are "up for grabs," even incontrovertible policy effects may be viewed very differently by partisans on each side, and policies have generally become less important in comparison with partisan-linked identities in determining how voters assess candidates.[48] As noted, moreover, the views of organized interests play an outsized role in shaping policymaking. How policies affect the political capacities and aims of those organized interests will thus be critical.

46 Suzanne Mettler, "Making What Government Does Apparent to Citizens: Policy Feedback Effects, Their Limitations, and How They Might Be Facilitated," *The Annals of the American Academy of Political and Social Science* 685, no. 1 (2019): 30–46, https://doi.org/10.1177/0002716219860108.

47 *See note 4.*

48 *See note 34.*

Employers' responses are particularly pivotal. If they see Medicare as an attractive means of insuring their workers, they are much more likely to climb on board. In the past, business opposition to social programs withered once employers realized they were a good deal. Although such dynamics are likely to be more muted in today's hyper-polarized context, a Medicare public option could appease or fragment key parts of the business community if a sizable share of employers now covering their workers saw the public option as an affordable alternative.

It is harder to be sanguine about the response of private insurers. Still, Medicare Advantage has attracted strong support from private insurers, and many insurers might well prefer a framework based on the Medicare model than the current ACA marketplaces (which are small in size and have not proved very attractive to the largest insurers). Insurer opposition could also be reduced by a robust effort to respond to potential displacement in the industry with retraining and other transitional assistance.

The fundamental question with insurers, however, is whether they will have the incentives and capacity to compromise the public option once it is in place. The history of Medicare's payment policies and the Medicare Advantage program provide some grounds for optimism; in general, Medicare has become more capable of restraining prices, and its system for paying plans has improved. Investing more in the administrative tools and powers of Medicare would increase the chance that this positive trend would continue.

Here, though, the capacities and incentives of policymakers are crucial. There is little prospect that the polarization of public officials will lessen in the near term, and thus legislative gridlock and persistent opposition efforts are likely to be a continuing barrier to salutary updating of all public policies. As the experience of the ACA suggests, "hardwiring" critical features of program design is essential to reduce the capacity of program opponents to undermine it over time. Such hardwiring, however, can undermine the ability of public officials to respond to changing circumstances, a problem that is particularly acute if the public option remains stuck in place alongside a dynamic market. There is no easy resolution of this dilemma, but it puts a premium on a governing structure for the public option that includes worker and consumer representatives and has the authority to pursue changes through fast-track procedures.

Equally important are up-front measures that increase the chance that the public option will grow in the future, such as dedicated financing that increases as enrollment does. If the public option is to start with a limited set of benefits, for example, the process by which these benefits are expanded should be written into law, or at least structured so that expansion is the most likely outcome. The tension between feasibility and expandability rears its head again here, but designers of a policy can improve the prospects for entrenchment and expansion even when opponents prevent them from hardwiring program growth into legislation. By thinking about sequencing as well as staging, advocates can improve their chance of putting in place initial legislative steps that create self-reinforcing political effects that push toward a better policy.

Finally, a look at existing proposals suggests that the comprehensiveness of the public option – how good its benefits are and how high its premiums might be – is something of a double-edged sword when it comes to policy feedback. For example, a more comprehensive benefit will be more popular for those enrolled, but it's also likely to provoke greater backlash from existing Medicare beneficiaries unless their benefits are similarly enhanced. For this reason, I have argued that a precondition for a successful Public Option 2.0 is a major commitment to upgrade Medicare's benefits for older and disabled Americans.

A more comprehensive benefit is also likely to attract more people and encourage more employers to drop private coverage. This is especially true if private workplace plans are required to provide similarly comprehensive benefits – employers required to upgrade their plans would surely be more likely to drop them. If the goal is to move quickly toward Medicare for All, all this would be a big plus. But it would make the public option more difficult to enact and potentially collapse private insurance so quickly that the law would provoke broad public and industry backlash. For this reason, among others, there's a case for gradual upgrading of both the standards for private plans and the generosity of public benefits (in the public option and Medicare, which should be integrated over time) – with this upgrading built into the initial law to the fullest extent possible.

The policy feedback effects of the public option thus depend crucially on a combination of program design and future political circumstances. Nonetheless, the public option would almost certainly grow in scope over time as it became familiar and gained citizen and business support. Employers' retreat from employment-based insurance is a long-term trend, and Public Option 2.0 proposals would create attractive opportunities for employers to insure their workers without directly providing coverage. Within the public framework, the balance of public and private plans is harder to forecast, but the public option would likely have at least as large a share of the market as traditional Medicare does (two-thirds). The result would not be Medicare for All – at least not without additional legislation – but it would be a system in which the public sector's coverage and price-setting power would encompass a sizable share of the market.

5.6 BROADER LESSONS FOR PUBLIC OPTION POLICIES

The rebirth of the public option has brought the nation full circle. As in the late 2000s, advocates of expanded coverage are debating once again how to overcome the hurdles imposed by the path-dependent development of our exorbitant and incomplete system. Unlike then, however, would-be reformers begin with a much more favorable policy situation. The ACA is battered but intact, and it has reduced the share of Americans without insurance dramatically. Moreover, Democrats have moved substantially to the left on health care, with the public option now seen as a basic building block of reform, not a potential add-on.

To some, in fact, the ground has shifted so much that the public option is no longer relevant. According to these advocates, Medicare for All is now within reach and the public option is overly timid. As I've argued, however, Medicare for All continues to face a steep uphill battle. As hard as it surely will be to enact a robust public option, it is much less likely to provoke backlash among the currently well insured (both Medicare beneficiaries and those happy with their workplace plans) or to face fierce opposition from the medical industry. And all available estimates suggest that even Public Option 2.0 plans will require far less up-front public spending, and hence new taxation, than will be needed to establish Medicare for All.

The proposals I have labeled "Public Option 2.0" are substantially different than the public option plans seriously considered in 2009 and 2010. All put in place strong measures to guarantee universal coverage and expand the reach of public cost controls over time. All emphasize the need for a level playing field between public and private plans – not the current tilted field seen in Medicare Advantage. And all aim to gradually move Americans out of employment-based plans and harmonize Medicare, Medicaid, and the public option over time. As a result, all these proposals are likely to move the nation substantially toward Medicare for All, though not as far as advocates of universal Medicare might like.

The basic trade-off posed by the public option (in health care, but likely in other policy domains, too) is between feasibility and expandability. Unlike complete public provision, public option proposals are less likely to face scorched-earth opposition from private competitors. But they're less likely to face such opposition precisely because they leave in place formidable private interests that will seek to use both their market and political power to gain an edge. Thus, a critical focus of those seeking to establish public options must be how to constrain competition so it delivers social value and insulate the public option from political efforts to limit its role.

This leads to a second fundamental conclusion: public options, much like political constitutions, are frameworks for contestation rather than fixed entities. Indeed, they are more likely to gain the support of affected interests when their future effects remain in doubt. Thinking about these "constitutional" elements of policy design reminds us that policymaking is an unfolding process, in which today's enactments shape the likelihood and character of subsequent ones. The public option opens up possibilities – not just in the moment, but also in the future.

6

The Irony of Health Care's Public Option

Allison K. Hoffman

6.1 INTRODUCTION

As the 2020 Democratic primaries heated up in September 2019, the Center for Deliberative Democracy gathered 523 voters, designed to be a representative sample of the electorate, in a room in Dallas, Texas for three days for an experiment called "America in One Room."[1] Researchers pre-polled the participants for their views on a range of controversial political issues, from immigration to the environment to health care. Then, over the weekend, these 523 "citizen delegates" immersed in conversation in small groups and plenary sessions and with field experts and candidates on these topics. At the end, they were asked their views again. On some topics their views changed wildly from beginning to end. One where it did not was health care's public option. At the beginning, just over 67 percent favored the idea that "[e]veryone should be able to buy a public plan like Medicare," and at the end just over 71 percent did. When asked the same idea with respect to people age 55 or older, the idea was even more popular: 72 percent at the start and 78.5 percent at the end.[2] People love the idea of a public health insurance option.

Yet, this idea might be more popular than warranted. At least a half century old, it has never had its day in the limelight. This chapter explains why if that moment ever comes, the public option will fall short of expectations that it will provide a differentiated, meaningful alternative and will spur health insurance competition.

Health care's public option bubbled up in its best-known form in California in the early 2000s and got increasing mainstream attention in the lead up to the 2010 health reform, the Patient Protection and Affordable Care Act (ACA).[3] Although it was not adopted into the ACA, the idea has reemerged with vigor once again as a cure to ACA shortcomings.

1 Center for Deliberative Democracy, *America in One Room* (2019), at https://cdd.stanford.edu/2019/america-in-one-room/.

2 Center for Deliberative Democracy, A1R Results (2020), at https://cdd.stanford.edu/mm/2019/10/A1R-Results-Participants-Overall-Issues-Scale-Collapsed-Oct2.pdf.

3 Helen A. Halpin & Peter Harbage, *The Origins and Demise of the Public Option*, 29 HEALTH AFF. 1117 (2010).

When people talk about health care's public option, they mean a public health insurance plan, typically based on Medicare that can compete in the market against private health insurance offerings. In their book, *The Public Option*, Ganesh Sitaraman and Anne Alstott refer to this type as a competitive public option, which they describe as having two key characteristics: that this option, first, "guarantees access to important services at a controlled price" and, second, coexists with private provision.[4] In this vein, proponents have argued that a public health insurance option could deliver better cost-control than private insurance, while also being able to offer members a broad choice of providers and quality control.[5]

Health care's public option died in the 2010 legislative process, but had it been enacted, it would have faced serious obstacles to produce the results its architects hoped. The assumption that people will select the public option if it is better than other options is belied by a mounting body of empirical literature showing how we struggle when choosing among health insurance options. Even more, political thorniness would almost certainly have prevented the public option from being a clear best alternative, which would have further impeded its ability to stand out in the crowd and to move the needle on the price and quality.

This chapter argues that for a public health insurance option to have the kind of transformative potential that Sitaraman and Alstott hope for from public options – to promote greater health equity and freedom – it needs to be more than an option among many, a competitive public option. It must be designed in a way that does not rely on people weighing it against other options available and selecting it over the competition when it is the best.

This chapter examines possibilities for health care's public option in three parts. It first explains the theory behind the ACA version of a competitive public option. It then considers the challenges this competitive public option would have faced had it become policy reality. Finally, it examines more effective ways that public health insurance might be integrated into a public/private hybrid system to achieve greater health equity.

6.2 THE "CLASSIC" HEALTH CARE PUBLIC OPTION

6.2.1 *The History*

To understand why the public option emerged, and why it has struggled to gain traction, it is helpful to recount the development of health insurance in the United States. This well-worn story is worth revisiting because it is still salient.

4 Ganesh Sitaraman & Anne L. Alstott, The Public Option 27 (2019). They explain: "Citizens can rely on the public option but also can turn to the marketplace for additional choices, combining public and private options in ways that work best for them." *Id.* at 23.

5 Jacob S. Hacker, Institute for America's Future, The Case for Public Plan Choice in National Health Reform 3 (2008).

The United States is unique among OECD nations when it comes to paying for health care, and not in a good way. Most countries' systems for health-care financing grew up in the early- to mid-twentieth century as medical care became more advanced and more expensive than most people could afford on their own.[6] In Europe, what emerged were public systems of health-care finance in two forms, often characterized broadly as Beveridge and Bismarkian systems.[7] The Beveridge approach was direct provision of health care by the government, as in England, where the government owns hospitals and employs medical professionals – aka "socialized medicine." Bismarkian systems, or social insurance, are ones where the government finances health care but the providers can be public or private. Over time, countries in Europe and beyond, such as Canada, developed variations on these themes. At the core, however, these systems embraced the basic idea that the government would take a central role in ensuring access to affordable health care for the entire population.

The United States charted a wholly different path. The beginning upsurge of health insurance in the United States was initiated by industry itself. As medical care became both more effective and expensive, people increasingly sought it. Hospitals feared not being paid for their work if they relied on patients to pay cash for services, nor did they want to have to confirm the financial solvency of every patient prior to caring for them.[8] Hospitals thus created prepaid health-care funds, beginning with Baylor University Hospital in the 1920s, that guaranteed people access to medical care up to a certain level, with prepayment.[9] These plans spread and eventually took on the name Blue Cross. Within a short period, Blue Shield followed, offering a similar structure for monthly prepayment of fees to groups of physicians in turn for guaranteed access to outpatient care. Unlike the health insurance of today, the Blues embraced some of the solidaristic characteristics that define systems elsewhere in the world, like charging all members of a community the same rate for membership regardless of their personal characteristics or health status.

A second – and the most defining – major development in the United States was the rise of employer-sponsored health insurance (ESI) during and after World War II (WWII). Increased reliance on employers as a source of health coverage in the United States coincided with the moment that many other countries were doubling down on the government's role. In England, for example, during WWII the government built health infrastructure to deal with an unmet need for medical services and this infrastructure served as the beginning of the National Health Service, established at the end of the war.[10]

6 Paul Starr, The Social Transformation of American Medicine 237–40 (1982).
7 *Id.*
8 *Id.* at 295–97.
9 *Id.*
10 Donald W. Light, *Universal Health Care: Lessons From the British Experience*, 93 Am. J. Pub. Health 25, 26 (2003).

In the United States, in contrast, in the years during and especially after WWII, ESI surged, bolstered by several public policies. A commonly told story is that the trend began with wage freezes during the war prompting employers to compensate with benefits instead of cash wages, but the growth in these plans was relatively small in this period.[11] More consistent with the timing of a major upsurge in adoption of ESI were a 1945 federal rule that required employers to leave wartime health benefits in place, a 1949 federal rule allowing unions to bargain for health benefits, and most importantly a 1954 rule by the Internal Revenue Service excluding dollars spent on health benefits by employers and employees from taxes.[12] This meant, by one estimate, that a dollar of compensation in cash wages only cost employers an average of $.66 if spent on health benefits. With all of these factors, ESI and the centrality of private insurance took hold. Today, half of all Americans have insurance through an employer.[13]

Public financing, however, maintained a key role. It began in small scale in the Veterans Health Administration and Indian Health Services. In 1965, after decades of attempts at universal, public health coverage, Medicare and Medicaid were signed into law by President Johnson. These programs established public programs to pay for medical care for populations seen as vulnerable and also least likely to have access to ESI – the elderly (Medicare) and poor children, pregnant women, and, later, people with disabilities (Medicaid).

People who didn't qualify for a form of public coverage and who didn't have private coverage available through an employer had limited options.[14] Some people could access charity care. Others paid out-of-pocket for health care, although doing so for anything other than the simplest care was out of the reach of most people. A final pathway was to buy health insurance directly from an insurer in the individual, or nongroup, insurance market, and doing so was thorny. In the individual market, insurers underwrote applicants and deemed many people with prior health problems as risky. Six to seven percent of the non-elderly population (about 15 million people) had individual-market coverage prior to the passage of the ACA.[15] Historically, this coverage was relatively more expensive, in part because administrative costs were as high as 15–20 percent of total costs. Individuals deemed risky were declined coverage.[16] As many as three in five people who applied for

11 David Blumenthal, *Employer-Sponsored Health Insurance in the United States—Origins and Implications*, 355 New Eng. J. Med. 82, 83 (2006).

12 *Id.* at 83.

13 *Health Insurance Coverage of the Total Population*, Kaiser Family Foundation (2017), www.kff.org/other/state-indicator/total-population/?currentTimeframe=0&sortModel=%7B%22colId%22:%22Location%22,%22sort%22:%22asc%22%7D.

14 Timothy S. Jost, *Access to Health Insurance and Health Benefits*, *in* Oxford Handbook of U.S. Health Law 149–50 (I. Glenn Cohen, Allison K. Hoffman, and William Sage, eds., 2017).

15 Paul Fronstin, *Sources of Health Insurance and Characteristics of the Uninsured: Analysis of the March 2009 Current Population Survey*, EBRI Issue Brief No. 334, September 2009, at 5.

16 *See, e.g.*, Melinda Beeuwkes Buntin et al., *The Role of the Individual Health Insurance Market and Prospects for Change*, 23 Health Aff. 79, 81 (2004); Sara R. Collins et. al., The Commonwealth

policies before the ACA could not afford the high premium prices or were denied coverage, and many people remained uninsured or underinsured.[17]

6.2.2 *The ACA and the Individual Insurance Market*

In the year before the ACA's passage, 16.3 percent of Americans were uninsured, including 18.4 percent of people under age 65, and many more were underinsured.[18] The goal of the ACA was to fill in the gaps between public coverage and ESI through two primary mechanisms: expansion of the Medicaid program to poorer Americans and regulation of the individual market to make it a source of affordable and meaningful coverage for everyone else without ESI or public coverage.

Here is where the public option came into play.

The ACA's strategy relied heavily on getting more people enrolled in private health insurance, for reasons both political and pragmatic.[19] Yet, the individual market was inhospitable to the goals of universal access and affordability, and early architects of the Obama reform had two responses to discipline the private insurance companies in this market: (1) regulate them and (2) create competition through a public option.

The first required a federalization of heath regulation and a complicated, multi-pronged approach. Prior to the ACA, most health insurance regulation, especially of the individual market, occurred at the state level, and there was little of it.[20] The ACA created federal rules for individual insurance, drawing lessons from the 2006 health reform in Massachusetts. Insurers were required to issue insurance to any

FUND, SQUEEZED: WHY RISING EXPOSURE TO HEALTH CARE COSTS THREATENS THE HEALTH AND FINANCIAL WELL-BEING OF AMERICAN FAMILIES 3–4 (2006).

17 Michelle M. Doty et al., *Failure to Protect: Why the Individual Insurance Market Is Not a Viable Option for Most U.S. Families*, COMMONWEALTH FUND PUB. no. 1300, 2009, at 1–3.

18 DEP'T OF HEALTH & HUMAN SERV., OFFICE OF THE ASSISTANT SEC'Y FOR PLANNING AND EVALUATION, OVERVIEW OF THE UNINSURED IN THE UNITED STATES: A SUMMARY OF THE 2011 CURRENT POPULATION SURVEY (2011), http://aspe.hhs.gov/health/reports/2011/cpshealthins2011/ib.shtml.

19 Politically many believed no law would have passed without the support of – or at least without active opposition from – the insurance industry. During the Clinton reform efforts, a coalition of health insurers, under the name Health Insurance Association of America (HIAA), financed negative advertising campaigns that hampered reform. JACOB S. HACKER, THE ROAD TO NOWHERE: THE GENESIS OF PRESIDENT CLINTON'S PLAN FOR HEALTH SECURITY 145–46 (1997). (The HIAA is now part of the group called America's Health Insurance Plans). How large of a negative impact these ads had is debated. *See* Paul Starr, *What Happened to Health Care Reform?*, 20 AMERICAN PROSPECT 20 (1994). In one now iconic advertisement, a couple named Harry and Louise lament that reform would result in few insurance choices and increased prices. Coalition for Health Insurance Choices, *Harry and Louise on Clinton's Health Plan*, YOUTUBE (1994), www.youtube.com/watch?v=Dt31nhleeCg .

20 McCarran-Ferguson Act, ch. 20, 59 STAT. 33 (1945) (codified as amended at 15 U.S.C. §§ 1011–1015 (2012)).Only six states required that insurers guarantee issue policies to all applicants, and only one-third of states regulated the variability in premium prices allowed among insured. *Individual Market Guaranteed Issue (Not Applicable to HIPAA Eligible Individuals)*, KAISER FAMILY FOUND., http://kff.org/other/state-indicator/individual-market-guaranteed-issue-not-applicable-to-hipaa-eligible-individuals/ (last visited September 26, 2019).

applicant ("guaranteed issue").[21] Medical underwriting was prohibited, and insurers could not consider preexisting conditions in determining eligibility or price.[22] In fact, premiums for a policy were allowed to vary based on only four factors: age, geography, family size, and tobacco use status.[23] Even if an insurer devised a way to cherry-pick out healthier applicants, the law intended to disgorge any resulting profits through reinsurance and risk-adjustment arrangements.[24] And the ACA also regulated benefits, requiring that all plans cover preventative care without cost sharing and a set of essential health benefits for individual-market plans, and prohibited limits on these benefits for most plans.[25]

So that these regulations did not exacerbate adverse selection, or the tendency of healthier people to wait to buy coverage until they need it, the law included an individual mandate that required that most Americans carry health insurance that offers "minimum essential coverage," or else pay a penalty.[26] As a carrot, the ACA provided for financial support to help lower-income individuals. Anyone who earns from 100 to 400 percent of the federal poverty level ($12,490 to $49,960 for a single person in 2020) and does not have another source of adequate insurance, such as through an employer or Medicaid, is eligible for subsidized premiums and in many cases also cost-sharing reductions to help pay for their out-of-pocket share of costs.[27]

6.2.3 *The ACA's (Foregone) Public Option*

In case the nearly 200 pages of the ACA devoted to the endeavor of regulating private insurance to achieve broader policy goals fell short, there was a second strategy: create competition through a public option.

The idea was to develop a public health plan, based either loosely or very closely on Medicare that would compete with private health plans in the exchanges – new marketplaces where people would go to compare and buy health insurance policies.

21 Patient Protection and Affordable Care Act § 1201, 42 U.S.C. § 300gg (2012).

22 *Id.*

23 *Id.*

24 *Id.* at § 1341–42, 42 U.S.C. § 18061–62 (2012). These provisions of the ACA are not working as smoothly as envisioned in early years of implementation because the contributions from insurers intended to cover these payments have fallen well short of the amount CMS owes insurers in claims. Timothy Jost, *Risk Corridor Claims by Insurers Far Exceed Contributions*, Health Aff. Blog (October 1, 2015), http://healthaffairs.org/blog/2015/10/01/implementing-health-reform-risk-corridor-claims-by-insurers-far-exceed-contributions/.

25 Patient Protection and Affordable Care Act § 1302, 42 U.S.C. § 18022; *Id.* at § 1001, 42 U.S.C. § 300gg-11 (2012), 42 U.S.C. § 300gg-13 (2012).

26 Patient Protection and Affordable Care Act § 1501, 26 U.S.C. § 5000A (2012). Some people are exempted from the penalty for reasons including religious objection or affordability, defined as when premiums cost over 8 percent of household income. *Id.*

27 *Id.* at § 1401, 26 U.S.C. § 36B (2012) (providing for "premium tax credits"); *Id.* at § 1402, 42 U.S.C § 18071 (2012) (providing for "cost-sharing reductions"). The employer plan must be "adequate" and "affordable." Adequate is defined as an actuarial value of at least 60 percent and affordable is when the employee's share of premium cost is under 9.5 percent of his or her income.

The public option was described by its proponents as simply one option among many, a public health insurance plan that would compete side-by-side with private plans and would win if the private options were not good enough. Presumably, if the public option offered a similar or better product for lower prices, people would choose it. As Jacob Hacker suggested: "public plan choice gives Americans the opportunity to choose for themselves how *they* value the strengths and weaknesses of a public, Medicare-like plan and competing private health plans."[28]

But this idea faced staunch resistance. Even advocates of market-based policy fought back, both on the details and on the concept as a whole. The public option was cast aside. Yet imagine for a moment that Congress had included a public option as part of the ACA. Would the world look different than it does today, and how?

6.3 ENVISIONING AN ALTERNATE FUTURE: THE ACA WITH THE PUBLIC OPTION

Had the public option survived the policy battles leading up to the passage of the ACA and become law, it would still have faced an uphill journey to fulfill the potential that Sitaraman and Alstott see in competitive public options (offering quality access at controlled prices *and* coexisting with private alternatives). There were two main possible ways health care's public option could have played out, and neither pathway would have fulfilled this vision; each would have fulfilled exactly one-half of it.

6.3.1 *The Two Pathways for a Public Option*

The first pathway would have led to everyone enrolling in the public option – what Jacob Hacker describes in his chapter as a back door to universal Medicare (Pathway 1). In Pathway 1, the public option would be based on Medicare. It would borrow Medicare's existing provider network and negotiated rates. This is the version its architects envisioned. Since the plans sold on the ACA's exchanges are standardized by regulation – they vary little on benefits and cost sharing structure – the way plans distinguish themselves is based on network, pricing, or perhaps name recognition or brand.

If the public option were built on Medicare's platform, it would easily have bettered private options on these dimensions in most geographies. Medicare has an extensive network of providers, who accept lower rates from Medicare than they do from private insurance, which pays rates to hospitals that are sometimes 50 percent higher than what Medicare pays.[29] Medicare also controls spending growth

[28] Hacker, *supra* note 5, at 2.
[29] MEDPAC, Report to the Congress: Medicare Payment Policy 14–15 (March 2018).

better than private plans.[30] The divergence between what Medicare and private insurers pay is increasing as consolidation among hospitals and other providers has enabled providers to demand significant rate increases from private plans.[31] Plus, Medicare's administrative rates are lower than those for private insurance, even considering that private insurance administrative rates for the individual market are limited under the ACA. All of this means that even if a public option plan paid providers a cut above Medicare's standard negotiated rates, it could offer similar benefits at much lower premium prices than private plans with a more comprehensive network of providers. It would simply be the better option.

Assuming people understood that the public option was clearly better – an assumption that should be taken with a grain of salt for reasons described below – everyone would have chosen the cheaper, better public option. Even if people chose only based on premium price, which evidence suggests is exactly what often happens on the ACA exchanges,[32] the public option would have won out. Over time, it would have displaced the private plans altogether and become the de facto coverage for anyone seeking a health plan on the ACA exchanges.

Pathway 1 would thus deliver on one half of the *competitive* public option vision. It would have provided guaranteed access at controlled prices, but eventually would not have coexisted with private plans at all, at least not side-by-side in a competitive structure.

Interest groups who opposed the public option – including insurers and medical providers and suppliers (pharmaceutical and medical device companies) whose reimbursement would be lower under Pathway 1 – saw the writing on the wall. During the ACA debates, they answered the mention of a public insurance plan option with cries of socialism.[33] They also demanded that if a public option were passed it had to compete without relying on the preexisting advantages of Medicare over private insurance.

The second possible way the public option could have, and likely would have, played out in the current political environment would have been that these interest groups' demands won out (Pathway 2). Imagine that a public option had to compete on "even ground," or "break even financially" (the latter of which even President Obama asserted)[34]. Although it's difficult to know exactly what that would have meant in practice, at the very least it would have prohibited the public option from coasting on the preexisting Medicare network and negotiated prices. If the public

30 *Id.*

31 *Id.*

32 Avalere Health, More Than 2 Million Exchange Enrollees Forgo Cost-Sharing Assistance (August 19, 2015), http://avalere.com/expertise/managed-care/insights/more-than-2-million-exchange-enrollees-forgo-cost-sharing-assistance [https://perma.cc/22M2-6C23].

33 Jacob S. Hacker, *The Road to Somewhere: Why Health Reform Happened*, 9 Persp. on Pol. 861, 864 (2010).

34 Michael O'Brien, *Steele: Public Option is Socialism*, The Hill (August 9, 2009), https://thehill.com/blogs/blog-briefing-room/news/57825-steele-public-option-is-socialism.

option did not have a clear pricing or network advantage – if it were not a clear winner – what would that have meant?

6.3.2 *The Problem of Choice*

In some of the examples that Sitaraman and Alstott profile in *The Public Option*, competitive public options are effective because they offer a genuinely meaningful alternative. Sometimes this alternative is one that is less expensive, or even free, as compared to pricier and probably fancier and more exclusive private options. This is the case with public pools – the inspiration for the cover of the print version of the book. Sometimes the alternative is part of a tiered system. With the USPS, they suggest, one can usually get reliable standard mail services, but for higher-end packing and shipping needs, Fed-Ex and UPS are the better go-to options.

The problem with health care's competitive public option is that in its more politically realistic form (Pathway 2), it would not have been easily differentiated in this way, and end users would have struggled to see its relative benefit. The public option would have offered nearly the same benefits as the private options, likely at a similar price. It might have been marginally better under close examination – maybe a better network of providers, maybe some extra benefits because of the ability of these plans to operate more slimly, maybe less administrative hassle for enrollees (or perhaps not), or maybe it would have provided an easier transition to Medicare once eligible. But none of these attributes would have been easy to detect, nor would they likely have driven someone's health plan selection.

The main problem, thus, with any politically realistic version of a competitive public option in health care is the problem of choice. Consumers are notoriously bad at deciphering differences among health plans and choosing wisely among them. This should be unsurprising when considering the nature of health plan choice. Fundamentally, buying health insurance demands having preferences about things that most people have never experienced before, like hospitalization or cancer care. Then they have to weigh this risk against spending on other goods and services.

Then someone must understand how such preferences translate into health insurance policy terms. Most people do not understand the basic features of health insurance plans that should shape their decisions – such as how much a plan costs and what benefits are covered.[35] In a survey of insured adults, only 14 percent correctly answered four simple multiple-choice questions about cost-sharing

[35] Deborah W. Garnick et al., *How Well Do Americans Understand their Health Coverage*, 12 HEALTH AFF. 204, 206 (1993) (finding that even though consumers largely understood whether their plans covered hospitalization or doctors' visits, they underreported that their plans covered services including mental health, alcohol and drug abuse treatment, or prescription drug and over-reported that their plans covered long-term care).

features, such as a deductible or copayment.[36] However, people overestimated their understanding of these insurance concepts, which suggests many would not seek help or education even if available.

Furthermore, choosing a health plan requires making calculations regarding deductibles, cost-sharing, and premiums that exceed many Americans' literacy and numeracy skills.[37] Even college-educated people show surprisingly high levels of error on simple arithmetic tests.[38]

Even putting aside these challenges, choosing health insurance has all of the telltale characteristics that impair rational decision-making, sometimes referred to as generating cognitive biases. People are overly optimistic about their own health,[39] which could prompt them to underinvest in health insurance. People also struggle to factor risk into decision-making – an element central, of course, to health insurance choices.[40] This is why young, healthy people often forgo buying health insurance, even if it's cheap.

Documenting the end result of all of these barriers, a volume of empirical work illuminates the many ways and reasons that we – regardless of education, income, or smarts – make poor choices among health plans. As described later, these poor choices persist when there is a clear, superior option. These poor choices persist even when options are simplified. And they persist even in the face of efforts to help people make better choices through decision-making supports, or nudges. As one set of researchers behind several studies that looked at how to help people make better decisions by simplifying health plan options or helping consumers through options concluded: "[T]he main barrier to financially efficient choice was not the number of options confronting employees, nor the transparency of their presentation, but rather the . . . lack of basic understanding of health insurance."[41]

36 George Loewenstein et al., *Consumers' Misunderstanding of Health Insurance*, 32 J. HEALTH ECON. 850, 855 (2013).

37 Wendy Nelson et al., *Clinical Implications of Numeracy: Theory and Practice*, 35 ANN. BEHAV. MED. 261 (2008) (providing an overview of research on health numeracy and the clinical implications for patients); Valerie F. Reyna et al., *How Numeracy Influences Risk Comprehension and Medical Decision Making*, 135 PSYCH. BULL. 943, 945–46 (2009) (reviewing studies showing links between innumeracy and poor health decisions); Ellen Peters & Irwin P. Levin, *Dissecting the Risky-Choice Framing Effect: Numeracy as an Individual-Difference Factor in Weighing Risky and Riskless Options*, 3 JUDGMENT & DECISION MAKING 435 (2008) (showing that lower levels of numeracy led to higher loss aversion). On health literacy, *see, e.g.*, ZSOFIA PARRAGH & DEANNA OKRENT, HEALTH LITERACY AND HEALTH INSURANCE LITERACY: DO CONSUMERS KNOW WHAT THEY ARE BUYING? (2015), www.allhealthpolicy.org/wp-content/uploads/2017/01/Health-Literacy-Toolkit_163.pdf (describing health literacy and summarizing studies on health and health insurance literacy).

38 Wendy Nelson et al., *supra* note 37, at 263.

39 *See* Neil D. Weinstein, *Unrealistic Optimism about Future Life Events*, 39 J. PERSONALITY & SOC. PSYCH. 806 (1980).

40 *See* Daniel Kahneman & Amos Tversky, *Prospect Theory: An Analysis of Decision Under Risk*, 47 ECONOMETRICA 263, 264 (1979) (showing that people tend to make choices inconsistent with their own expected utility when dealing with risky options).

41 Saurabh Bhargava & George Loewenstein, *Choosing a Health Insurance Plan: Complexity and Consequences*, 314 JAMA 2505, 2506 (2015).

A few select examples from the many studies showing the extent that we struggle when selecting a health plan can illuminate this problem. For example, one study simulated the purchase of an ACA plan, using participants who passed a screening test for basic insurance literacy.[42] Even these more-literate-than-average respondents selected the best choice only about half of the time, and Wharton business school participants got it wrong over one-quarter of the time.[43]

Among enrollees in the University of Michigan's employee health plan, over one-third of workers selected a plan that was identical to another in every way except that it had a more restricted provider network.[44] No one would be better off enrolled in this plan. Importantly, this kind of network size variation is exactly what might differentiate a private and public option on a health insurance exchange. Another study of a large US firm found that a majority of employees chose a worse option and, as a result, they paid on average 24 percent more than they should have on premiums.[45] Lower-income employees were more likely to make a bad choice.

Similar results occur in Medicare when beneficiaries choose among private prescription drug plans. One study found that 73 percent of enrollees could have chosen a plan with lower premiums with no risk of spending more on prescription drugs over the course of the year.[46] Another estimated that only about 10 percent of enrollees choose their least-expensive option.[47]

On the ACA marketplaces, a significant share of people choose plans with the lowest monthly premiums but that make them ineligible for cost-sharing reductions, which reduce their deductibles and copayments when they use medical care.[48] People who select these plans will likely spend more in the long run.

42 Eric J. Johnson et al., *Can Consumers Make Affordable Care Affordable? The Value of Choice Architecture*, 8 Plos One e81521.

43 *Id.*

44 Anna D. Sinaiko & Richard A. Hirth, *Consumers, Health Insurance, and Dominated Choices*, 30 J. Health Econ 450, 453 (2011).

45 Saurabh Bhargava et al., *Choose to Lose: Health Plan Choices from a Menu with Dominated Options*, 132 Q. J. Econ. 1319, 1325 (2017)("Taken collectively, results from the experiments suggest that the demand for dominated plans does not predominantly reflect the informed preferences of consumers or the consequences of menu complexity, but instead involves a failure of consumers to accurately evaluate and compare plans.")

46 Jason Abaluck & Jonathan Gruber, *Heterogeneity in Choice Inconsistencies Among the Elderly: Evidence from Prescription Drug Plan Choice*, 101 Am. Econ. Rev. 377, 379 (2011). They find that individuals consider premiums, instead of total out-of-pocket costs, in making decisions. *Id.*

47 Florian Heiss et al., *Plan Selection in Medicare Part D: Evidence from Administrative Data*, 32 J. Health Econ 1325, 1377–78 (2013).

48 Vicki Fung et al., *Nearly One-Third of Enrollees in California's Individual Market Missed Opportunities to Receive Financial Assistance*, 36 Health Aff. 21 (2017); Avalere Health, More than 2 Million Exchange Enrollees Forgo Cost-Sharing Assistance (August 19, 2015), http://avalere.com/expertise/managed-care/insights/more-than-2-million-exchange-enrollees-forgo-cost-sharing-assistance.

Others choose health plans that are not aligned with their own stated medical needs and preferences.[49] In a study simulating the purchase experience on ACA exchanges, only one-third of respondents chose the cost-minimizing plan, based on their own anticipated medical care need.[50] Forty-three percent over insured, on average overspending by 24 percent or $1,324 on premiums, and nearly a quarter underinsured.[51] The authors of this study estimated that if all people buying plans on the ACA exchanges had similar error rates as the study population, "the result would be roughly $7.1 billion of excess spending each year, borne by a population with low to moderate incomes."[52]

This quick and only partial yet representative review of research on health plan selection is simply meant to illustrate that if the public option were not an obvious best alternative – and probably even if it were –people would not necessarily select it. If, in turn, the public option failed to gain significant market share, it would not exert pressure on the private insurers to offer better quality or lower-priced plans.

Thus, at the end of the day, the public option would coexist with private plans. Yet, it would not serve the other promise that Sitaraman and Alstott see in competitive public options, that of ensuring guaranteed universal access at controlled prices.

That's not to say that having an undifferentiated public option would have no benefit. In 2018, there were 37 percent of counties where only one private insurer participates on the ACA exchange, which results in 17 percent of enrollees having only one choice of insurer.[53] In these regions, evidence suggests health plans have higher premiums.[54] In these areas, the mere presence of a public option might hold down premiums and premium growth. Such benefits are laudable, but far short of the transformative vision that the public option's architects had for it.

Further, the marginal gains from a competitive public option would have come at a cost. The public option would have further justified preserving the existing system and problems with it. Injecting this option into the existing ACA exchanges would perpetuate, and perhaps even validate, this structure that is causing fundamental problems of inequity and regulatory bloat in health care.

49 Andrew J. Barnes et al., *Determinants of Coverage Decisions in Health Insurance Marketplaces: Consumers' Decision-Making Abilities and the Amount of Information in their Choice Environment*, 50 Health Svcs. Rev. 58, 67 (2014) (finding in a simulation based on purchasing actual ACA exchange plans that 40 percent of respondents choose a plan that would cost them at least $500 more than another option, based on their self-reported health needs).

50 Saurabh Bhargava et al., *The Costs of Poor Health (Plan Choices) & Prescriptions for Reform*, 3 Behavioral Sci. & Pol'y 1 (2017). This study varied plans only by cost. It told respondents that benefits were equal among plans and did not mention network differences. *Id.*

51 *Id.* at 7–8.

52 *Id.* at 10.

53 Rachel Fehr, Cynthia Cox, & Larry Levitt, Kaiser Family Foundation, Insurer Participation on ACA Marketplaces 2014–2019 (2018), www.kff.org/health-reform/issue-brief/insurer-participation-on-aca-marketplaces-2014–2019/.

54 Jessica Van Parys, ACA *Marketplace Premiums Grew More Rapidly in Areas with Monopoly Insurers than in Areas with More Competition*, 37 Health Aff. 1243 (2018).

6.3.3 *The Problem of Market-Based Bureaucracy*

This regulatory bloat is the beginning of the more structural problems with a competitive individual health insurance public option. While the promise of markets is that they are nimble and less bureaucratic than direct regulation, market-based approaches to health insurance have produced exactly the opposite: massive regulatory scaffolding to establish choice infrastructure and ongoing technocratic tinkering to try to fix the market's flaws and poor decision-making. Elsewhere, I've called this reality health care's market bureaucracy.[55]

The ACA's exchanges have cost billions of dollars and have demanded extensive regulatory investments and, at the end of the day, only provide coverage to 10 million people, less than 3 percent of the population.[56] The federal government spent nearly 5 billion dollars on state grants to establish exchanges and continues to spend 1–2 billion dollars annually to operate healthcare.gov, the federally funded exchange.[57] The effort to overhaul healthcare.gov after it failed to work on its initial launch cost $1.7 billion, compared in an initial budget of $93.7 million.[58]

States with their own exchanges must fund a large part of their ongoing operations. California estimated it would spend $534 million, excluding federal grants, by the end of FY2017 on administration of Covered California with ongoing annual costs of over $350 million, funded out of plan assessments.[59] Even a smaller state like Vermont will spend about $50 million annually to run its state exchange.[60]

Costs also include opportunity costs. The efforts needed to bolster and refine the exchanges have consumed health insurance regulators – at both the state and the federal level. They have commanded oversized technocratic analysis of exchanges and their successes and shortcomings, with some of the most talented researchers and think tanks consumed by this task.[61]

55 Allison K. Hoffman, *Health Care's Market Bureaucracy*, 66 UCLA L. Rev. 1926 (2019).

56 *Six Years of ACA Exchange Effectuations in One Graph: 2014–2019*, ACA Signups (August 13, 2019), http://acasignups.net/19/08/13/six-years-aca-exchange-effectuations-one-graph-2014–2019 (reporting about 10 million ACA exchange effectuations, meaning monthly enrollments for someone who both selected a plan and paid for it, effectuating enrollment).

57 Annie L. Mach & C. Stephen Redhead, Congressional Research Service, Federal Funding for Health Insurance Exchanges (October 29, 2014), www.fas.org/sgp/crs/misc/R43066.pdf.

58 The Failed Launch of www.healthcare.gov, HBS Digital Initiative, https://rctom.hbs.org/submission/the-failed-launch-of-www-healthcare-gov/ (last visited March 2, 2019).

59 Covered California, Proposed Fiscal Year 2018–2019 Budget 3 (May 7, 2018), https://board.coveredca.com/meetings/2018/05–17/CoveredCA_2018–19_Proposed_Budget-5–17-18.pdf.

60 *Department of Vermont Health Access (DVHA) Budget Document, State Fiscal Year 2016, at* 88.

61 *See* Allison K. Hoffman, *Cost-Sharing Reductions, Technocratic Tinkering, and Market-Based Health Policy*, 46 J. L. Med. & Ethics 873 (2019) (offering one example of such analysis with respect to cost-sharing reductions). From 2010–mid 2017, a constant stream of research studies and news articles obsessed over the functioning of the exchanges. For example, New England Journal of Medicine published 35 articles focused on the exchanges, Health Affairs 280 articles that mention and 140 that focus on the exchanges, and over 800 law review articles have discussed the exchanges, 250 of which focus on them in depth. Original research (on file with author).

For example, the Department of Health and Human Services proposed, revised, and issued hundreds of pages of federal regulations to implement the exchanges.[62] From the passage of the ACA through the end of the Obama Administration, the Centers for Medicare and Medicaid Services (CMS) promulgated twenty-four new rules and generated sixty-four guidance documents with respect to the exchanges alone.[63] An entirely new office, the Center for Consumer Information and Insurance Oversight, was established within CMS in part to implement them.[64] In parallel, state regulators have been doing the same.

Even more, sociologically, this labored creation and preservation of a market-based structure reinforces the idea that choice of health plan is sacred and should be a primary goal, even if the choice of plan it enables offers little meaning or value. By becoming part of this market bureaucracy, the public option would reinforce the value that is at its very core: choice defined in a narrow, microeconomic sense. Ironically, as compared to public options in other domains like swimming pools or shipping services that can improve access or quality, a public health insurance option would perpetuate prioritizing choice as a value over high-quality, universal, and affordable access. In some domains, as Sitaraman and Alstott assert, a competitive public option might simultaneously advance values of equity and freedom or autonomy, but when it comes to health insurance and when freedom is defined as market choice, these two values are at odds.

6.4 A MORE TRANSFORMATIVE PATH AND THREE MODELS OF NONCOMPETITIVE PUBLIC OPTIONS FOR HEALTH CARE

Even though the ACA-style competitive public health insurance option is certain to disappoint, public health insurance can coexist with private health insurance in achieving universal access to affordable health care. But the most productive ways they can coexist are not in a competitive model.

If we think of freedom in collective terms, it can be advanced if a public option enables everyone access to health care that would improve life opportunities. With this framing, the public option could fill in glaring holes in our current system, or it

62 As one example, the 2019 annual ACA exchange market rule received over 400 comments, about one-third of which came from industry participants, including Anthem, PhRMA, and DaVita. HHS Notice of Benefit and Payment Parameters for 2019, 82 Fed. Reg. 51052 (November 2, 2017); *Cf.* Ryan Bubb & Richard H. Pildes, *How Behavioral Economics Trims its Sails and Why*, 127 Harv. L. Rev. 1595, 1605 (2014) ("Soft paternalistic measures run the risk of being less visible than more traditional regulations and mandates, which could make the political dynamics more prone to capture rather than less").

63 *The Center for Consumer Information & Insurance Oversight: Regulations and Guidance*, Centers for Medicare & Medicaid Services: CMS, www.cms.gov/CCIIO/Resources/Regulations-and-Guidance/index.html#Health-Insurance-Marketplaces (last visited September 25, 2019) (counting listings under "Health Insurance Marketplaces" through calendar year 2016).

64 *The Center for Consumer Information & Insurance Oversight*, Centers for Medicare & Medicaid Services: CMS, https://www.cms.gov/cciio/ (last visited July 18, 2017).

could be the key to more fundamental reform, by replacing the heavy reliance on private health insurance for baseline access.

This final section is a brief sketch of more productive ways to employ a public health insurance "option." Many of these ideas have long existed in policy discussions and have been amplified leading up to the 2020 election, as experts consider the best path forward to achieve the dual goals of guaranteed access at controlled prices.

6.4.1 *Baseline Coverage*

One way public health insurance and private health insurance can coexist is with public health insurance as a baseline plan to cover basic health needs. This approach is undoubtedly the surest way to achieve Sitaraman and Alstott's vision of what public options can uniquely deliver: guaranteed access at a controlled price. A baseline plan is available to all. The government sets payment rates for goods and services, working to keep spending as low as possible while maintaining sufficient supply of providers.

Health-care systems all around the world follow this model, in countries such as Canada, France or England. The details can take many forms. Benefits can be more or less extensive. This, in turn, defines the nature of its relationship with private supplemental coverage that fills in what is not covered. Medicare for All is one idea in this mold, and the details would determine how the public and private coverage coexists. A more comprehensive version, like the model advanced by Senator Bernie Sanders, is not a baseline model because it would leave little role for private insurance, but a more politically realistic version of Medicare for All would likely be similar to what other countries do.

Private insurance would thus serve the kinds of roles it does elsewhere – supplemental coverage to fill in gaps if the public coverage does not pay for the full costs of care, or complementary coverage to cover goods and services not publicly financed at all. For example, in the existing Medicare program, original public Medicare is a baseline. It pays on average about 60 percent of the total health-care costs of the enrolled population, and 90 percent of Medicare enrollees have a secondary plan to fill in the gaps.[65] Current enrollees use private coverage in two ways. Some people buy a private supplemental plan, which they layer on top of original Medicare. Others choose a private Medicare Advantage plan as a replacement for traditional, fully public Medicare, and this privately administered plan covers everything that

[65] Paul Fronstin et al., Emp. Benefit Research Inst., No. 351, Issue Brief: Funding Savings Needed for Health Expenses for Persons Eligible for Medicare 3 (2010) (describing that Medicare paid for 64 percent of enrollees health-care costs in 2007); Ben Umans & K. Lynn Nonnemaker, The Medicare Beneficiary Population 1 (2009) ("Only one in 10 beneficiaries relies solely on the Medicare program for health-care coverage. The rest have some form of supplemental coverage to help with medical expenses.").

original Medicare would and fills in the gaps.[66] Either way, a lion's share of health care costs is publicly financed, directly or in the form of payments to private Medicare Advantage insurers.

A less transformative version of a baseline plan would be to offer a baseline to everyone, but to allow certain people to opt out, on a temporary or permanent basis. A more permanent opt out might allow people with incomes above a certain level to opt for private coverage as their primary coverage, as in Germany.[67] But as Germany illustrates, this approach can be thorny because it invites in inequity in access, where people who opt out might buy into the better doctors, quicker access, and higher quality care.

Although a universal baseline approach would best serve the goal of health equity, it is the hardest to achieve politically. Efforts at universal, public health-care financing have been proposed and defeated repeatedly in the United States over the past century.[68] It may prove impossible to create a hybrid system with public coverage as a baseline in a country where there is already a strongly embedded private system (although starting from scratch can be done, as Taiwan demonstrated). Hybrid systems may work best in domains where the public option exists first and the private ones fill in later, as in primary education or libraries. Yet, even then, there are significant challenges to maintain a balance between the two when the boundaries of play overlap or are not well demarcated.

6.4.2 *Gap-Filler*

Another way to use public health insurance productively is as a gap-filler for everyone who does not have an alternative. For example, Medicare or Medicaid could be made available to anyone who does not currently meet the criteria for these programs and who does not have quality access to ESI or a subsidized private health insurance plan on an exchange.

A more ambitious version of this idea would be to subsume the ACA's exchange population as well. In the end, half of the population would have private coverage through ESI and the other half would have public coverage of some flavor – Medicare, Medicaid, CHIP, VHA, and IHS. The public coverage would still vary by program, so it would lack any uniform policy characteristic, but it would at least ensure that people did not fall through the cracks and the government could attempt to control spending for at least half of the population. In this version, public and

66 Some enrollees choose private Medicare coverage, known as Medicare Advantage. One-third of all Medicare enrollees choose these private plans that fill in cost-sharing gaps and often also pay for some services not covered by original Medicare, such as dental or vision care. Gretchen Jacobson et al., *A Dozen Facts about Medicare Advantage in 2019*, Kaiser Family Foundation (June 6, 2019), www.kff.org/medicare/issue-brief/a-dozen-facts-about-medicare-advantage-in-2019/.

67 *Health Insurance Options in Germany – 2020*, How to Germany (January 2020), https://www.howtogermany.com/pages/healthinsurance.html.

68 Paul Starr, Remedy and Reaction (2011).

private would coexist population-wide, with people sorted roughly into one or the other. It would offer the flexibility Hacker discusses in Chapter 5 and the potential, even if small, for private insurance innovation. The greatest challenge would be to ensure that the two paths remain equitable.

6.4.3 *The Creeping Public Option*

A compromise between a universal baseline and a gap-filler is to start with gap-filling and to expand over time. This was the initial vision that the architects of Medicare had in the 1960s – that it would first cover older Americans and would over time expand to cover the whole population.[69] This vision is also what led opponents to universal, public coverage to advocate for simultaneous passage of Medicaid.[70] They bet (correctly) that once the elderly, pregnant women, and children were covered, it would reduce motivation for any monumental expansion of public insurance.

A creeping expansion, however, could still happen now. Candidates in the Democratic presidential primaries in 2019, including then Senators Kamala Harris and Elizabeth Warren, proposed creeping public options. Legislation introduced by Representatives Rosa DeLauro and Jan Schakowsky, and informed by Jacob Hacker (Chapter 5), proposes to use Medicare first to fill in existing gaps.[71] It also gives employers the option to enroll their employees in public coverage instead of offering ESI. Over time, it envisions Medicare would grow in its reach by enrolling all newborns, which over a generation would eventually create a universal baseline program and could take any of the forms of private and public coexistence described earlier.

Even if the creep stops short of universal, a public option that covers many Americans could improve health equity and the health-care system significantly. In fact, the larger and more heterogenous of a population a public option reaches, the more durable it will be politically and the more people will be invested in its success, as illustrated by high popular and political support for Medicare.[72]

These kinds of proposals for creeping public options recognize the challenge of transitioning from the current system to one where a public, baseline option serves a broader social function and benefit. They also will face deep resistance from the same parties whose livelihood will be threatened or transformed if public insurance expands – namely, private insurers and providers and suppliers whose reimbursement rates will be squeezed. They may, in fact, be no more politically feasible than a direct step to Medicare for All and much more complex, growing the market bureaucracy even more.

69 Theodore Marmor, The Politics of Medicare 152 (1970).
70 *Id.* at 53.
71 Medicare for America Act, H.R. 2452, 116th Cong. (2019).
72 Mollyann Brodie et al., *Medicare as Reflected in Public Opinion*, ASA: American Society on Aging, www.asaging.org/blog/medicare-reflected-public-opinion (last visited September 25, 2019).

6.5 CONCLUSION

A public option that is more than just a cog in a competitive marketplace – a piece of the market-based bureaucracy – offers more potential to achieve greater equity and opportunity for Americans. In fact, rolling out a public option as part of a neoliberal policy framework is somewhat ironic. It seeks to serve particular end goals – ensuring high-quality health care at controllable prices – while also perpetuating a system that itself has been detrimental to achieving these same goals.

That said, pushing the competitive feature aside enables imagining possible futures where public and private stand side-by-side or, more aptly, layered and working together to ensure equitable and affordable access to medical care that improves people's life opportunities. This imagining is not terribly hard. Countries all around the world manage to make it happen in a variety of different models. But getting from our current models, and mindsets, to these more equitable ends is no easy lift.

7

Promoting Quality and Equality through Early Education and Care

Kimberly J. Morgan

Americans are regularly presented with examples of the horrific consequences of US childcare, when children are harmed, sometimes fatally, in unsafe settings. These episodes draw attention to instances of malpractice, neglect, and even violence in US childcare centers. What tends not to rise to the level of public attention is the quotidian reality of early childhood education and care in the United States: that the quality of too many programs is at best mediocre (Barnett and Frede 2017, 153–4). This is the case despite the high cost of these services to parents, creating challenges for many to afford decent care but especially burdening low- and moderate-income families. The consequences of this expensive, variable-quality system reverberate across US society, depressing women's workforce participation, undermining the potential gains for children of early education, and reproducing class, racial, and gender inequalities.

The root cause of this situation is US reliance on private markets and limited demand-side subsidies to provide early childhood education and care (ECEC) services.[1] Public aid for childcare and preschool consists of means-tested assistance or programs that reach only a fraction of the population and tax subsidies that fail to cover much of the cost of these services. Parents therefore rely on a market that exists largely because of the low pay received by those employed in this sector, which in turn depends on the low educational requirements for those working in these jobs. One of the many consequences is high staff turnover in ECEC centers, preventing the development of skills and knowledge about the care and education of children. The system is mutually reinforcing, as raising standards for staff education and training would raise pay and lower turnover but render these services prohibitively expensive for most parents, given the lack of public subsidies. The result is a landscape of expensive and flawed ECEC services that fail parents, children, ECEC workers, employers, and society as a whole.

[1] The term ECEC is common among experts and policymakers in OECD countries, reflecting efforts to overcome the traditional bifurcation between care and educational programs. The former often were oriented around helping mothers work, while the latter downplayed that goal and instead focused on a child's education. Today, many policymakers aspire to create unified ECEC systems that promote both objectives.

How did we arrive at this point? And what might we do to improve the situation? This paper explores how public options in ECEC can remake our current market-based system into one that lays the foundations for a most just and equitable society. As defined by Sitaraman and Alstott (2019, 27), a public option "guarantees access to important services at a controlled price" but "coexists . . . with private provision of the same service." One important rationale for government involvement in social provision, they argue, is to foster equality of opportunity, creating the conditions for people to help themselves succeed in our market economy. Early childhood education and care is fundamental to this goal, but only if programs are safe, enriching, affordable, and widely available. What is needed is an ECEC system that can promote both quality and equality. A public option is the best way to achieve this.

7.1 A BRIEF HISTORY OF MARKETS IN US ECEC PROVISION

The first time the federal government became involved in early childhood education and care was during the Great Depression, when the government instituted federal subsidies for nursery school programs as a way to keep school staff employed. In the 1940s, these and other centers received Lanham Act funding to support women working in war-time industries. The centers were closed at the end of the war, however, so that women would leave the labor force and make room for returning veterans (Michel 1999, chap. 4). Even so, as in other areas of the welfare state (Howard 1997; Hacker 2002), congressional decision-makers in the 1950s carved out some tax breaks so that working parents could deduct childcare costs as a business expense. The assumption guiding policymakers at the time, however, was that men would be the main breadwinners and women would be at home caring for children, even though many families did not conform to this vision (Coontz 1993).

By the late 1960s, however, there was a growing social and political movement to expand access to early education and care. Civil rights activists and child development specialists joined forces to create Head Start – a program that offers education and health services for disadvantaged, preschool-aged children. Despite bipartisan support for 1971 legislation that would have built on the Head Start model and created a national childcare system, President Nixon issued a vitriolic veto of the bill that was a stinging rebuke of Congress. Unbeknownst at the time, the veto not only dashed immediate hopes for a federally subsidized system, but also signaled a turning point in the history of US ECEC provision. Head Start survived the attack, and the federal government expanded tax deductions for childcare costs in an effort to further promote a market of childcare programs. Otherwise, not only was significant, direct support to ECEC off the table, but social conservatives also mobilized opposition in the 1970s and 1980s against policies that encouraged mothers' employment (Morgan 2001, 239–40). Moreover, intensified conflict over welfare reform contributed to the racialization of public assistance and anything associated with it, including federal spending on childcare (Gilens 1999).

Efforts to expand federal ECEC spending since that time have produced moderate increases in means-tested assistance, usually in the form of services aimed at bolstering workforce participation of low-income parents. Aside from Head Start, the Child Care Development Block Grant (CCDBG) is the main source of federal ECEC spending (Table 7.1), mainly through the Child Care Development Fund (CCDF), followed by specialized grants that provide food, home visits, support to children with disabilities, and so forth. The number served by these programs is limited: in 2016, for instance, only 15 percent of the 13.3 million children eligible for childcare subsidies actually benefitted from them (Office of the Assistant Secretary for Planning and Evaluation, 2019). The number of children served by the CCDF has declined over the past decade, dropping from 1.69 million (served monthly) in 2010 to 1.32 million in 2017 (Child Care Aware of America 2019, 30). One reason for the decline is likely that growing numbers of providers refuse to accept federal subsidies because they have failed to keep up with the real cost of care (Child Care Aware of America 2019, 32–33). Head Start also reaches only a portion of eligible children – by some estimates, just half of those eligible who are African

TABLE 7.1 *Spending on Major Federal Childcare Programs (2018)*

	FY2018 (millions)	Eligibility
Head Start	$9,863	Family income below 100 percent of the federal poverty line.
Childcare and Development Block Grant	$8,130	Family income below 85 percent of state median income, states usually set lower. Parents must be at work, in training, or in school.
MIECHV	$400	States must prioritize certain families, such as those with low incomes.
Preschool Development Grant	$250	Family income below 200 percent of the federal poverty line.
IDEA (preschool and part C)	$851	For children with disabilities and/or developmental delays.
CCAMPIS	$50	Children of low-income postsecondary students, usually with a Pell Grant.
FACE	$16	Indian parents and children in Bureau of Indian Education-funded school.
CACFP	$3,638	Generally low-income children, also elderly or disabled adults.
CDCTC	$4,690	Taxpayers with dependent care expenses.
Dependent Care Exclusion	$900	Taxpayers with expenses eligible for employer-sponsored-dependent care assistance.

Source: Committee on Ways and Means 2018, Table 9–1.

American, 38 percent of Hispanic or Latino children, and 36 percent of Asian children (National Research Council 2018, 125).

There has been significant expansion in state-level prekindergarten programs since the start of the 2000s, and there are now 61 programs in 44 states and the District of Columbia that enroll almost 1.6 million children (National Institute for Early Education Research 2019, 11). However, enrollment has stagnated since the Great Recession, and thus nationally these programs serve only about one-third of four-year-old and 6 percent of three-year-old children (Figure 7.1), and there are tremendous differences between states in access and the quality of these programs (National Institute for Early Education Research 2019, 10). The truncation of direct public support for ECEC is notable in comparative perspective: as Figure 7.2 shows, the United States is nearly at the bottom of OECD countries in public spending on childcare and preschool education.

With most lacking access to public services, families have relied on private markets that are partially subsidized by tax breaks. The Child and Dependent Care Tax Credit (CDCTC) allows parents to deduct a portion of their care expenses on a sliding scale according to income, but this credit is nonrefundable and thus of little use to parents with low incomes.[2] Twenty-three states also have child and dependent care tax credits, and twelve of these are partially or fully refundable

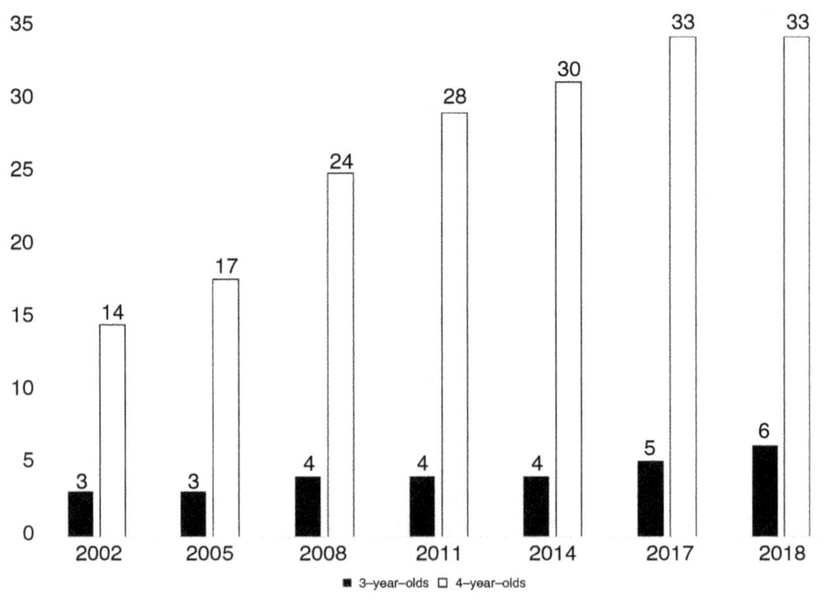

FIGURE 7.1 Percentage of children in state publicly funded pre-K programs
Source: National Institute for Early Education Research 2019.

[2] Parents can deduct up to $3,000 in expenses for one qualifying dependent, and $6,000 for two or more qualifying dependents, but this amount is then multiplied by a percentage that is linked to a person's income. The maximum credit rate is 35 percent.

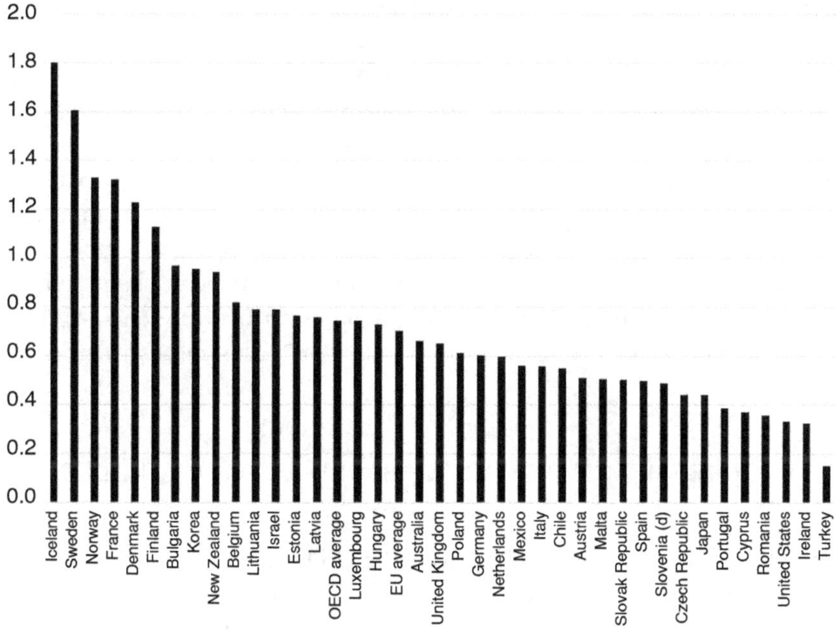

FIGURE 7.2 Public spending on childcare and early education as a percent of GDP, 2015 or latest available
Source: OECD Social Expenditure Database. See original source for details on specific countries. www.oecd.org/els/family/database.htm

(National Academies of Sciences, Engineering and Medicine 2018, 74). About 56 percent of firms offer their employees flexible spending programs that allow an individual to shield up to $5,000 of dependent care costs from taxes, while around 7 percent provide childcare on-site or nearby for their employees, but at a cost to parents (National Academies of Science, Engineering and Medicine 2018, 76). These funds, and parental demand, have helped support expansion of a market of childcare providers, so that even though the US lacks the publicly funded programs that are now prevalent in other countries, significant numbers of US children are in ECEC programs. According to a 2016 survey, around 60 percent of children below the age of five (and not yet in kindergarten) were in some kind of nonparental care, with 59 percent in a center-based program, and 22 percent cared for by a nonrelative in a private home (Corcoran and Steinley 2019, 5).[3]

What does the ECEC market look like? In addition to public pre-K, most programs are provided by nongovernmental entities that operate on either a for-profit or nonprofit basis. The former range from mom-and-pop operations, often in private homes, to large chains, such as Kinder Care or Bright Horizons. Nonprofit

[3] Children can be in more than one type of care, and this is reflected in data from this survey.

centers are also highly varied, and include those programs run by religious denominations, universities, elementary schools, and community-based organizations. All told, there are some 54,000 commercial facilities and 21,000 centers run by nonprofits, with a combined annual revenue of roughly $41 billion (Child Care Services 2019). Another form of private care is more individualized: nannies, au pairs, and babysitters that care for children, sometimes through joint arrangements with multiple families. For school-aged children requiring afterschool or summertime care, there also are wide array of programs, of varying auspices.

In sum, lacking public alternatives, most parents have turned to a large and varied marketplace to find care and educational programs for their preschool-aged children. What could be wrong with such a system? The short answer: almost everything.

7.2 THE IMPACT OF MARKET-BASED ECEC ON QUALITY AND EQUALITY

To get a handle on the many limitations of the US ECEC system, it is necessary to review why policymakers and scholars around the world increasingly favor government involvement in ensuring widespread access to good quality ECEC programs. One rationale concerns child development: the first five years of a child's life are critical from the standpoint of neurological development, and thus environmental conditions and experiences during that period lay the foundations for lifelong capabilities. As one influential scientific panel concluded, "Virtually every aspect of early human development, from the brain's evolving circuitry to the child's capacity for empathy, is affected by the environments and experiences that are encountered in a cumulative fashion, beginning early in the prenatal period and extending throughout the early childhood years" (Institute of Medicine and National Research Council 2000, 6). Services available during early childhood can shape cognitive as well as social development, with potentially lasting effects on the capacities for lifelong learning (OECD 2017, 31). For instance, good quality ECEC programs have been shown to have positive effects on math skills, language, literacy, and social behavior in the short term, with more mixed but suggestive evidence of long-term consequences for school completion, employment, criminality, and health (Yoshikawa, Weiland, and Brooks-Gunn 2016; Heckman and Karapakula 2019).

A prerequisite for these positive effects, however, is *quality*. The greatest developmental gains for children come from high-quality services, whereas poor quality programs can negate these benefits (Gambaro, Stewart, and Waldfogel 2014, 3–6; Melhuish 2015, 10). What is a quality program? Child development experts generally capture quality by structural and process measures (Ishimine and Tayler 2014, 273; Slot 2018) – the former includes child-staff ratios, maximum group size requirements, health and safety regulations, and requirements concerning staff qualifications and continuing professional development, while the latter captures the interactions between staff and children. There is some relationship between structural and process quality (Eurofound 2015, 18–26). Growing recognition about the importance of ECEC quality has led to significant investments in these programs across advanced industrialized states, and initiatives by the European Commission, OECD, and other international organizations, to draw attention to this issue (Schleicher 2019; Morgan forthcoming).

Quality programs can, in turn, promote *equality* through a variety of pathways. One set of impacts is on gender equality, as women's employment choices are shaped in part by availability of good quality and affordable ECEC services. Research on the United States and other countries shows that cost, availability, and quality can all factor into parents' decisions when it comes to paid work, with effects in particular on mothers' labor market participation (Hegewisch and Gornick 2011, 128–129). The ramifications of leaving the workplace can be enduring: during lengthy periods of time out of the labor market, human capital degrades, making it more difficult to reenter the workforce later on. The result is a penalty on mothers' earnings that is more pronounced in countries lacking childcare and other supports to mothers' employment (Budig, Misra, and Boeckmann 2012).

As mothers' employment affects the financial well-being of households, ECEC access also has broader economic consequences. The era during which one earner could support a family on one income is well past in most advanced industrialized states, as good paying blue-collar jobs have disappeared, unionization rates have fallen, and job insecurity has increased, including for many white-collar workers. In the United States, wage growth has largely stagnated since 2000 for all except those in at least the 90th percentile of the income distribution (Economic Policy Institute 2019). Today, 15 percent of households with children under age eighteen are headed by a single parent, and these households are at particular risk for poverty (Census Bureau 2019). Of the 17.5 percent of children living in poverty, 58.2 percent of them are in households headed by single mothers (Children's Defense Fund 2017). The reality today is that most households depend on the market incomes of the adults living within them, whether it is a two-parent or single-parent family. Supporting paid work is thus essential to the financial well-being of families. Not only does access to affordable, good quality ECEC programs support mothers' employment, but these services also can potentially be a source of employment, often for women, as teachers and caregivers.

Finally, promoting broad-based access to quality ECEC programs affects equality of opportunity through its effects on child development. The income-based gap between children in their cognitive capabilities is already apparent when children begin school and tends not to widen very much thereafter. This suggests that the critical period for intervention is *before* the compulsory school age (Yoshikawa, Weiland, and Brooks-Gunn 2016, 22). As Valentino (2018, 79) sums up the available research on the topic, "achievement gaps between Black and Hispanic children and their White peers and between children from lower socioeconomic backgrounds and their higher socioeconomic counterparts are about two-thirds of a standard deviation at the start of kindergarten … the equivalent of about three years of learning in later grades."

Promoting equality of opportunity through ECEC programs has positive consequences not only for societal well-being but also for the economy as a whole. The potential effects are both short-term and long-term. In the immediate term, assuring parents access to affordable, good-quality care reduces staff turnover and absenteeism. One economic analysis of parents lacking adequate care for children under age three found that the average cost to parents in lost earnings was $3,350, adding up to $37 billion annually, while the yearly cost to businesses was $13 billion (reflecting less revenue and the cost of recruiting new employees). With families paying less in income and sales taxes, the annual cost to taxpayers is $7 billion (Belfield 2018). The longer-term economic effects are a source of greater debate, owing to the difficulties of calculating the lasting consequences of investments in ECEC for the productivity to workers or reduced crime rates. That said, conservative estimates hold that for every dollar invested in preschool education there is a return of around three to four dollars (Karoly 2016).

Recognition of the manifold and multiple benefits of ECEC have spurred expansions of these programs across OECD countries. Even in countries that traditionally shied away from supporting mothers' employment, recognition of the economic and social realities fueling women's labor force participation, coupled with growing awareness of the importance of early education for children, has led governments of varying ideological stripes to expand access to ECEC programs. Not all of these initiatives have put as much emphasis on the quality of these programs as they should, and some countries have developed systems rooted in market forces and demand-side subsidies (Morgan 2012). Overall, however, there is growing recognition that ECEC is a fundamental feature of what has been called a "social investment" approach to social policy that invests in human capital and prioritizes access and quality in public services in order to promote equality (Morel, Palier, and Palme 2012).

The market-based ECEC system in the US does not uniformly promote quality and equality. With limited public subsidies, access to programs is highly stratified by income, a reflection of the fact that parents themselves pay much of the cost. One estimate holds that parents pay about 46 percent of ECEC costs, while public funds cover 52 percent and private funds the rest (National Research Council 2018, 56–57), but this is total spending and does not reflect the realities facing individual families who, often with minimal subsidies, struggle to pay for expensive care. In 2018, the average annual cost of childcare in the Northeast reached $26,102 (compared to $13,214 for college tuition), while in the South the average cost was $18,442 (while annual college tuition cost $9,706) (Child Care Aware of America 2019, 12). This represents a hefty, if not impossible, portion of annual income. An OECD analysis found that, after taking into account tax breaks and other subsidies, middle-income and low-income two-earner and single-parent families in the United States paid 30 percent of their earnings on childcare, compared to the OECD average of 17 percent for two-earner families and 11 percent for low-income single-parent households.[4]

Although parental choices with regard to ECEC reflect a variety of economic and cultural factors, much research concludes that cost is a major determinant of utilization (National Research Council 2018, 120–122). Use of ECEC services rises with socioeconomic status, measured by income and education (see Figure 7.3), and studies have shown that increasing subsidies reduces these gaps in programs use. Access to *quality* care also is highly dependent on income and also stratifies the population based on race or ethnicity: in the United States, poor and/or minority children are less likely to have access to good quality ECEC programs, compared to white and/or non-poor children (Karoly et al. 2008, 147–150; Valentino 2018). But quality is a problem that plagues the entire market-based US system. As Barnett and Frede (2010, 22) sum up the situation, "few of the preschool programs children

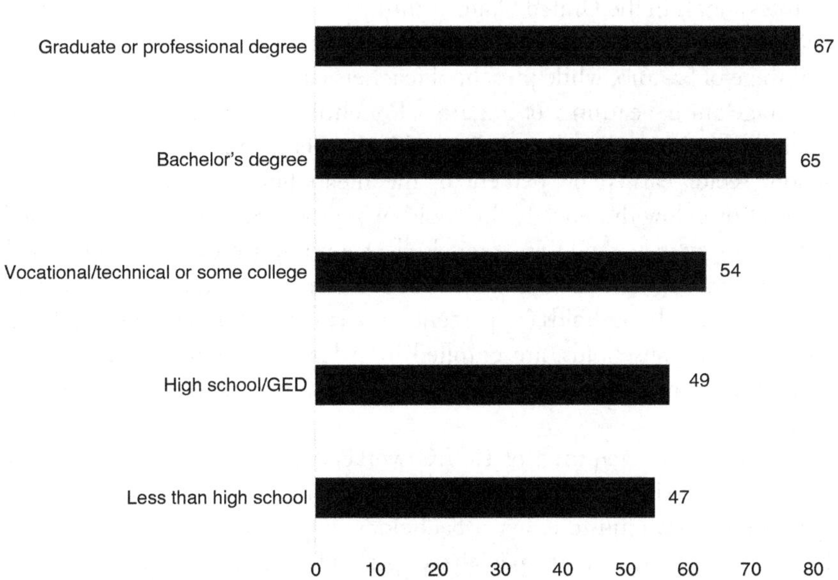

FIGURE 7.3 Participation of children below age five (and not yet in kindergarten) in center-based care, by Parental Education Level (2016)
Parental education is the highest level attained for either parent or nonparental guardian living in the household. Source: Corcoran and Steinley 2019, p. 8.

[4] The analysis concerns a two-income family earning 167 percent of average earnings and with two children in full-day care, and a single-earner family with two children and with an income of 50 percent of average earnings. OECD Family Policy Database: www.oecd.org/els/family/database.htm.

attend are of high quality. Most might be rated as mediocre. A significance percentage provides little support for learning and development."

One might wonder how it is that a service parents pay so much for remains inferior in quality. The answer lies in the economics of ECEC programs, in which labor costs amount to 70 percent of operating costs (Child Care Services 2019). As most centers depend heavily on parental fees for revenue, the price parents pay is directly tied to the wages of ECEC staff (Whitebook 1999). To maintain profitability, centers must find ways to keep these costs down or else parents will seek out cheaper forms of care, like babysitters or relatives. Large chains reap some economies of scale, but the ECEC market overall is characterized by considerable fragmentation and the predominance of small operations. Given the low subsidies and state-level regulations on the number of staff required per child, the way ECEC services survive is to squeeze the wages and benefits of their employees, which in turn assumes that the employees are not highly educated or trained or else they would find other forms of employment (Child Care Services 2019).

As a result, the US ECEC market's existence hinges on very low-paid staff that are ill-trained, too often not supported in their work, and unlikely to stay in the position for very long. ECEC workers are "some of the most erratically trained and poorly paid professionals in the United States" (Phillips, Austin, and Whitebook 2016, 140). In 2018, the mean hourly wage for childcare workers was $11.83, resulting in a mean annual wage of $24,610, while preschool teachers earned an average wage of $16.54 (and average annual earnings of $34,410).[5] For childcare workers, their earnings are less than half the mean hourly wage in the United States ($24.98), while those in the preschool sector earned 66 percent of the mean hourly wage. This represents incomes at or below the poverty threshold, which was $25,100 for a family of four in 2018.[6] Many who work in this sector also lack employer-provided benefits, such as health insurance (National Research Council 2018, 37), and more than half of childcare workers' households (53 percent) and 43 percent of preschool and kindergarten teachers' households, are enrolled in at least one public support program (compared to 21 percent for all workers) (*Early Childhood Workforce Index* 2018, chap. 3, 14).[7]

The qualifications required of ECEC workers vary markedly by state, type of center, and job position, but generally are not very high. State-funded prekindergarten programs often require either a bachelor's degree (59 percent currently have such a requirement) and/or specialized prekindergarten training (81.9 percent require this) (NIEE 2019, 11), while the Head Start program requires that at least

5 Available at the Bureau of Labor Statistics, www.bls.gov/oes/current/oes399011.htm and www.bls.gov/oes/2018/may/oes252011.htm.

6 For the forty-eight contiguous states and Washington DC. https://aspe.hhs.gov/2018-poverty-guidelines.

7 The four programs included in the analysis are the federal Earned Income Tax Credit; Medicaid and Children's Health Insurance Program; Supplemental Nutrition Assistance Program (food stamps); and Temporary Assistance for Need Families.

half of teachers have a bachelor's or advanced degree in early childhood education. In 2013, about 66 percent of staff working with preschool-aged children had a BA degree (National Research Council 2015, 424). While this still falls below the recommendations of the Institute of Medicine and National Research Council that all preschool teachers have a BA and training in early childhood education (NIEE 2019, 14), it is nonetheless better than the situation in other childcare centers. Only one state has a similar educational/training requirement for other center-based programs, while seventeen states require less than a high school degree or GED (National Research Council 2015, 424). Teachers in these centers are not required to have any prior experience in early childhood in forty-one states (National Research Council 2015, 425).

Low wages and a frequent lack of benefits lead to high rates of employee turnover in ECEC programs. Whether one comes to this line of work with specialized training or not, experience and continuing professional development programs (if they exist) can help develop skills and coping mechanisms for working in what can be a stressful environment. Yet, turnover remains high in this sector, at around 30–40 percent per year, with staff often complaining of low pay, workplace stress, and the lack of benefits (National Research Council 2015, 471; Child Care Services 2019). Turnover rates are highest in for-profit centers, whether they be chains, franchises, or independent operations, when compared to other nonprofit and publicly sponsored centers, and it is also in those for-profit centers that both the pay and qualification levels of the staff are the lowest (Whitebook, Phillips, and Howes 2014, 26–30).

All of these features of the ECEC system reinforce inequalities in US society. Not only is class inequality reinforced by disparities in the access of poor children to high quality developmental services, but these disparities reinforce achievement gaps between minority groups. To reiterate the point made earlier: some of the children who would especially benefit from access to good quality ECEC programs are less likely to access them, and in the United States that has particular implications for low-income minority children. The precise role of access disparities in shaping these differences remains a subject of continuing research, yet, we know that some of the groups of children that would most benefit from enriching, developmental care, or early education are less likely to access it (Karoly et al. 2008, 147–150; Ladd 2017). The expansion of public pre-K and other targeted programs has improved access to children from lower- and middle-income families, but disparities in access based on income are still significant, as is true for children from Latino families (Chaudry and Datta 2017, 9, 11).[8]

The US ECEC system also contributes to gender inequality. After rising rapidly during the 1970s and 1980s, women's employment rates have stagnated in the US since the 1990s, in contrast to trends in many other advanced industrialized states (Figure 7.4). The high cost of childcare is one factor that has depressed US mothers' employment (Kubota 2018). And the treatment of the ECEC workforce also

[8] This analysis is of three- and four-year-olds.

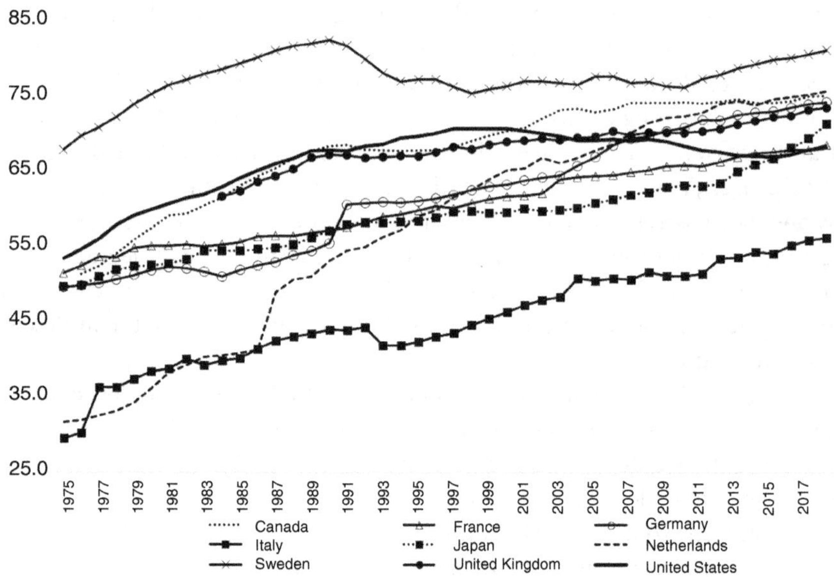

FIGURE 7.4 Labor force participation rates of women, ages 15–64, 1975–2018
Source: OECD.stat.

contributes to, rather than potentially mitigating, both gender and economic disparities. Employees in ECEC programs are overwhelmingly female and have relatively low education and skills. They also are disproportionately racial and ethnic minorities: around 40 percent of the ECEC workforce, in centers and registered home-based care, consists of people of color, which is true of half of unlicensed home-based care providers (*Early Childhood Workforce Index*). It is on the backs of these low-paid and often underappreciated workers that our market-based ECEC system operates.

7.3 WHAT A PUBLIC OPTION COULD LOOK LIKE

A public option can rectify many of these problems and could take various forms. One type of public option could be modeled after our public schools, with universal access to publicly run programs alongside private programs that continue to operate for those parents who prefer them. This approach, outlined by Sitaraman and Alstott (2019, chap. 10), would involve a first layer of services for children below the age of three, followed by universal pre-K programs that could be integrated with local public schools. Access would be guaranteed, being either free of charge, as is the case with public schools, or available to parents according to sliding-scale fees based on income. Another approach would build on our existing system of ECEC providers but use quality-enhancing regulations as well as supply-side subsidies to ensure services that are affordable and of good quality. Private, nonsubsidized services could also continue to offer their own programs, but many would likely agree to higher program standards and requirements in return for public subsidies.

One can also envision a mix of these two approaches: directly provided programs as well as subsidized private providers who are required to meet the same kinds of standards as the publicly provided programs in terms of facilities requirements, curriculum, staff qualifications and pay, and training. One example of a mixed model is the Department of Defense (DoD) childcare system for military personnel, which employs 23,000 childcare workers and provides for around 200,000 children (Kamarck 2018). The backbone of the military system is government-provided centers that must meet high standards for the quality of their facilities and staff training and pay. To supplement the DoD-provided centers, there also is a fee assistance program in which DoD makes direct payments to civilian ECEC providers.[9] The latter are required to meet many of the same high standards as the military's centers, including the requirement that they be accredited by a nationally recognized accreditation body.[10] For both DoD-provided ECEC and that offered by subsidized, civilian providers, parental fees are set according to income and the overall cost to parents is significantly below that paid for nonsubsidized care in private markets (Kamarck 2018, 12).

Whether through direct government provision or through subsidies to existing providers, the key is to intervene on the supply-side to make sure that ECEC programs are broadly available and of good quality. In theory, we might imagine a system in which generous and refundable demand-side subsidies – refundable tax credits or vouchers – ensure that lower- and moderate-income people have most of the cost of their services covered. Combining this with strict regulations on quality should ideally then enable a subsidized market of private, for-profit providers that will compete for parents' dollars. In practice, there are grounds for skepticism that such a system would be sustainable, for many of the reasons that Sitaraman and Alstott (2019, 187–191) outline. Providers may just raise prices to gobble up parents' vouchers, and the variable price of care across the country would make it difficult to tailor the voucher to the right cost. Volatility in individual incomes, particularly pronounced among lower income people, adds further complexity to figuring out how to create a voucher or refundable tax credit that equitably supports parents with ECEC costs. To these technical challenges, I would add a political one that is particularly pertinent in the United States, where organized interests often mobilize to influence policy in their favor. Private providers exist to maximize profits and, as was noted earlier, the economics of ECEC is relentless on this score. Staff costs are everything and there are few productivity gains to be had (unless we are willing to

9 This includes DOD-operated child development centers and family childcare, services run in people's homes that are certified by the DOD and thus required to meet many of the same requirements as the childcare centers. There also is school-aged childcare.

10 www.childcareaware.org/fee-assistancerespite/militaryprograms/

turn our children over to robots). Facing strict requirements on staff pay, educational requirements, and strictures on class sizes and staff–child ratios, for-profit firms in the US context will lobby hard to reduce these requirements.

By intervening on the supply side through either direct provision or subsidies to providers, policymakers could then also increase requirements for the education, training, and continuing professional development of those working in these centers. Decoupling pay from parental fees is critical to enabling a transformation of these jobs into decently paid, opportunity-enhancing forms of employment. Staff not only could earn a livable wage but have opportunities for training and other programs that provide a career ladder. Some states have already sought to develop such ladders through ECEC programs, so that low-skilled staff can gain support for continuing education that enables them to advance into more skilled and better remunerated positions in the ECEC workforce. Such initiatives could also be thought of as a public option for ECEC education and training: publicly provided or publicly subsidized programs for those seeking employment in the ECEC field.

However, as long as these positions in ECEC programs offer low pay and often inadequate or nonexistent benefits, many will jump off these ladders and seek out other forms of employment. Severing the connection between parental fees and the pay received by ECEC staff has been crucial to the success of the military ECEC program in delivering quality care at a reasonable cost. In the words of one Army official in charge of the system, "We broke the link between parent fees and personnel costs. You have the fair share fees on the one side, and you have the appropriate wage [for providers] on the other, and the armed services make up the difference" (cited in Covert 2017). That is the essence of a public option in ECEC.

7.4 CONCLUSION: JOINING THE REST OF THE ADVANCED INDUSTRIALIZED WORLD

The United States was not alone in using social policy to support single-earner families in the post-WWII decades. To the contrary, governments in many advanced industrialized countries, including Australia, Germany, Japan, the Netherlands, New Zealand, and Switzerland, shied away from investments in public ECEC programs out of a belief that such responsibilities were better left to families and local voluntary organizations. In the past three decades, however, policymakers in these countries came to realize that the world had changed around them. Women were working, there were more single-parent families, and traditional neighborhood structures were no longer available to provide supportive environments for young children. Demographic aging highlighted the importance of helping parents combine work and family, so that women's workplace aspirations would not clash with their desire to have children, leading to zero-sum trade-offs that depress fertility rates. And research showed the critical importance of investments during the early years of children's lives for maximizing their lifelong potential. Leftists and neoclassical economists alike all came to realize that one of the most important things government can do is ensure there are safe and stimulating learning environments for all young children.

It is well past time for the United States to join much of the advanced industrialized world in developing a public ECEC option. Such programs can provide developmentally stimulating programs to young children that also enable parents to be in paid employment. Access to these services is especially important for children experiencing various forms of disadvantage owing to low family income, migrant status, and/or disability. ECEC also can provide employment, often for less-skilled and/or lower-income women. In short, ECEC programs can help fight poverty, promote equal opportunity, and foster societal well-being, and in so doing they embody the many goals of the public option.

REFERENCES

Barnett, W. Steven and Ellen C. Frede. 2010. "The Promise of Preschool: Why We Need Early Education for All." *American Educator* 34, no. 1 (Spring): 21–40.

Barnett, W. Steven and Ellen C. Frede. 2017. "Long-Term Effects of a System of High-Quality University Preschool Education in the United States." In *Childcare, Early Education and Social Inequality: An International Perspective*, edited by Hans-Peter Blossfeld, Neven Kulic, Jan Skopek, and Moris Triventi, pp. 152–172. Cheltenham, UK: Edward Elgar.

Belfield, Clive R. 2018. *The Economic Impacts of Insufficient Child Care on Working Families*. Ready Nation: Council for a Strong America. www.strongnation.org/

Budig, Michelle J., Joya Misra, and Irene Boeckmann. 2012. "The Motherhood Penalty in Cross-National Perspective: The Importance of Work–Family Policies and Cultural Attitudes." *Social Politics: International Studies in Gender, State & Society* 19, no. 2 (Summer): 163–193.

Census Bureau (2019). *America's Families and Living Arrangements: 2019*. www.census.gov/data/tables/2019/demo/families/cps-2019.html

Chaudry, Ajay and A. Rupa Datta. 2017. "The Current Landscape for Public Pre-Kindergarten Programs." In *The Current State of Scientific Knowledge on Pre-Kindergarten Effects*, 5–18. National Institute for Early Education Research. http://nieer.org/research-report/current-state-scientific-knowledge-pre-kindergarten-effects

Child Care Aware. 2019. *The US and the High Price of Child Care: An Examination of a Broken System*. www.childcareaware.org/our-issues/research/the-us-and-the-high-price-of-child-care-2019/

Child Care Services. 2019. First Research Industry Profile. Dun & Bradstreet, November 18.

Children's Defense Fund. 2017. *Child Poverty in America*. www.childrensdefense.org/wp-content/uploads/2018/09/Child-Poverty-in-America-2017-National-Fact-Sheet.pdf

Committee on Ways and Means. 2018. Green Book: Background Material and Data on the Programs within the Jurisdiction of the Committee on Ways and Means. U.S. House of Representatives. https://greenbook-waysandmeans.house.gov/2018-green-book

Coontz, Stephanie. 1993. *The Way We Never Were: American Families and The Nostalgia Trap*. New York, NY:Basic Books.

Corcoran, Lisa and Katrina Steinley. 2019. *Early Childhood Program Participation, Results from the National Household Education Surveys Program of 2016*. Washington DC: National Center for Education Statistics, Institute of Education Sciences, U.S. Department of Education. https://nces.ed.gov/pubsearch/pubsinfo.asp?pubid=2017101REV

Covert, Bryce. 2017. "The U.S. Already Has a High-quality, Universal Childcare Program — in the Military." https://archive.thinkprogress.org/universal-military-childcare-9bb2b54bd154/

Early Childhood Workforce Index 2018. Berkeley, CA: Center for the Study of Child Care Employment. https://cscce.berkeley.edu/early-childhood-workforce-2018-index/

Economic Policy Institute. 2019. *Top 1.0% of Earners See Wages up 157.8% Since 1979*. www.epi.org/blog/top-1–0-of-earners-see-wages-up-157–8-since-1979/

Eurofound. 2015. *Early Childhood Care: Accessibility and Quality of Services*. Luxembourg: Publications Office of the European Union.

Gambaro, Ludovica, Kitty Stewart, and Jane Waldfogel. 2014. "Introduction." In *An Equal Start? Providing Quality Early Education and Care for Disadvantaged Children*, edited by Ludovica Gambaro, Kitty Stewart, and Jane Waldfogel, pp. 1–28. Bristol, UK: Policy Press.

Gilens, Martin. 1999. *Why Americans Hate Welfare: Race, Media, and the Politics of Antipoverty Policy*. Chicago: University of Chicago Press.

Hacker, Jacob S. 2002. *The Divided Welfare State: The Battle over Public and Private Benefits in the United States*. Princeton: Princeton University Press.

Heckman, James J. and Ganesh Karapakula. 2019. *The Perry Preschoolers at Late Midlife: A Study in Design-Specific Inference*. NBER Working Paper No. 25888 (May).

Hegewisch, Ariane and Janet C. Gornick. 2011. "The Impact of Work-Family Policies on Women's Employment: A Review of Research from OECD Countries." *Community, Work & Family* 14, no. 2: 119–138.

Howard, Christopher. 1997. *The Hidden Welfare State: Tax Expenditures and Social Policy in the United States*. Princeton: Princeton University Press.

Institute of Medicine and National Research Council. 2000. *From Neurons to Neighborhoods: The Science of Early Childhood Development*. Washington DC: The National Academies Press. https://doi.org/10.17226/9824.

Ishimine, Karin and Collette Tayler. 2014. "Assessing Quality in Early Childhood Education and Care." *European Journal of Education Research, Development and Policy* 49, no. 2 (June): 272–290.

Kamarck, Kristy N. 2018. *Military Child Development Program: Background and Issues*. Washington, DC: Congressional Research Service.

Karoly, Lynn A. 2016. "The Economic Returns to Early Childhood Education." *Future of Children* 26, no. 2 (Fall): 36–55.

Karoly, Lynn A., Bonnie Ghosh-Dastidar, Gail L. Zellman, Michael Perlman, and Lynda Fernyhough. 2008. *Prepared to Learn: The Nature and Quality of Early Care and Education for Preschool-Age Children in California*. Santa Monica, CA: Rand Corporation.

Kubota, So. 2018. "Child Care Costs and Stagnating Female Labor Force Participation in the U.S." Unpublished ms., Hitotsubashi University. https://drive.google.com/file/d/18ywB-GrgYcYtocKIBJ7v9ttbUE8UnA2e/view

Ladd, Helen F. 2017. "Do Some Groups of Children Benefit More Than Others from Pre-Kindergarten Programs?" In *The Current State of Scientific Knowledge on Pre-Kindergarten Effects*, pp. 31–36. Washington, DC: Brookings Institution. www.brookings.edu/wp-content/uploads/2017/04/duke_prekstudy_final_4-4-17_hires.pdf

Melhuish, Edward. 2015. *Provision of Quality Early Childcare Services*. Discussion Paper for Early Childcare Services, Czech Republic. Peer Review. November 10 –11. https://ec.europa.eu/social/main.jsp?catId=1024&langId=en&newsId=2335&moreDocuments=yes&tableName=news

Michel, Sonya. 1999. *Children's Interests/Mothers' Rights: The Shaping of America's Child Care Policy*. New Haven: Yale University Press.

Morel, Nathalie, Bruno Palier, and Joakim Palme, eds. 2012. *Towards a Social Investment Welfare State? Ideas, Policies, Challenges*. Bristol, UK: Bristol University Press.
Morgan, Kimberly J. 2001. "A Child of the Sixties: The Great Society, the New Right, and the Politics of Child Care." *Journal of Policy History* 13, no. 2 (March): 215–250.
Morgan, Kimberly J. 2012. "Promoting Social Investment through Work-Family Policies: Which Nations Do It and Why?" In *Towards a Social Investment Welfare State? Ideas, Policies, Challenges*, edited by Nathalie Morel, Bruno Palier, and Joakim Palme, pp. 153–180. Bristol, UK: Bristol University Press.
Morgan, Kimberly J. (forthcoming). "Social Investment or Child Care on the Cheap? Quality, Workforce, and Access Considerations in the Expansion of Early Childhood Education and Care." In *The World Politics of Social Investment*, edited by Julian Garritzman, Silja Hauersermann, and Bruno Palier. New York, NY: Oxford University Press.
National Institute for Early Education Research. 2019. *The State of Preschool 2018*. http://nieer.org/state-preschool-yearbooks/2018–2
National Research Council. 2015. *Transforming the Workforce for Children Birth Through Age 8: A Unifying Foundation*. Washington, DC: The National Academies Press. https://doi.org/10.17226/19401.
National Research Council. 2018. *Transforming the Financing of Early Care and Education*. Washington, DC: The National Academies Press. https://doi.org/10.17226/24984
OECD. 2017. *Starting Strong 2017: Key OECD Indicators on Early Childhood Education and Care*. Paris: OECD.
Office of the Assistant Secretary for Planning and Evaluation. 2019. *Factsheet: Estimates of Child Care Eligibility and Receipt for Fiscal Year 2016*. Washington, DC: U.S. Department of Health and Human Services.
Phillips, Deborah, Lea J.E. Austin, and Marcy Whitebook. (2016). "The Early Care and Education Workforce." *Future of Children* 26, no. 2 (Fall): 139–158.
Schleicher, Andreas. 2019. *Helping Our Youngest to Learn and Grow: Policies for Early Learning*, International Summit on the Teaching Profession. Paris: OECD Publishing. http://dx.doi.org/10.1787/9789264313873-en
Sitaraman, Ganesh and Anne Alstott. 2019. *The Public Option: How to Expand Freedom, Increase Opportunity, and Promote Equality*. Cambridge, MA: Harvard University Press.
Slot, Pauline. 2018. *Structural Characteristics and Process Quality in Early Childhood Education and Care: A Literature Review*. OECD Education Working Papers no. 176.
Valentino, Rachel. 2018. "Will Public Pre-K Really Close Achievement Gaps? Gaps in Prekindergarten Quality between Students and Across States." *American Education Research Journal* 55, no. 1: 79–116.
Whitebook, Marcy. 1999. "Child Care Workers: High Demand, Low Wages." *Annals of the American Association of Political and Social Science* 563, no. 1 (May): 146–161.
Whitebook, Marcy, Deborah Phillips, and Carollee Howes. 2014. *Worthy Work, STILL Unlivable Wages: The Early Childhood Workforce 25 Years after the National Child Care Staffing Study*. Berkeley, CA: Center for the Study of Child Care Employment.
Yoshikawa, Hirokazu, Christina Weiland, and Jeanne Brooks-Gunn. 2016. "When Does Preschool Matter?" *The Future of Children* 26, no. 2 (Fall): 21–35.

8

Revamping Public Energy

Shelley Welton[*]

As unusually strong Santa Ana winds whipped through California in fall 2019, the state's utilities faced a bind: cut power for millions, or risk their transmission infrastructure sparking another devastating and deadly fire? In the end, both occurred, and California was alternately ablaze and in the dark throughout the fall. This impossible predicament was, many said, a harbinger of things to come: climate change exposing the precarity of seemingly advanced economies, as centuries of fossil fuel emissions reveal their bite.[1]

The California fires also prompted renewed debate over control of utilities under changing climate conditions – particularly as evidence mounts that deferred grid maintenance in favor of shareholder payments was a contributing cause of the wildfires.[2] San Jose launched calls for a public takeover of California's largest utility, Pacific Gas & Electric (PG&E).[3] San Francisco had already put in a bid to buy its portion of PG&E's grid.[4] These proposals are the latest iteration of a growing conversation about whether private control of electric

* Assistant Professor, University of South Carolina School of Law.

1 *See, e.g.*, Reis Thebault et al., *High-Voltage PG&E Power Line Broke Near Origin of Massive Fire in California Wine Country*, WASH. POST (October 25, 2019), www.washingtonpost.com/nation/2019/10/24/fast-moving-wildfire-ignites-northern-california-wine-country-prompting-evacuations/.

2 Dale Kasler, *PG&E Gets Blamed for Another Deadly 2017 Wildfire, This Time from "Sagging Power Lines.,"* SACRAMENTO BEE (October 9, 2018), www.sacbee.com/news/california/fires/article219731815.html; David Roberts, *California's Deliberate Blackouts Were Outrageous and Harmful. They're Going to Happen Again.*, VOX (October 24, 2019), www.vox.com/energy-and-environment/2019/10/16/20910947/climate-change-wildfires-california-2019-blackouts.

3 John Woolfolk, *San Jose Leads Cities, Counties Calling for Ratepayer Takeover of PG&E*, MERCURY NEWS (November 5, 2019), www.mercurynews.com/2019/11/05/san-jose-leads-cities-counties-calling-for-ratepayer-takeover-of-pge/.

4 Shanti S. Nair, *PG&E Turns Down San Francisco's $2.5 Billion Offer to Buy Assets*, REUTERS (October 11, 2019), www.reuters.com/article/us-pg-e-us-sanfrancisco-assets/pge-turns-down-san-franciscos-2–5-billion-offer-to-buy-assets-idUSKBN1WQ2SO.

utilities is compatible with the scale of the energy transition demanded by climate change.

The aim of this chapter is to clarify the debate between public and private energy options in the context of climate change – and to mount a case for why public energy's longstanding theory and praxis suggest several promising roles for public options in the clean energy transition. Many are familiar with the role that public energy played in bringing electricity to rural America during the New Deal, when investor-owned utilities refused to expand service to rural areas because they were insufficiently profitable. To fill the gap, Congress created the Tennessee Valley Authority (TVA) and other federal public power entities to produce cheap power, and simultaneously provided low-cost loans to local communities to form rural electric cooperatives or municipal utilities to build lines to deliver this power.[5] The long-term result of these public investments has been widespread (though lamentably still imperfect) access to reliable, affordable power across the United States.[6]

However, the fact that public options proved critical in electrifying America has limited bearing on their potential to help with the central challenge facing the US power sector today: the need to decarbonize energy supply to respond to climate change. Recent scientific alarm bells have suggested that the United States has a limited window – perhaps a couple of decades – to transform its energy system to 100 percent clean energy before the planet overheats to catastrophic levels.[7] In response, young activists have sparked a vibrant movement for a "Green New Deal" to jointly tackle climate change and inequality, while several US states have adopted their own 100 percent clean energy targets.[8]

5 *See* Tennessee Valley Authority Act of 1933, ch. 32, 48 Stat. 58 (1933) (codified as amended at 16 U.S.C. § 831 (2012)); Rural Electrification Act of 1936, ch. 432, 49 Stat. 1363 (May 20, 1936) (codified at 7 U.S.C. § 901).

6 On the imperfect realization of access, see Laurel Morales, *For Many Navajos, Getting Hooked Up to the Power Grid Can be Life-Changing*, NPR Shots (May 29, 2019), www.npr.org/sections/health-shots/2019/05/29/726615238/for-many-navajos-getting-hooked-up-to-the-power-grid-can-be-life-changing (reporting that 10 percent of Navajos living in the Navajo Nation, "the largest Native American reservation in the U.S.," are without electricity). On ongoing affordability challenges, see Diana Hernández & Stephen Bird, *Energy Burden and the Need for Integrated Low-Income Housing and Energy Policy*, 2 Poverty & Pub. Pol'y 5, 6 (2010) (discussing the difficult choices that many American families must make between paying for food or electricity each month).

7 *See* Intergovernmental Panel on Climate Change, Summary for Policymakers, *in* Global Warming of 1.5°C: An IPCC Special Report on the Impacts of Global Warming of 1.5°C Above Pre-Industrial Levels and Related Global Greenhouse Gas Emission Pathways, in the Context of Strengthening the Global Response to the Threat of Climate Change, Sustainable Development, and Efforts to Eradicate Poverty (2018).

8 *See* H.R. Res. 109, 116th Cong. (1st Sess. 2019); Julia Pyper, *Tracking Progress on 100% Clean Energy Targets*, GTM (November 12, 2019), www.greentechmedia.com/articles/read/tracking-progress-on-100-clean-energy-targets (reporting that "[s]even states, as well as Puerto Rico and the District of Columbia, have passed 100 percent clean energy transition laws," and several others have executive orders to the same effect).

Some have suggested that public options could play an important role in this new effort at infrastructure transformation; others have doubted their suitability to this suite of challenges.[9]

To bring the terms of this debate into focus, this chapter first traces the roles that public options play across the energy system today. It then parses the ways in which public options might enhance the transformation of energy supply, transmission, and delivery, highlighting where in the system public options are most likely to achieve their theoretical potential to remediate climate change, and where risks may outweigh potential rewards.

8.1 THE PUBLIC ENERGY LANDSCAPE TODAY

Any conversation about public options in energy must begin from an understanding of how significant they already are in the US energy system. The key components of the electricity system are supply (generation), transmission and distribution (the poles and wires), and procurement and delivery (sales to end-use customers). Nearly a century after the New Deal, and even as the energy sector has increasingly embraced competition,[10] public options continue to perform all three of these functions (see Figure 8.1). On the supply side, federally owned power projects, such as the TVA, supply generation and transmission services to many publicly owned utilities and cooperatives, some of whom also own their own generation facilities. On the distribution and sales side, these publicly owned utilities (typically owned by a municipality, but sometimes by a rural power district) serve 14.4 percent of Americans, while cooperatives serve another 13 percent.[11]

When theorists and policymakers speak of public "options," they generally mean public alternatives that can coexist alongside private ones: for example,

9 *Compare The Green New Deal*, BERNIESANDERS.COM [hereinafter *The Green New Deal*], https://berniesanders.com/en/issues/green-new-deal/ (last visited December 13, 2019) (championing a robust public ownership role), *with* Mark Paul, *Can Public Ownership of Utilities be Part of the Climate Solution?*, FORBES (September 13, 2019), www.forbes.com/sites/washingtonbytes/2019/09/13/can-public-ownership-of-utilities-be-part-of-the-climate-solution/#5fb7b1232296 (quoting Elizabeth Warren as disagreeing with public ownership of utilities as a climate change solution).

10 See William Boyd, *Public Utility and the Low-Carbon Future*, 61 UCLA L. REV. 1614 (2014), on the evolution of the sector over the twentieth century.

11 AM. PUB. POWER ASS'N, 2019 STATISTICAL REPORT 16 (2019) [hereinafter APPA], www.publicpower.org/system/files/documents/2019-Public-Power-Statistical-Report.pdf. Technically cooperatives are not "public," because they are member-owned, whereas municipal utilities and public utility districts are owned by the local government itself. But they similarly aspire to democratic management.

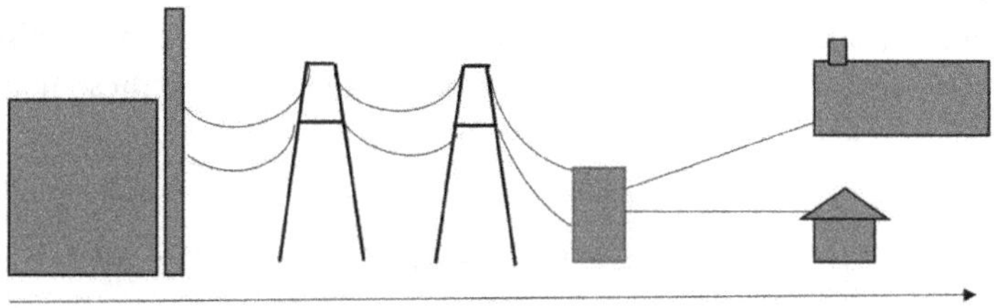

FIGURE 8.1 Schematic of US Electricity System, with relevant ownership shares[12]

a public community pool in the same town as several private, membership-based pool clubs; or public libraries that might share the same block with bookstores.[13] This genre of public options maximally preserves individual choice: join the country club or swim for free; borrow the book or buy the book – up to you.

Public options in energy function differently. The transmission and distribution networks are presumed to be natural monopolies, because it would be duplicative and ugly to build two sets of poles and wires in the same place. Accordingly, only a single entity – public or private[14] – serves a given locale. That means that the choice of whether to have a publicly or privately owned grid must be made at the collective, community level (except in rural places that private companies refuse to serve, in which case there is no choice). Public ownership of these energy assets is thus a democratic but clunky form of a public option, because it requires majority vote (or, in some places, city council approval) plus protracted negotiations to

12 Picture adapted from Analytical Study Methods for Reducing Power Losses in Mesh Power Grids Using Optimization Techniques for Sizing and Location of Decentralized Generators, www.researchgate.net /figure/Traditional-power-system-structure-1_fig22_320626855 (last visited December 13, 2019). Data from *Electricity 101*, ENERGY.GOV, www.energy.gov/oe/information-center/educational-resources/electricity-101 (last visited December 13, 2019); APPA, *supra* note 11, at 23 (cooperatives and publicly owned power sales); U.S. ENERGY INFO. ADMIN., ELECTRIC POWER ANNUAL 2018 tbl.2.1 (October 2019), www.eia.gov /electricity/annual/html/epa_02_01.html (retail energy-only providers).

13 *See* GANESH SITARAMAN & ANNE L. ALSTOTT, THE PUBLIC OPTION: HOW TO EXPAND FREEDOM, INCREASE OPPORTUNITY, AND PROMOTE EQUALITY 2 (2019).

14 When I say "private," I mean the term as shorthand for investor-owned. Many of these corporations are publicly traded.

switch between public and private options.[15] In contrast, on the generation side, most of the country now has electricity markets where generators compete to sell power[16] – such that public options in electricity generation can coexist more closely with private ones, since they can compete side-by-side in these markets in many states.

8.2 CLIMATE CHANGE AND THE ENERGY SYSTEM

For the last seventy years, the ownership patterns described earlier have remained relatively stable.[17] Limited switching between public and private systems has occurred, mostly via small municipal systems selling their assets to private utilities – but flip-flopping between the two ownership structures is rare.[18] Recently, however, the wisdom of this mottled system has been thrown into question by theorists, politicians, and community activists. The central reason for this renewed interest in questions of utility ownership is climate change – which challenges every component of the electricity system.

8.2.1 *Supply*

To decarbonize the electricity system – a task often called the "linchpin" of responding to climate change[19] – will require a radical shift in the sources of electricity. The generation mix today is approximately 62 percent fossil fuels (27 percent coal and 35 percent natural gas); 19 percent nuclear power, and 16 percent renewable.[20] In the next decade, or two, or three (depending on which expert's discounting practices and relative degree of technological optimism you favor), 100 percent of that electricity will need to be produced by clean sources – as the sector also doubles in size to electrify transportation.[21]

[15] *See, e.g.*, SYNAPSE ENERGY ECON., AN ANALYSIS OF MUNICIPALIZATION AND RELATED UTILITY PRACTICES 12 (September 30, 2017), https://doee.dc.gov/sites/default/files/dc/sites/ddoe/publication/attachments/An%20Analysis%20of%20Municipalization%20and%20Related%20Utility%20Practices.pdf.

[16] *See* William Boyd & Ann E. Carlson, *Accidents of Federalism: Ratemaking and Policy Innovation in Public Utility Law*, 63 UCLA L. REV. 810, 837–38 (2016).

[17] *See* SYNAPSE ENERGY ECON., *supra* note 15, at 8 (finding that of the 900 "munis" in existence, only 2 percent municipalized since 1990).

[18] *See* Shelley Welton, *Public Energy*, 92 N.Y.U. L. REV. 267, 90 (2017)(charting the rise and fall of municipal utilities over the twentieth century).

[19] Jesse D. Jenkins et al., *Getting to Zero Carbon Emissions in the Electric Power Sector*, 2 JOULE 2498 (2018).

[20] Hydropower and wind each produce around 7 percent; solar energy makes up only 1.6 percent. *See What is U.S. Electricity Generation by Energy Source?*, U.S. ENERGY INFO. ADMIN., www.eia.gov/tools/faqs/faq.php?id=427&t=3 (last visited December 13, 2019).

[21] *See* Alexandra B. Klass, *Expanding the U.S. Electric Transmission and Distribution Grid to Meet Deep Decarbonization Goals*, 47 ENVTL. L. INST. 10,749, 10,751 (2017).

8.2.2 *Transmission and Distribution*

Transmission infrastructure does not need to transform as radically as generation to respond to climate change. Existing transmission can carry electrons produced from clean energy sources as easily as electrons from dirty sources. However, the sector faces two key challenges of its own. First, considerably more transmission infrastructure must be built to connect new renewable resources to population centers.[22] Second, as revealed by tragedies like California's wildfire crisis or Puerto Rico's destruction under Hurricane Maria, the electricity grid – with its reliance on physical interconnectedness of delicate wires – is uniquely susceptible to damage from the kinds of disasters that climate change is rendering worse and more frequent.[23] In response, the grid must either be hardened to become less susceptible to such damage, or become more "distributed" or localized – so that it can function without long-distance interconnectedness, at least for periods of time.[24]

8.2.3 *Procurement and Sales*

The energy sector under climate change must also grow more adept at managing not just supply, but also demand. No longer passive recipients of central-station power, consumers must increasingly participate in the electricity system. Through rooftop solar panels, energy storage, electric vehicles, and electricity management technologies, households and businesses can play an important role in creating a cleaner, leaner, and more resilient system.[25] But investor-owned utilities often resist the policy and pricing changes that would be required to achieve this more interactive grid, since they typically earn profits from investing in precisely the infrastructure that these reforms are designed to reduce.[26]

8.3 PUBLIC OWNERSHIP VERSUS PUBLIC UTILITY: CONFRONTING HISTORICAL EVIDENCE

When public energy options are broached as climate change solutions, a common first reaction is to inquire how the public options already in

[22] *See* Alexandra B. Klass & Elizabeth J. Wilson, *Interstate Transmission Challenges for Renewable Energy: A Federalism Mismatch*, 65 Vand. L. Rev. 1801 (2012).

[23] *See* Alyson Kenward & Urooj Raja, Climate Central, Blackout: Extreme Weather Climate Change and Power Outages 3–4 (2014), http://assets.climatecentral.org/pdfs/PowerOutages.pdf.

[24] Kate Anderson et al., *Increasing Resiliency through Renewable Energy Microgrids*, 2 J. Energy Mgmt., no. 2, at 24 (August 2017), www.nrel.gov/docs/fy17osti/69034.pdf.

[25] *See* Sharon B. Jacobs, *The Energy Prosumer*, 43 Ecology L.Q. 519 (2017).

[26] *See* Michael P. Vandenbergh & Jim Rossi, *Good for You, Bad for Us: The Financial Disincentive for Net Demand Reduction*, 65 Vand. L. Rev. 1527, 1530 (2012).

existence are responding to climate change. This part tackles the comparative question between public and private utilities today, before explaining why this inquiry is of limited relevance to an exploration of public options' potential future role.

The contrast painted above between public and private options in electricity in some ways splits the sector too dramatically: investor-owned utilities are some of the most heavily regulated companies in the United States, where the law treats them as "public utilities" to be managed in the public interest. States and the federal government carefully scrutinize the rates that private utilities charge to ensure that they are just, reasonable, and nondiscriminatory.[27] In contrast, most states – and the federal government – exempt publicly owned utilities from these requirements on the theory that democratic control will provide similar checks on access and affordability.[28]

Over time, theories of both public utility regulation and democratic accountability have worked reasonably well: Private and public powers are competitive on price and complaints of discriminatory service are rare in both.[29] The comparability of public and private options in energy might be taken as affirmation of the "yardsticking" theory that led President Franklin D. Roosevelt to champion public energy in the 1930s, whereby private utility performance could be measured against public options to keep prices and service quality in check.[30]

But even as yardsticking has worked well to impose price discipline, it has failed to drive sectoral transformation. At a snapshot level, public power's comparative record on climate change is unimpressive. Despite resistance, a majority of states have placed clean energy requirements on private utilities through mandates that dictate an ever-cleaner private energy sector – in some cases, demanding 100 percent clean energy within the next few decades.[31]

27 *See* 1 Alfred E. Kahn, The Economics Of Regulation: Principles And Institutions 3 (1988) (describing the four principal components of public utility regulation: control of entry, price-fixing, prescription of quality and conditions of service, and an obligation to serve all applicants under reasonable conditions).

28 *See* Jim Cooper, *Electric Cooperatives: From New Deal to Bad Deal?*, 45 Harv. J. on Legis. 335, 345 (2008).

29 The American Public Power Association (APPA) reports that in 2018, publicly owned utilities charged an average of 11.8 cents/kilowatt-hour for residential customers, whereas investor-owned utilities averaged 13.5 cents/kilowatt-hour. APPA, *supra* note 11, at 20; *see also* John D. Donahue, The Privatization Decision: Public Ends, Private Means 76 (1989) (collecting comparative studies and noting that "[n]o study even hints at superior private efficiency"); Welton, *supra* note 18, at 330 n.10 (collecting studies).

30 Franklin D. Roosevelt, *Campaign Address in Portland, Oregon on Public Utilities and Development of Hydro-Electric Power*, Am. Presidency Project (September 21, 1932), www.presidency.ucsb.edu/ws/?pid=88390.

31 *See* Pyper, *supra* note 8.

Many of these policies exempt public power and cooperatives.[32] Relatedly, publicly owned utilities remain more reliant on coal – the dirtiest fossil fuel – than investor-owned utilities, and have taken more limited steps to develop new renewable energy generation.[33] At the federal level, the TVA has long since lost its progressive luster, as it has worked to block renewable energy and teamed up with private utilities to lobby against federal climate change regulation.[34]

There are several reasons that publicly owned utilities have proven even more sclerotic than their private counterparts on clean energy. Many are locked into long-term purchase agreements for fossil fuel-based electricity, or own long-lived fossil assets that they are loath to retire before the end of their useful life.[35] If they retire assets or end these contracts early, there are no shareholders to help bear the costs, which instead fall entirely on community members.[36] Other publicly owned utilities are simply responding to local priorities. In communities where climate change is not high on the agenda, one can hardly be surprised under a theory of democratic control that the publicly owned utility (or cooperative) mirrors this deprioritization.[37]

However, in places where climate change *is* a political priority, publicly owned power entities have responded impressively. Many city-run utilities in communities with ambitious climate change goals are decarbonization pioneers, including Austin Energy, San Antonio's CPS Energy, the Sacramento Municipal Utility District, Seattle City Light, the Burlington Electric Department, and the City of Aspen Utilities.[38] These examples suggest that public energy has the potential to play the same kind of transformative role in a Green New Deal that it did in the New Deal, by performing a new

[32] *See State Renewable Portfolio Standards and Goals*, NAT'L CONFERENCE OF STATE LEGISLATURES (November 1, 2019), www.ncsl.org/research/energy/renewable-portfolio-standards.aspx.

[33] *See* APPA, *supra* note 11, at 4 (showing, percentagewise, more coal and less wind and solar generation by publicly owned utilities).

[34] *See, e.g.*, Daniel Tait & Joe Smyth, *TVA Attempts to Chain Local Power Companies to Longer Contracts in Effort to Prevent Defection Risk*, ENERGY & POL'Y INST. (September 22, 2019), www.energyandpolicy.org/tva-local-power-companies-defection/ (describing barriers that TVA has erected to local communities' efforts to adopt renewables); Stephen Smith & Maggie Shober, *TVA Deceives the Public and the Press with Misleading Claim of Solar Commitment*, CLEANENERGY.ORG (September 19, 2019), https://cleanenergy.org/blog/tva-deceives-the-public-and-the-press-with-misleading-claim-of-solar-commitment/.

[35] See NAT'L RURAL ELEC. COOPERATIVE ASS'N, COMMENTS ON STANDARDS OF PERFORMANCE FOR GREENHOUSE GAS EMISSIONS FROM EXISTING SOURCES: ELECTRIC UTILITY GENERATING UNITS, DOCKET NO. EPA-HQ-OAR-2013-0602, AT 66–67 (December 1, 2014) (on file with author).

[36] *Id.*

[37] *See, e.g.*, Wilmon H. Droze, *The TVA, 1945-80: The Power Company, in* TVA: FIFTY YEARS OF GRASS-ROOTS BUREAUCRACY 66, 81 (Erwin C. Hargrove & Paul K. Conkin eds., 1981) (describing the TVA's investments in coal and nuclear generation as driven by its "mission to provide low-cost electricity").

[38] *See* Welton, *supra* note 29, at 332–38.

yardsticking function that measures not only affordability, but carbon content. But public energy can only play this role more broadly if tasked to do so – as it has been in the communities described earlier.

The more interesting question going forward, then, is this: If charged with a clean energy mission, can public power deliver? Can it deliver better than investor-owned, commission-regulated utilities, and in what ways and on what terms?

8.4 WHAT SHOULD BE PUBLIC? WEIGHING BENEFITS AND RISKS

The fact that climate change drives new calls for public options in energy makes this sector different from many others in which public options are proposed as gap-fillers, focused on expanding coverage to those currently underserved by the private market (as in health care, banking, and early childhood education – and as public power and rural electric cooperatives did in the electricity sector in the first half of the twentieth century). The central challenge to be solved in electricity today is not coverage, but sectoral transformation. Moreover, many of the calls for public options in energy are concerned with more than just bare decarbonization: public provisioning is often proposed as a way of accomplishing multifaceted goals that relate broadly to making the economy more equitable as it shifts to run on new sources of energy. A new theory is required to explain how public energy options might aid in accomplishing these new objectives – a theory capable of explaining how public options can function as agents of change.

To construct such a theory, it is important to disaggregate the roles that public options might play in electricity generation, transmission and distribution, and procurement. To this end, this part analyzes the rationales animating the most prominent proposals for public energy ownership. It also explores the pragmatic benefits and risks of each. It concludes there is a rank order of the potential gains from public options that is inverse to their costs and risks. Local public procurement options offer both the greatest potential upside and the least potential risk. In contrast, expanded federal power administrations carry the most political and economic risk – at least without design modifications – for reasons explained earlier.

8.5 CLEAN ENERGY-FOCUSED FEDERAL POWER ADMINISTRATIONS

One proposed public option is expanding the network of federal power administrations to drive clean energy construction across the country. Most notably, presidential hopeful Bernie Sanders called for the expansion of federal power marketing administrations to every state, which along with a refocused TVA would buildout

$1.52 trillion in renewable energy generation and $852 billion in energy storage capacity.[39] Because such proposals would require Congressional buy-in, the critical point of comparison is how these federal authorities stack up next to their chief private sector alternative: a federal mandate on private companies to achieve 100 percent clean energy.

The most appealing element of federal power administrations is their not-for-profit structure, which is well-suited to the nature of renewable energy production. Unlike fossil fuels, which require considerable expenditures to unearth, wind and sun are there for the taking. For this reason, renewable energy's variable costs – the costs of producing it once infrastructure is in place – are close to zero.[40] Renewable energy operators thus do not necessarily need to generate substantial long-term revenue – unless managed by a private corporation that must demonstrate such returns to attract investors.[41]

To date, US renewable energy policy has focused on providing private renewables' developers extra revenue streams outside the market to make renewable energy "financeable" by guaranteeing a healthy long-term rate of return.[42] But instead of funneling money to the private sector to build renewables, in-house production by a government authority, backed by low-cost government financing, might prove cheaper and faster. These savings could then be passed on to municipal and cooperative utilities – or investor-owned utilities – in the form of low-cost power supply contracts. Alternatively, revenue derived from market-rate sales of publicly owned renewables might be spent on other public energy projects – including transmission buildout, public building retrofits, mass transit, electric vehicle infrastructure, and other pressing decarbonization initiatives.[43] Federally owned projects could also help transform the nature of energy work – for example, by providing high-wage, unionized jobs – a mission that private renewables companies appear none too eager to embrace.[44]

39 *The Green New Deal*, *supra* note 9; *see also* Kate Aronoff et al., A Planet to Win: Why We Need A Green New Deal 53 (2019). Britain's Labour Party has made similar proposals. *A Green Industrial Revolution*, Labour, https://labour.org.uk/manifesto/a-green-industrial-revolution/ (last visited December 13, 2019).

40 *See* Joshua C. Macey & Jackson Salovaana, *Rate Regulation Redux*, 168 U. Pa. L. Rev. [manuscript 3–4] (forthcoming 2020).

41 *See* Andreas Malm, Fossil Capital: The Rise of Steam Power and the Roots of Global Warming 369–70 (2016) (quoting BP and Shell executives regarding the difficulty of making money on the sun).

42 *See* U.S. Dep't of Energy, Pub. No. DOE/EE-1509, Leveraging Federal Renewable Energy Tax Credits (2016), www.energy.gov/sites/prod/files/2016/12/f34/Leveraging_Federal_Renewable_Energy-Tax_Credits_Final.pdf; Edward Holt et al., Nat'l Renewable Energy Lab., Technical Report No. NREL/TP-6A20-51904, The Role of Renewable Energy Certificates in Developing New Renewable Energy Projects (June 2011).

43 *See* Aronoff et al., *supra* note 39, at 59.

44 *See, e.g.*, Lauren Kaori Gurley, *This Solar Energy Company Fired Its Construction Crew After They Unionized*, Vice (November 21, 2019), www.vice.com/en_us/article/evjenn/this-solar-energy-company-fired-its-construction-crew-after-they-unionized.

Can the climate-change-denying, solar-power-blocking TVA really be remade in this mold? Critics question the political feasibility and practicality of such efforts, as compared to simply continuing to spur private investment in clean energy.[45] These concerns are reasonable – although more market-based climate proposals have to date equally confronted political feasibility challenges.[46] My predominant concern is less with this duel over which strategy might ultimately prove more politically feasible, and more with the scale of operations proposed. Although sympathetic to the idea of more publicly owned generation, I nevertheless find myself asking: Why *federal*? Why must public clean energy options be of the nature and size of the TVA?

Our track record on federal mega-projects suggests some reason to doubt their efficacy in achieving the kind of multifaceted social goals that proponents of these new authorities advance. As historians have documented, the TVA's size contributed to the least appealing elements of its history. The architects of the TVA emphasized "grassroots administration" and "democratic planning" as guiding principles for development in the Tennessee Valley.[47] But especially in the building of power projects, the TVA came to prioritize project completion as the measure of success, abandoning much of its initial commitment to the agency's democratic ideals.[48] The losers of this strategy were, as one researcher describes it, "the most vulnerable: poor farm tenants, African and Native Americans, and farmers forcibly removed from their lands."[49]

Those advocating for new TVA-like clean energy entities are well aware of the limitations of the original form.[50] To avoid repeating these mistakes, Green New Deal proponents have called for new infrastructure development to occur through "democratic and participatory processes that are inclusive of and led by frontline

45 Lisa Friedman, *Sanders's Climate Ambitions Thrill Supporters. Experts Aren't Impressed*, N.Y. Times (November 14, 2019), www.nytimes.com/2019/11/14/climate/bernie-sanders-climate-change.html; *see also* Richard Lowitt, *The TVA: 1933-45*, *in* TVA: Fifty Years of Grass-roots Bureaucracy, *supra* note 37, at 35, 46 (describing the "heavy price in expensive litigation" that the TVA had to endure during its first several years).

46 *See, e.g.*, Ryan Lizza, *As the World Burns*, New Yorker (October 3, 2010) (describing the failure of federal cap-and-trade legislation); Theda Skocpol, Naming the Problem What It Will Take to Counter Extremism and Engage Americans in the Fight Against Global Warming 11 (2013) (similar).

47 *See* Atif Ansar, *The Fate of Ideals in the Real World: A Long View on Philip Selznick's Classic on the Tennessee Valley Authority (TVA)*, 36 Int'l J. Project Mgmt. 385, 389 (2017); David E. Lilienthal, TVA: Democracy on the March 19 (1944) (prioritizing "democratic methods" and "active daily participation of the people themselves" in "the TVA experience").

48 Ansar, *supra* note 47, at 392; *see also* Philip Selznick, TVA and the Grassroots: A Study in the Sociology of Formal Organization 7 (1966) (discussing how ends overpowered means in the TVA's orchestration); Gail Radford, The Rise of The Public Authority: Statebuilding and Economic Development in Twentieth-Century America 111–12 (2013).

49 Ansar, *supra* note 47, at 392; *see also* Richard Lowitt, *The TVA: 1933-45*, *in* TVA: Fifty Years of Grass-roots Bureaucracy 35, 52, 58–59 (Erwin C. Hargrove & Paul K. Conkin eds., 1981) (on discrimination in the TVA).

50 *See, e.g.*, H.R. Res. 109, 116th Cong., at 5 (1st Sess. 2019).

and vulnerable communities and workers."[51] These are commendable promises – but they have been made and broken before. How to design federal clean energy authorities to resist these tendencies is thus a critical institutional puzzle that needs solving.

One possibility for mitigating the risks of these federal programs might be to decentralize them. Renewable energy development does not require projects on the scale of the TVA's Muscle Shoals or Tellico Dam – it is considerably more modular.[52] For this reason, it may not be necessary to recreate TVA-like behemoths to drive renewable energy infrastructure development across the country. Why not instead design a scheme with more inherent democratic potential?

For example, taking a cue from the Rural Electrification Act, a federal program could offer low-cost loans to municipal, state, and not-for-profit renewable energy projects that communities develop from the bottom up. This more flexible approach to public generation options would accomplish many of the same yardsticking objectives as massive federally owned projects, with fewer humanitarian risks. And to capture a wider range of goals, such a program could include priority loans or favorable terms for low-income communities and communities of color, as well as stipulating worker protections.

To be sure, a more chaotic, bottom-up process might make planning and orchestration of the clean energy buildout more complex. However, more localized projects come with a substantial upside: they might expedite siting and infrastructure approval processes. Absent substantial reform of current state-centered energy siting regimes, local opposition to TVA-style renewable energy projects might prove a substantial wrench in the works of such an organization.[53] On the flip side, research shows that community involvement and bottom-up planning substantially enhance public acceptance of renewable energy infrastructure and the transmission needed to support it.[54] Decentralization thus might ultimately speed up construction of renewable energy projects, while offering a buffer against federal agency tunnel vision.

[51] H.R. Res. 109, 116th Cong., at 10, 12 (1st Sess. 2019).

[52] For example, utility-scale solar is often defined as any project greater than 5 megawatts – whereas Wilson Dam at Muscle Shoals has a capacity of 653 megawatts. *Compare* MARK BOLINGER & JOACHIM SEEL, LAWRENCE BERKELEY NAT'L LAB., EMPIRICAL TRENDS IN PROJECT TECHNOLOGY, COST, PERFORMANCE, AND PPA PRICING IN THE UNITED STATES ii (2018), https://emp.lbl.gov/sites/default/files/lbnl_utility_scale_solar_2018_edition_report.pdf, *with Wilson*, TENN. VALLEY AUTH., www.tva.gov/Energy/Our-Power-System/Hydroelectric/Wilson-Reservoir (last visited December 13, 2019).

[53] See Michael B. Gerrard, *Legal Pathways for a Massive Increase in Utility-Scale Renewable Generation Capacity*, 47 ENVTL. L. INST. 10,591 (2017); J. B. Ruhl, *What Happens When the Green New Deal Meets the Old Green Law?* (March 27, 2019), www.acoel.org/post/2019/03/27/What-Happens-When-the-Green-New-Deal-Meets-the-Old-Green-Laws.aspx.

[54] See Richard Cowell et al., Acceptance, Acceptability and Environmental Justice: The Role of Community Benefits in Wind Energy Development, 54 J. ENVTL. PLAN. & MGMT. 539 (2011); Alastor M. Colby et al., *Public Attitudes and Participation in Wind Turbine Development*, 11 J. ENVTL. ASSESSMENT POL'Y & MGMT 69 (2009); Chad Walker & Jamie Baxter, *Procedural Justice in Canadian Wind Energy Development: A Comparison of Community-Based and Technocratic Siting Processes*, 29 ENERGY RES. & SOC. SCI. 160 (2017).

8.6 PUBLIC OWNERSHIP OF THE GRID

A second public option floated by many communities is takeover of the grid itself – the poles and wires that deliver power from generators to customers. This could be done at various scales, but is most often discussed at the city or state level. When done by a city, such takeovers are referred to as grid "municipalization." Boulder, San Francisco, and Chicago are among the cities to recently consider municipalizing.[55] At the state level, in addition to California's recent threats, state representatives in Maine have introduced legislation that would replace the state's two largest investor-owned utilities with a "Maine Power Delivery Authority."[56]

There are three key theories advanced in favor of public grid ownership. First, many hope for better service at lower cost. Costs may be reduced through a combination of lower borrowing rates (via low-interest bonds, rather than commercial interest rates) and the elimination of the need to pay shareholder dividends.[57] These savings might be funneled into necessary grid maintenance and upgrades to prepare for the effects of climate change (the same maintenance that PG&E deferred for decades, in favor of shareholder payouts).[58] They might also help pay for the buildout in transmission infrastructure necessary to integrate adequate renewable energy.

Second, publicly owned transmission and distribution companies allow cities or states to more easily accomplish climate-related goals. Many cities pursue public control over the grid as a means of obtaining control over procurement – that is, the decisions about where the community's energy comes from. Utilities often thwart city-level renewable procurement goals by refusing to arrange special clean energy supplies, and fight against city- or state-led initiatives to install rooftop solar panels and pursue aggressive energy efficiency improvements.[59] Municipal (or state) grid ownership eliminates this resistance, thus giving governments a key tool for making good on decarbonization objectives.

55 Catherine Morehouse, *Chicago Considers Municipalizing ComEd*, UtilityDive (July 25, 2019), www.utilitydive.com/news/chicago-considers-municipalizing-comed/559505/

56 H.P. 1181, 129th Leg., 1st Reg. Sess. (Me. 2019).

57 *See, e.g.*, Robert Wasserstrom, Opinion, *The Promise of Public Power, and What it Means for Maine*, Bangor Daily News (May 1, 2019), https://bangordailynews.com/2019/05/01/opinion/contributors/the-promise-of-public-power-and-what-it-means-for-maine/; Letter from Mayor Sam Liccardo, City of San José et al., to The Honorable Marybel Batjer et al., President, California Public Utilities Commission (November 4, 2019) [hereinafter California PUC Letter], https://rtoinsider.com/wp-content/uploads/Mayor-CPUC-Letter-final-11.5.19.pdf.

58 *See supra* note @.

59 *See* Hiroko Tabuchi, *Rooftop Solar Dims Under Pressure from Utility Lobbyists*, N.Y. Times (July 8, 2017), www.nytimes.com/2017/07/08/climate/rooftop-solar-panels-tax-credits-utility-companies-lobbying.html; Vandenbergh & Rossi, *supra* note 26; Max T. Brozynski, *Decarbonizing Power and Transportation at the Urban Scale: An Analysis of the Austin, Texas Community Climate Plan*, 43 Sustainable Cities & Soc'y 41, 42 (2018) (describing how Austin avoided these challenges by controlling its own utility).

Third, given the hard questions that grid management will increasingly raise about who to black out and when for the sake of safety and fire prevention, some argue that a public grid takeover would "allow[]the public to have greater role in determining decisions that increasingly have come to define matters of life and death."[60]

Some of these theoretical benefits could prove vulnerable under real-world pressures. Will cities and states be able to resist the desire to funnel grid earnings into other government projects (the equivalent of shareholder dividends)? Will publicly owned grid operators really slash their own earnings through strategic investments in energy efficiency and other demand reduction strategies? Will political pressures to keep costs low overwhelm the pressing need for transmission and renewable energy investments? Do politicians actually want to own the "life and death" decisions around blackouts and wildfire prevention? These are fair questions – the answers to which depend upon local political winds.

At the same time, the price of grid ownership is dear. Boulder, Colorado is in year nine of its struggle to purchase its grid from the private utility Xcel Energy. Along the way, it has waged several court battles, endured five years of adjudication at the Colorado Public Service Commission, and spent millions on studies and referenda.[61] In November 2019, the city offered Xcel $94 million to purchase the company's electric utility assets, which the city reports "is nearly double the original cost of the company's assets, less depreciation."[62] Under a best-case scenario, city representatives estimate that the final referendum required to authorize the terms of the agreement might take place in 2021[63] – making municipalization an expensive ten-year-process before operations even get up and running.

Whether city ownership will be worth the price and delay is difficult to weigh ex ante – but the money and time spent on these efforts obviously has substantial opportunity costs. Moreover, for cities like Boulder where municipalization is driven by climate change goals, full grid takeover may not be necessary. As the final part of this chapter explains, there are easier ways for a community to gain control over its energy supply.

Before turning to this final public option, however, a few words connecting federal power authorities and grid ownership are warranted. Although less discussed, a federal role might prove most transformative in ownership of the transmission grid. Experts

60 California PUC Letter, *supra* note 57.

61 Alex Burness, *Boulder's Long Road to its Elusive Right to a Municipal Electric Utility*, Daily Camera (April 22, 2017), www.dailycamera.com/2017/04/22/boulders-long-road-to-its-elusive-right-to-a-municipal-electric-utility/.

62 Sam Lounsberry, *Boulder Offers Xcel $94 Million for Assets Necessary to Form Municipal Utility*, Denver Post (November 22, 2019), www.denverpost.com/2019/11/22/boulder-offers-xcel-94m-for-assets-necessary-to-form-municipal-utility/.

63 Sam Lounsberry, *Boulder Gains State Approval to Transfer Some Xcel Assets in Municipal Utility Effort*, Daily Camera (October 10, 2019), www.dailycamera.com/2019/10/10/boulder-gains-state-approval-to-transfer-some-xcel-assets-in-municipal-utility-effort/.

have calculated that the costs of a renewable energy transition will be dramatically lowered –and its physical accomplishment substantially eased – by a more interconnected grid, which can balance the inherent intermittency of renewable resources across the country.[64] If a new TVA-like entity could be charged with only one mission, it should be this: construct a federally funded backbone of high-speed transmission lines to facilitate the nationwide integration of renewable energy projects. To successfully accomplish this mission, Congress would also have to override state and local project approvals and siting processes – one of the main roadblocks to such a network.[65] Such an override would be contentious, but this is one infrastructure project where it is worth stepping on some federalist toes for the greater collective good.

8.7 PUBLIC OPTIONS IN ELECTRICITY PROCUREMENT

There is a final component of the energy system that can be made public with considerably less effort: electricity procurement and sales to end-use customers. Procurement decisions determine whether a community's electrons will come from renewable energy or coal, and where such energy generation is located. Therefore, public control over procurement functionally translates into public control over generation – at least in terms of controlling the resource mix, although not the profit motive.

Historically, procurement was a task bundled together with grid ownership and all accomplished by a single utility, be it public or private. Utilities would either self-supply by building and running their own generation plants, or would enter into contracts to purchase the electricity they needed from other utilities.[66] But with the advent of competitive electricity markets has come the possibility for a new form of public procurement, called Community Choice Aggregation (CCA). Where permitted by state statute, CCA arrangements allow a community to vote to "break up" with their private monopoly utility and make their own electricity purchases instead. At the same time, CCAs leave operation of the poles and wires to the incumbent private utility. That means that CCAs can turn to competitive energy markets to select particular types of energy they want to purchase – or particular locales for such energy – without having to orchestrate the full grid takeover required to municipalize electricity service. For this reason, they are often referred to as "public power lite."[67] CCAs are currently allowed in nine states: California, Massachusetts, Illinois, New Jersey,

64 *See* Lori Bird & Michael Milligan, *Lessons from Large-Scale Renewable Energy Integration Studies* (Nat'l Renewable Energy Lab., Conference Paper, NREL/CP-6A20-54666, June 2012), www.nrel.gov/docs/fy12osti/54666.pdf (reviewing studies reaching this conclusion).

65 *See* Ashira Pelman Ostrow, *Grid Governance: The Role of a National Network Coordinator*, 35 Cardozo L. Rev. 1993 (2014); Klass & Wilson, *supra* note 22.

66 *See* Paul L. Joskow, *Lessons Learned from Electricity Market Liberalization*, Energy J. (special issue) 9, 10–11 (2008).

67 Herman K. Trabish, *As CCAs Take Over Utility Customers, Local Renewable Generation Emerges as the Next Big Growth Driver*, UtilityDive (October 8, 2019), www.utilitydive.com/news/as-ccas-take-over-utility-customers-local-generation-emerges-as-the-next-b/564422/.

New York, Ohio, Rhode Island, New Hampshire, and Virginia.[68] Communities in these states can elect to create a CCA either by referendum or city council vote.[69] Residents are then automatically enrolled in the CCA, but can elect to Opt out and receive service from their traditional utility if dissatisfied with the CCA.[70] In this way, CCAs are a more classic "public option" than municipalization, because they provide individual choice regarding participation.[71]

Some cities turn to CCAs for the simple reason of managing costs, and they have often been able to deliver power at lower rates than the incumbent utility.[72] But increasingly, cities are turning to CCAs as an explicit climate change strategy, particularly as the price of renewable energy has plummeted.[73] For example, the city of Newton, Massachusetts recently entered into a CCA arrangement that decreased electricity rates by around 2 cents per kilowatt hour, while providing customers with 60 percent renewable energy content – as compared to the state-mandated 14 percent required of investor-owned utilities.[74]

One advantage of CCAs, then, is their climate-oriented yardsticking function. Utilities often resist renewable energy mandates by decrying their cost or technological infeasibility. CCAs put the lie to overblown protests, illustrating that more rapid progress on decarbonization is possible and affordable. In total, US CCAs in 2017 procured around 8.9 million megawatt-hours of renewable energy above and beyond state-mandated purchases – amounting to 9 percent of US voluntary renewable energy purchases.[75]

But the case for local control over energy procurement goes beyond yardsticking. Responding to climate change necessitates reimagining the ways in which humans might live together, in modern comfort, without using the atmosphere as a giant dumping ground. Cities prove a key physical and political space for testing and contesting various low-carbon ways of living, through their authority over housing and land use, transportation, local economic development, and public spaces.[76]

68 Six other states are considering CCAs: Colorado, Connecticut, New Mexico, Nevada, Oregon, and Utah. *See* Eric O'Shaughnessy et al., Nat'l Renewable Energy Lab., Technical Report No. NREL/TP-6A20-72195, Community Choice Aggregation: Challenges, Opportunities, and Impacts on Renewable Energy Markets (February 2019) [hereinafter "NREL CCAs"]; Shawn Marshall & Peter Millman, Community Choice Aggregation, Presentation on behalf of Lean Energy (May 2019) (on file with author).

69 *See* Local Gov't Comm'n, Community Choice Aggregation Fact Sheet 1 (May 2015), www.lgc.org/resources/community-design/lpu/may2015/.

70 Researchers estimate that 85 percent to 95 percent of consumers choose to remain with their CCA. *See* NREL CCAs, *supra* note 68, at 8.

71 *Cf.* Sitaraman & Alstott, *supra* note 13.

72 Advocates assert 3–10 percent average bill savings from CCAs, as compared to incumbent utilities. *See* Marshall & Millman, *supra* note 68.

73 *See* NREL CCAs, *supra* note 68, at 15.

74 *See* Marshall & Millman, *supra* note 68.

75 NREL CCAs, *supra* note 68, at v, 4, 12.

76 *See* Jedediah Purdy, This Land is Our Land: The Struggle for a New Commonwealth 82 (2019) ("We are creatures of our built environment, an infrastructure species"); Katherine A. Trisolini, *All*

Assuming control over energy procurement as well allows a city to weave together many of these issues in potentially transformative ways.

For example, political control over energy supply allows communities to address jointly the related challenges of decarbonizing electricity and transportation – the two biggest sectoral contributors to climate change in the United States.[77] Most experts believe the best way to decarbonize transportation is to electrify it.[78] But getting people to adopt electric vehicles has proven structurally challenging because they require new charging infrastructure and provoke "range anxiety." At the same time, some question whether a future of private electric vehicles – with the materials they require to produce, and the traffic snarls they still create – is even the right goal.[79] A city that has control over its energy, zoning, and housing policy can build an urban infrastructure that empowers its population to transition to more sustainable, high-quality forms of transportation. Already, several CCAs in California are pursuing electric vehicle and electric bus projects as a way of uniting their approaches to decarbonizing electricity and transportation.[80]

More broadly, cities that control energy procurement can integrate decarbonization and social justice in ways that prove challenging within the bounds of public utility law. A city might use revenue from its energy sales to fund a retrofitting and renewable energy initiative on public housing – thus jointly reducing electricity demand and energy poverty. Or a city might prioritize the siting of community-scale solar energy at local brownfield locations because of the jobs and community revitalization benefits such projects provide, even if buying utility-scale solar from the next state over would be cheaper.[81] Such programs would parallel rural electrification efforts during the New Deal, while also potentially tackling the structural racism that the New Deal largely failed to remediate.

CCAs thus have broad potential to help communities build new models of how life post-climate crisis might be lived – a potential that inheres in their public nature and could not be replicated by a private utility of the same size. At the same time, CCAs' political and economic costs are lower than those of federal power authorities or public grid ownership. Utilities of course still resist CCA efforts, since they allow a city to control decisions that cut into utilities' bottom line,

Hands on Deck: Local Governments and the Potential for Bidirectional Climate Change Regulation, 62 Stan. L. Rev. 669 (2010) (tracing the many controls cities have over climate change).

77 *Sources of Greenhouse Gas Emissions*, U.S. EPA, www.epa.gov/ghgemissions/sources-greenhouse-gas-emissions (last visited December 13, 2019).

78 *See* Brozynski, *supra* note 59, at 43.

79 *See* Aronoff et al., *supra* note 39, at 129–32.

80 NREL CCAs, *supra* note 68, at 15–16; Cal. Pub. Utility Comm'n, Cal. Community Choice Ass'n, Comments on the California Consumer Choice Project Workshop 7, www.cpuc.ca.gov/uploadedFiles/CPUC-Public_Website/Content/Utilities_and_Industries/Energy_-_Electricity_and_Natural_Gas/CA%20Community%20Choice%20Aggregators.pdf (last visited December 13, 2019).

81 *See* NREL CCAs, *supra* note 68, at 15 (gathering examples of communities that have prioritized local energy in their CCAs).

including energy efficiency and incentives for on-site generation and storage.[82] But because the incumbent utility retains its position as the grid operator, billing manager, and opt-out service provider, it has less at stake – as evidenced by the fact that 750 communities have managed to adopt CCA arrangements in the past several decades.[83] Of course, CCAs only work where authorized by state legislation. Perhaps, though, municipal resources are better spent winning one battle at the state legislature to authorize CCAs, rather than individualized, piecemeal battles to municipalize the grid city-by-city.

There are, to be sure, risks to CCAs as well. First, they may be poorly run and fail. But here the cost of failure is relatively low – residents simply revert back to their utility. Two other concerns are more substantial: CCAs may balkanize energy decision-making, and they may flourish best in wealthier communities, leaving others stuck behind with the retrograde utility.[84] These are real risks, and they become more acute in places where CCAs come to dominate the energy landscape, as in California, where regulators now project that by 2025 an astounding 85 percent of load will no longer be supplied by investor-owned utilities.[85] For this reason, I would not necessarily champion a move to a 100 percent CCA-controlled model of energy procurement, at least not without policies in place to coordinate decarbonization efforts and share system costs and benefits equitably across localities. But most of the country is far from encountering these risks and can safely focus on CCA authorization and promotion.

Ultimately, CCA experiments produce potentially far-ranging benefits – especially under political conditions that do not yet favor federal climate action. These local projects can serve as proof positive of ways to weather the coming climate storms, thereby propelling popular acceptance of greater action at the state, national, and international levels. At least, that is the promise that makes these public options particularly worth the risk.

8.8 CONCLUSION

The robust range of public options in our current energy system has worked remarkably well to produce reliable, affordable power for tens of millions of Americans underserved by private utilities. The next generation of public options

82 *See* Herman K. Trabish, *Join or Die: How Utilities Are Coping with 100% Renewable Energy Goals*, UTILITYDIVE (December 13, 2017), www.utilitydive.com/news/join-or-die-how-utilities-are-coping-with-100-renewable-energy-goals/512664/.

83 *See* NREL CCAs, *supra* note 68, at iv.

84 *See* CAL. PUB. UTIL. COMM'N, CALIFORNIA CUSTOMER CHOICE: AN EVALUATION OF REGULATORY FRAMEWORK OPTIONS FOR AN EVOLVING ELECTRICITY MARKET 8, 20–21 (May 2018) (showing CCAs clustered on the coast and "nearly absent from the Central Valley").

85 CAL. PUB. UTILITY COMM'N, CONSUMER AND RETAIL CHOICE, THE ROLE OF THE UTILITY, AND AN EVOLVING REGULATORY FRAMEWORK 3 (2017). This figure includes CCAs and large companies choosing to self-supply. *Id.*

in energy must respond to a new charge: transformation of the system away from fossil fuels, toward clean technologies that power new low-carbon ways of living together. Community control over energy procurement provides a potent tool for effectuating this transformation in communities that already have adequate political will. As more states and eventually the federal government join course, either private utilities must rapidly transform themselves into partners, or else a broader range of public options across the energy system should be seriously considered as a way to inject both discipline and creativity into the clean energy transition.

9

A Public Option in Banking

Postal Banking

Mehrsa Baradaran

There are many services and utilities that would benefit from a public option because markets are either monopolized or failing. Whatever the merits of the public option in other fields, the banking system is undemocratic without a public option. This is because most basic banking services – deposit-taking, financial transactions, lending – operate using a federal government platform, network, or guarantee. Federal government support is not a mere subsidy because the federal infrastructure does not simply enhance bank profits, but it makes the entire modern banking enterprise possible. In other words, this framework not only enhances, but enables modern banking markets. Most of this support, like FDIC insurance, is invisible to the average consumer and usually unnecessary, while some of this support is implicit and rare like the bank bailouts. All of it is meant to induce public trust and participation in the banking sector. Scholars have called banks "a franchise" and courts have called them "instrumentalities" of the federal government.[1] Banks are granted a charter to operate by the federal government, which allows them to "plug in" to the government payments and credit structure. Thus, the hidden monopoly power in the banking sector is the federal government, making it essential to provide access to all.

Insofar as banks operate in tandem with government credit and payments facilities, it stands to reason that they must make their services available to all. Yet they are not currently under any such mandate of accessibility. This is due both to the fact that banks have become more enmeshed with the federal infrastructure over time, especially after the Progressive Era and the operational legislation and institutional framework inaugurated by the New Deal. More recently, an erosion of legal requirements on banks has enabled banks to abandon lower-profit regions and customers under the guise of "inefficiency" and market competition.[2] Thus, the

[1] *See Starr Int'l Co. v. Fed. Reserve Bank of* N.Y., 742 F.3d 37, 40 (2d Cir. 2014) (FRBs are instrumentalities of the federal government and the operating arms of its central bank); Robert C. Hockett & Saule T. Omarova, *The Finance Franchise*, 102 CORNELL L. REV. 1143, 1147 (2017).

[2] Mehrsa Baradaran, *Banking and the Social Contract*, 89 NOTRE DAME L. REV. 1283, 1285–86 (2014); For a modern example, see Jeanna Smialek et al., *Banks Want Efficiency. Critics Warn of Backsliding.*, N.

United States has a federally sponsored banking system that is exclusionary. Those who are excluded are the most financially vulnerable individuals and communities who are forced to pay the most for services. Thus, a public option in banking is essential to making the system democratic.

This chapter will make the case for postal banking as a public option available to all Americans. Ganesh Sitaraman and Anne Alstott define a public option as a service provided by the government that is available to all, competes in a free market, and charges all people the same amount for the same services.[3] This chapter proposes a public option in banking using the post office as the point of delivery. Postal banking could include a range of financial services, but imperative to full financial inclusion would be to provide access to the payments system or in other words, simple checking services. Postal banking could also offer a public option in small credit. Payday lending is a large and fairly new industry that provides high-cost small loans to the most vulnerable Americans. The industry has evaded state and federal regulation thus far, both due to high demand for loans, successful lobbying efforts by the industry, and the failure of the Trump administration's Consumer Financial Protection Bureau (CFPB) in enforcing payday regulations adopted by the Obama administration. Offering a public option for credit reduces the need to regulate usury and push for the elimination of payday lenders. Instead of forcing private lenders to adopt a low interest rate or alternatively allowing the status quo wherein low-income borrowers have no option but to borrow money at crushingly high interest rates. A public option in lending could alleviate some of those harsh penalties for many low-income Americans who must rely on these loans. Lending has many risks as well as rewards, and this chapter will also discuss some of the drawbacks of a public option and suggest how some of those obstacles can be averted.

Crucially, postal banking is not a new idea nor is it a radical departure from history. The United States had a successful postal banking system from 1910 until 1966 as do many other countries worldwide. The post office has had a historic connection with banking services as both are essentially public goods and necessary for participation in commerce. Postal banking in America was among a slate of Progressive Era policies adapted to create more egalitarian markets. At a crucial turning point in American banking policy, policymakers tackled inequality and banking instability. This was in the early 1900s, but in many ways, economic conditions are similar today. What the progressive reformers understood and what modern politics has forgotten is that credit policy is public policy. To the extent that certain communities are excluded from mainstream banking institutions, their exclusion is a problem of public policy and not a gap in the market.

Y. Times (August 20, 2019), www.nytimes.com/2019/08/20/business/bank-regulation-federal-reserve.html.

3 Ganesh Sitaraman & Anne L. Alstott, The Public Option: How to Expand Freedom, Increase Opportunity, and Promote Equality (2019).

9.1 BANKING AS A PUBLIC UTILITY

When confronting the power of banking trusts and monopoly power over credit, Justice Louis Brandeis proposed that certain industries were especially suited for a public utility nature. Banking or railroads, for example, were considered service essential to full participation in commerce. In these cases, Brandeis offered an alternative to create a public utility. Such a utility could either compete with the market or offer an alternative. Brandeis believed banking to be among the industries that might be considered a public utility because, as he explained "deposit banking should be recognized as one of the businesses 'affected with a public interest'."[4] This was because banks gained their market power and their profits through the use of "other people's money." President Roosevelt did not make banks a public utility, but his administration did embed public duties in all the legislation governing banks during the New Deal.[5] Many of those laws have been eroded since even as banks are ever more reliant on public services for their operations.

Today, each aspect of banking, including deposits, loans, and simple financial transactions, relies on a robust network of government support.[6] Each time a bank sends or accepts money, they are using the Federal Reserve's payments system.[7] Banks can take and lend customer deposits and engage in fractional reserve lending (and the magic money multiplier effect this enables) only because customer deposits are insured by the FDIC. Unlike all other corporations, banks pay virtually nothing for their funding (customer deposits) because of this federal government subsidy.[8] And when the FDIC fund goes into the red – as it did in 2008 – these deposits are backstopped by the full faith and credit of the US Treasury.[9] On the asset side, most mortgages and student loans are guaranteed, bundled, or subsidized by the FHA or

4 Louis D. Brandeis, Other People's Money 64 (1914).

5 For a more robust discussion, see Mehrsa Baradaran, How the Other Half Banks: Exclusion, Exploitation, and the Threat to Democracy 211 (2015); Baradaran, *supra* note 2, at 1297–98.

6 *See* Justin Pritchard, *Understanding the FDIC*, The Balance (April 29, 2020), www.thebalance.com/what-is-the-fdic-315786 [https://perma.cc/B2TZ-CDA9].

7 Carol Coye Benson et al., Payments Systems in the U.S.: A Guide for the Payments Professional **XX** (3rd ed. 2017).

8 Banks do pay into the FDIC insurance fund through premiums, but most scholars agree that the premiums are underpriced. Furthermore, it is not just the actual funds that are paid out in the event of a failure that is of importance here. It is the fact that bank deposits are backed by the full faith and credit of the federal government making them a safe repository for their customers' funds. "Until the early 1990s, the FDIC levied flat-rate insurance premiums on banks as a function of deposits, but not the banks' risk. In 1991 the FDICIA required that the FDIC introduce risk-based premiums. However, to date, the range of premiums is much narrower than the range of risk exposures of the FDIC to individual bank failures. Under the Deposit Insurance Funding Act of 1996, when the FDIC reserve fund exceeds 1.25 percent of deposits, the 'safest' of banks pay no deposit insurance premium meaning that recently more than 90 percent of banks holding over 90 percent of total bank assets paid NO premiums." Joe Peek & James A. Wilcox, *The Fall and Rise of Banking Safety Net Subsidies*, *in* Too Big to Fail: Policies and Practices in Government Bailouts 177–78 (Benton E. Gup ed., 2004).

9 *Id.*

the Government Sponsored Entities (GSE's) Fannie Mae, Freddie Mac, Ginnie Mae, and Sallie Mae.[10] These entities purchase almost every mortgage and student loan in the country and resell them to investors. And when these institutions fail, they too have the implicit backing of the federal government.[11] These GSEs enable banks to lend exponentially more loans than what their customer deposits would allow.[12] At the crux of our banking system, then, is a state-enabled credit system.

Deposits and loans – assets and liabilities – are all supported by the federal government. And that's just the tip of the iceberg. When an individual has a liquidity crisis or can't pay a bill, she or he has to go to a payday lender and take out an emergency small loan at around 400 percent APR.[13] In contrast, when a bank has a liquidity crisis, they are able to go to the Fed's discount window, which provides banks loans at 0.5 percent higher than the Federal Funds rate, which is currently set at 2.0 percent[14] None of this takes into account the government bailout, the staggering magnitude of which went on full display after the 2008 financial crisis.[15] Using its § 13(3) émergency lending powers, the federal government bailed out a failing banking industry with over a trillion dollars of equity infusions, loans, guarantees, asset purchases, and other forms of financial support.[16] The help came on very favorable terms with interest rates not available on the market. The

[10] Sallie Mae ceased being a GSE, and became fully privatized, when Congress terminated its charter on December 29, 2004. At that point, the GSE became SLM Corporation, "a fully private sector corporation." U.S. Dep't of Treasury, Lessons Learned from the Privatization of Sallie Mae 1 (2006), www.treasury.gov/about/organizational-structure/offices/Documents/SallieMaePrivatizationReport.pdf [https://perma.cc/F5Z4-RSDE]. A table on page 3 of the above mentioned Treasury report distinguishes the former GSE-Sallie Mae from the fully privatized SLM corporation. Notable differences include: (1) the GSE's charter was created by an act of Congress; (2) the president appointed the GSE's board members; (3) the GSE could borrow up to $1billion from the Treasury, whereas the SLM corporation cannot borrow from the Treasury; (4) the GSE's debt was eligible for federal open market purchases; (5) the GSE was exempt from SEC registration and financial and other filings with the SEC; and (6) the GSE was exempted from federal, state, and local income taxes. *Id.* at 3.

[11] Fannie Mae and Freddie Mac were spun off of the federal government and privatized, which meant that they were run by a board of shareholders. It did not mean that they operated in normal markets. The market still treated them like government entities, meaning that they did not contemplate their failure. When they did fail because of the excessive risks their managers took, the government bailed them out without flinching. *See id.*

[12] *Id.*

[13] CFPB, *What is a Payday Loan* (June 2, 2017), www.consumerfinance.gov/ask-cfpb/what-is-a-payday-loan-en-1567/.

[14] *See* Kimberly Amadeo, *Federal Reserve Discount Window and How It Works*, The Balance (November 26, 2018), www.thebalance.com/federal-reserve-discount-window-3305923 [https://perma.cc/L97W-4Z2B]; Bd. of Governors of the Fed. Res. Sys., Monetary Policy, www.federalreserve.gov/monetarypolicy/openmarket.htm [https://perma.cc/ST3K-3TRM].

[15] *See* Peek & Wilcox, *supra* note 8, at **XX**.

[16] The actual amount of the bailout is difficult to determine because much of it was in guarantees. The special inspector general for TARP estimated a total potential support package of $23.7 trillion, or over 150 percent of the U.S. GDP. However, many of these guarantees were never used. Johnson & Kwak, 13 Bankers: The Wall Street Takeover and the Next Financial Meltdown 174 (2011).

arrangement was so good that the CEO of one of the largest bailed out banks, upon seeing the terms of the deal, remarked, "This is very cheap credit!"[17]

Then there are the unprecedented waves of asset purchases and money pumped through banks, ostensibly so that the money will pass through financial institutions and make it to the public.[18] Three rounds of quantitative easing have left the Fed still holding over four trillion dollars in bank assets and the continuing interest on reserves that are still ongoing. Another less well-known example of monetary policy is Interest On Excess Reserves ("IOER"). In a payment that seems to violate what people may assume to be the laws of the market and basic common sense, the Federal Reserve pays billions of dollars in interest to banks on their reserves.[19] In just one year, the Federal Reserve paid about $7 billion in interest to commercial banks, including more than $100 million to Goldman Sachs and more than $900 million to JPMorgan Chase. The point of this payment is that it will "pass through" the banks to the depositor, but the IOER is in fact not being passed on but being absorbed by the bank as profits, and thereby increasing inequality.[20] Because excess reserves pay higher interest than Treasury bills, there is no reason banks would pass up a risk-free, high-interest opportunity. Each dollar held on reserve is a dollar not lent for real estate, infrastructure, or business operations in the American economy.[21]

All this federal government support sets the banking sector apart from other business that must create its own wealth without the use of other people's money or cheap loans when they fall short. Banks and the government (and by extension the people) should have a mutually beneficial arrangement that consists of the government providing market-enabling structures and trust-inducing deposit insurance and banks, in return, playing their essential role in financing the expansion of the economy and serving the needs of their customers and local communities. The

[17] David Wessel, In Fed We Trust: Ben Bernanke's War on the Great Panic 240 (2009).

[18] *See* Peek & Wilcox, *supra* note 8, at 169–70.

[19] Due to the massive amounts of money created by QE, bank reserves swelled to over $1.7 trillion as of October 2018. This overage is called excess reserves and even though it was created by the federal reserve, banks earn interest on these reserves. These reserves comprise a substantial portion of the nation's monetary base. The Federal Reserve is using this payment, called an "administered rate" as its primary monetary policy tool post QE. Fed. Res. Bank of St. Louis, Required Reserves of Depository Institutions (2018), https://fred.stlouisfed.org/series/REQRESNS [https://perma.cc/6BEF-MX4A]. Banks are required to hold roughly 10 percent of their deposits in reserves at the central bank. The required reserves on just customer deposits would equal roughly $189 billion. *See* Walker F. Todd, *The Problem of Excess Reserves, Then and Now*, 8, 15 (Levy Econ. Inst., Working Paper No. 763, 2013).

[20] This policy, which was meant to encourage lending by banks, has turned into a subsidy that in fact discourages lending because banks can earn more by "lending" customer deposits to the Federal Reserve than they can pursuing consumer or business loans. Excess funds can be rolled over at no cost and liquidated on the same day, making excess reserves more attractive than lending. Morgan Ricks, *Money as Infrastructure*, 2018 Colum. Bus. L. Rev. 757–62 (2018); Symposium, Darrell Duffie & Arvind Krishnamurthy, Pass through Efficiency in the Fed's New Monetary Policy Setting 4 (August 25, 2016) (unpublished paper) (on file with the Federal Reserve Bank of Kansas City).

[21] Todd suggests that the Federal Reserve sell about $180 billion in mortgage-backed securities or longer maturity Treasury securities per year in order to prevent future inflation. Todd, *supra* note 19, at 15–16.

relationship can be described as a social contract or an implicit promise or exchange made by the government and the banks.[22] Viewed from this lens, it becomes clear that this level of government support to the banking sector must mean that the government and by extension "the people" must be entitled to demand a banking sector that serves all of us.

9.2 A PUBLIC OPTION IN BANKING

The phrase "public option" entered the political lexicon during the health-care debates as an option among the other forms of health-care provisions.[23] However, the concept of a public option has been around since the founding of the country.[24] A public option is when the government enters a market and offers a product or service to compete with private companies. Government-funded health insurance would have been a public option. More common public options include public libraries, public pools, or the US Post Office. The government offers these services either through subsidies or at cost (as is the case with the post office). Private companies like bookstores or UPS can compete with the public option, but consumers can make a choice to use the public option. Broadly conceived, public options already exist in banking. The Federal Reserve's payments system is a public option.[25] It competes with private payments providers, but banks can choose to use the Fed's payments system. Adam Levitin and Susan Wachter have also called the US housing finance system a public option and argue that federal government credit institutions and subsidies created the American mortgage.[26] As Thomas Herndon and Mark Paul explain, "the creation of a stable mortgage structure during the New Deal provides an excellent case study of how public options can be used to regulate in the public interest by shielding households from risk."[27]

[22] There is a long and rich philosophical discussion about the social contract between individuals and society. In general, social contract theory posits that individuals consent to surrender some natural liberty in exchange for protection or other benefit conferred by society. The relationship between the government and banks is similar. The social contract between individuals and the state has been taken up by Hobbes, Kant, Rousseau, Rawls, and others. Paul Tucker, Deputy Governor, Bank of England, Remarks at the British Bankers' Association Annual International Banking Conference, Regimes for Handling Bank Failures – Redrawing the Banking Social Contract (June 30, 2009), www.bis.org/review/r090708d.pdf [https://perma.cc/NH6W-KHTU].

[23] *See* Margot Sanger-Katz, *The Difference Between a "Public Option" and "Medicare for All"? Let's Define Our Terms*, N.Y. Times (February 19, 2019), www.nytimes.com/2019/02/19/upshot/medicare-for-all-health-terms-sanders.html [https://perma.cc/6K8B-HG7M].

[24] The Post Office was established during the Postal Act of 1792. Andrew Glass, *Washington Signs the Postal Act: Feb. 20, 1792*, Politico (February 20, 2008), www.politico.com/story/2008/02/washington-signs-the-postal-act-feb-20–1792-008592.

[25] *See* Bd. of Governors of the Fed. Reserve Sys., Payment System Risk, www.federalreserve.gov/paymentsystems/psr_about.htm [https://perma.cc/9K5L-QQ4P].

[26] *See* Adam J. Levitin & Susan M. Wachter, *The Public Option in Housing Finance*, 46 U.C. Davis L. Rev. 1111, 1119 (2013).

[27] Thomas Herndon & Mark Paul, A Public Banking Option 17 (2018), http://rooseveltinstitute.org/wp-content/uploads/2018/07/Public-Banking-Option-final.pdf [https://perma.cc/7HN3-EZJE].

The federal government also provides deposit insurance for banks.[28] Banks pay premiums for the insurance, which makes deposit insurance resemble other public options, but FDIC insurance is not an "option." All banks must buy in to the scheme. Still, the innovation of a public and federal insurance scheme was crucial in stabilizing the banking sector and avoiding near-constant panics, runs, and crises.[29] Despite many attempts at private deposit insurance, only federal insurance has been an effective antidote to runs.[30]

What I am proposing is a different sort of public option – a bank account and small credit option to compete with the check cashing and payday lending alternatives. In a way, a public option is the path not taken during the Progressive Era and in the New Deal reforms that followed it. The Progressive coalition, made up of Southerners and farmers, pushed for small community institutions instead of large federal ones.[31] For instance, in their fight against monopolies, they preferred to break apart big companies and form smaller ones tied to each community.[32] FDIC insurance itself was such a bargain.[33]

Reforming the banking sector could have taken a variety of forms: one was FDIC insurance that was first proposed by William Jennings Bryan, the Democrat who most embodied the progressive spirit at its height. FDIC insurance would stabilize banking by diminishing runs, but crucially, it would favor small local banks. The other option was the Republican option at the time, proposed by Teddy Roosevelt – another icon of the Progressive era, but a Republican, who proposed postal banking as a potential reform after the Panic of 1907.[34] Postal banking was not adopted in Teddy Roosevelt's administration, but he did set the ball rolling. Congress enacted the United States Postal Savings System (USPSS) in 1910 and President Taft signed the Act into law.[35] Thus, offering postal banking is not a new enterprise, but a reconsideration of a path not taken during the New Deal.

Franklin Delano Roosevelt adopted many of the progressive reformers' agenda items and New Deal reformers viewed banking through the lens of a public utility.[36]

28 *See* Fed. Deposit Ins. Corp., Deposit Insurance FAQs, www.fdic.gov/deposit/deposits/faq.html [https://perma.cc/6VY4-U5ET].

29 *See* Richard Scott Carnell et al., The Law of Financial Institutions (5th ed. 2013); Richard S. Grossman, Unsettled Account: The Evolution of Banking in the Industrialized World since 1800 246–50 (2010).

30 *See* Roger Lowenstein, *There's a Reason for Deposit Insurance*, N.Y. Times (March 23, 2013), www.nytimes.com/2013/03/24/business/deposit-insurance-and-the-historical-reasons-for-it.html [https://perma.cc/49K5-WLJ4].

31 *See* Mehrsa Baradaran, *Jim Crow Credit*, 9 U.C. Irvine L. Rev. 887, 888, 900 (2019).

32 *See id.* at 887–88.

33 *See id.* at 901.

34 *See* Theodore Roosevelt, President of the US, Seventh Annual Message (December 3, 1907) (transcript available in the University of Virginia Miller Center).

35 See Appendix B for the roll call vote results. 45 Cong. Rec. S2, 7766–68 (June 9, 1910).

36 *See* Jane W. D'Arista, The Evolution of U.S. Finance Volume II: Restructuring Institutions and Markets 204 (1994); Jeff Manza, *Political Sociological Models of the U.S. New Deal*, 26 Ann. Rev. of Soc. 297, 298 (2000).

Yet Roosevelt chose FDIC insurance instead of Treasury-backed deposit accounts (postal banking) to stabilize the banking sector.[37] Postal banking remained viable and was even deployed by Roosevelt to help fund the war and alleviate the government debt from the Great Depression, but the public utility option – or the public option through postal banks – was left on the table as an abandoned progressive idea.[38]

Postal banking could have proved to be as effective as FDIC insurance in stabilizing the banking sector. Both were federal government supports of the banking sector – a federal backstop that could stop runs. FDIC insurance was a fund that would guarantee all deposits, but it was ultimately backed by the US Treasury. Postal banking was a public option – or a utility model of Treasury banking.[39] Accounts held by the postal banks were directly backed by the US Treasury; therefore, the postal banks were immune to runs. They were immune not just because of the direct Treasury backstop, but because these banks did not engage in fractional reserve lending – the deposits were held as Treasury bonds or they circulated as excess liquidity in local banks.[40] In either case, there was never a run on postal banks.[41] In fact, recent economic research reveals that postal banking helped ease the general panic conditions during the Great Depression.[42] Panicked depositors fleeing from failing banks used postal banks as a safe alternative, which helped ameliorate the liquidity crisis in the banking sector.[43]

9.3 MODERN POSTAL BANKING

The basic idea of modern postal banking is a public bank that would offer a wide range of transaction services, including small lending.[44] The post offices could offer these services at a much lower cost than banks and the fringe industry because they can use natural economies of scale and scope to lower the costs of the products.[45] Their existing infrastructure significantly reduces overhead costs, and they do not have profit-demanding shareholders and thus would be able to offer products at cost.[46] As for communities without access to safe credit and banking services, the

37 *See* D'ARISTA, *supra* note 36, at 65.
38 *Id.*
39 *Id.* at 65-68.
40 *Id.*
41 *Id.*
42 *See* Mehrsa Baradaran, *A Short History of Postal Banking*, SLATE (August 18, 2014), https://slate.com/news-and-politics/2014/08/postal-banking-already-worked-in-the-usa-and-it-will-work-again.html [https://perma.cc/F6M5-22CA].
43 *See* Steven Sprick Schuster et al., *An Empirical History of the United States Postal Savings System* 12–13 (NAT'L BUREAU OF ECON. RESEARCH, Working Paper No. 25812, 2019), https://ssrn.com/abstract=3306033 [https://perma.cc/ZT2K-MZE3].
44 *See* Mehrsa Baradaran, *It's Time for Postal Banking*, 127 HARV. L. REV. F. 165, 166 (2014).
45 *Id.*
46 *Id.* at 167, 172.

post office remains as one of the only public institutions that still serves these communities regardless of profits. The post office offers money orders, and many customers use money orders in lieu of a checking or savings account.[47] Researchers Terri Friedline and Mathieu Despard concluded in their "Mapping Financial Opportunity" project that postal banking can best help rural areas that are banking deserts.[48]

Public options have recently begun to be studied in the legal and economic literature.[49] Law Professors Morgan Ricks, John Crawford, and Lev Menand have suggested that the Federal Reserve should offer accounts directly to all individuals and businesses through a *FedAccount*, which they claim could be offered through the post office.[50] They argue that "restricting central bank accounts to an exclusive clientele (banks) is no longer justifiable on policy grounds if indeed it ever was."[51] Their proposal for a public account at the Federal Reserve would extend to all businesses, individuals, and organizations.[52] They state that based on the myriad public subsidies that banks receive from the Federal Reserve's monetary policy, providing a public option would put people in a similar position as the banks.[53] After all, banks make billions per year just in interest payments on reserves (IOER) that they do not pass on to customers.[54] Both postal banking and *FedAccounts* could be designed to create revenue for the post office and the Federal Reserve.[55] Herndon

47 *Id.*

48 Terri Friedline & Mathieu Despard, Mapping Financial Opportunity: Final Report 8–9 (2017), https://aedi.ssw.umich.edu/sites/default/files/publications/Mapping-Financial-Opportunity.pdf [https://perma.cc/V5AF-2FLF].

49 *See, e.g.*, Ganesh Sitaraman & Anne L. Alstott, The Public Option: How to Expand Freedom, Increase Opportunity, and Promote Equality (2019); Herndon & Paul, *supra* note 27; Baradaran, *supra* note 44; Levitin & Wachter, *supra* note 26; Morgan Ricks et al., *FedAccounts*, Vand. L. Res. Paper 18–33 (December 2, 2018).

50 *See* Ricks et al., *supra* note 49, at 1, 5.

51 *Id.* at 1.

52 *Id.*

53 Special privileges for banks: In addition to US depository institutions, *see* 12 U.S.C. § 342, the Federal Reserve is authorized to maintain accounts for the US Treasury, *see* 12 U.S.C. § 391, certain government-sponsored enterprises in the residential mortgage area, see 12 U.S.C. §§ 1435, 1452(d) & 1723a(g), foreign governments, banks, and central banks, see 12 U.S.C. §§ 347(d) & 358, certain international organizations, such as the International Monetary Fund and the World Bank, see 22 U.S.C. § 286(d), and certain designated financial market utilities, see 12 U.S.C. § 5465, as well as assorted other governmental and government-sponsored entities that we omit here. We just say "banks" in the main text for expositional convenience.

54 *See* Morgan Ricks, *Money as Infrastructure*, 2018 Colum. Bus. L. Rev. 757, 794, 798 (2018).

55 For revenue projections for the post office, *see* U.S. Postal Serv., Office of Inspector Gen., Providing Non-Bank Financial Services for the Underserved 16 (2014). As for Fed Accounts, as Ricks, Crawford, and Menand explain, the FedAccounts would increase revenue. "Central banks' asset portfolio returns typically exceed their interest payments and other expenses by a wide margin. These earnings are called 'seigniorage': fiscal revenue from money creation. The amounts are large. The Fed remitted $98 billion, $92 billion, and $90 billion in earnings to the US Treasury Department in 2015, 2016, and 2017, respectively. Because FedAccounts would probably greatly expand the Fed's balance sheet (see Part III.A), these remittances could easily double or triple, even after accounting for the costs of maintaining millions of retail accounts." Ricks et al., *supra* note 49, at 16–17.

and Paul also propose a public banking option with two components: First, their public option would create a new public bank with basic deposit and transaction services and "'plain vanilla' consumer financial services, such as small-dollar loans, auto loans, and mortgages." Second, a public bank would "manage an online financial services marketplace, where public services would directly compete with private services."[56]

One promising path toward effectuating a public option is to repurpose an old democratic institution: the post office. American banks long ago deserted most impoverished communities. But post offices, even two centuries later, have remained – still rooted in their original egalitarian mission. As America's oldest instrument of democracy in action, the Post Office can once again level the playing field and in the process. This is not a new or radical idea. The United States had a robust postal banking system from 1910 until 1966, and most other countries have offered or are still offering postal banking accounts.[57] The idea has recently gained traction in the United States as well. I proposed postal banking in a 2012 article and have been actively involved in its promotion since.[58] The Postal Service Inspector General issued a 2014 White Paper studying the issue.[59] Senator Warren endorsed postal banking in 2015, and was followed by Senators Sanders and Gillibrand – both of whom have proposed legislation to this effect.[60] The 2016 Democratic National Platform included postal banking.[61] The postal workers unions also negotiated a postal banking pilot in their contract negotiations in 2015.[62] As of this writing, the postmaster general has not supported postal banking and legislation has not been passed, but efforts to enact such reform are ongoing.

9.4 FINANCIAL INCLUSION

The most important argument in favor of postal banking is that it has the potential to bank the unbanked and expand access to savings accounts that could diminish the need for fringe banking services. Postal banking can provide transactional services and small loans without life-crushing fees and interest. Critically, by making

56 Herndon & Paul, *supra* note 27, at 20–21.

57 For more information, see Mehrsa Baradaran, How the Other Half Banks: Exclusion, Exploitation, and the Threat to Democracy (2015).

58 Mehrsa Baradaran, *How the Poor Got Cut Out of Banking*, 62 Emory L. J. 483 (2013).

59 U.S. Postal Serv., *supra* note 55.

60 *See* Kevin Wack, *Postal Banking is Back on the Table. Here's Why That Matters*, Am. Banker (April 26, 2018), www.americanbanker.com/opinion/postal-banking-is-back-on-the-table-heres-why-that-matters [https://perma.cc/9ZRX-9DBM] [note: I have worked on most of the senate and house legislation dealing with postal banking].

61 Democratic Platform Comm., 2016 Democratic Party Platform 11, https://democrats.org/wp-content/uploads/2018/10/2016_DNC_Platform.pdf [https://perma.cc/9TYG-TDXW].

62 *See* Dave Johnson, *Postal Workers and the Public Want a Postal Banking Public Option*, HuffPost (February 19, 2015), www.huffpost.com/entry/postal-workers-and-the-pu_b_6717096 [https://perma.cc/E8DD-DTDW].

banking available to those deserted by a government-supported banking system, the state can minimize the threat to democracy posed by the heavily subsidized, exclusionary, and powerful banking sector.

Without bank accounts, many Americans do not save – or they store their savings at home under the proverbial mattress.[63] More than 40 percent of Americans do not have even $500 in savings and would need to borrow if they had a shortfall – over 60 percent would need to borrow $1000 if they faced a financial emergency.[64] Many Americans do not save because they do not earn enough even while working full time, but even if they have money to save; most accounts are not accessible to those with small savings.[65] Cash savings are vulnerable to theft and loss.[66] Research abroad has demonstrated that increased access to a savings account enhances economic welfare and other important outcomes.[67] Having a safe, low-cost, and easy savings account could lead to more savings, which could diminish the need for payday loans when families hit a snag.[68] When individuals can dip into savings, they are less likely to need payday loans. A postal savings account made possible through a local postal branch could significantly ease the burden on many families leading to more savings. There is some evidence for this historically. When the postal savings accounts were first established in 1910, they became very popular with immigrants living in urban areas who had previously stored their earnings in "stocking banks."[69] Most of the deposits into the early savings banks came from the home hiding places of these immigrants.[70] Historian Sheldon Garon has contrasted the low savings rates in the United States versus higher rates in Germany and Japan and has surmised that the difference had much to do with the strong network of postal banks that remained

63 Pew Charitable Trs., Drowning in Debt: A Health Impact Assessment of How Payday Loan Reforms Improve the Health of Minnesota's Most Vulnerable (2016), www.pewtrusts.org/-/media/assets/external-sites/health-impact-project/hip-2016-payday-lending-report.pdf [https://perma.cc/S7V6-VBZN].

64 Bd. of Governors of the Fed. Reserve Sys., Report on the Economic Well-Being of U.S. Households in 2017 – May 2018, www.federalreserve.gov/publications/2018-economic-well-being-of-us-households-in-2017-dealing-with-unexpected-expenses.htm.

65 Sarah Holder, *Why Cleveland Wants to Bring Back Postal Banking*, CityLab (June 4, 2019), www.citylab.com/equity/2019/06/cleveland-post-office-banking-cash-check-predatory-lending/590557/; Derek Thompson, *Why Don't Americans Save More Money?*, The Atlantic (April 19, 2016), www.theatlantic.com/business/archive/2016/04/why-dont-americans-save-money/478929/.

66 Holder, *supra* note 65; Thompson, *supra* note 65.

67 Dean Karlan et al., *Impact of Savings Groups on the Lives of the Poor*, 114 Proc. of the Nat'l. Acad. of Sci. of the U.S. 3079 (2017).

68 *Id.*

69 *See* Baradaran, *supra* note 42.

70 The *Times* reports a figure of 28 million, but by the end of the year, the Post Office Annual Report states that deposits totaled $33 million. *Postal Savings System Practically Self Sustaining*, N.Y. Times (May 25, 1913), https://timesmachine.nytimes.com/timesmachine/1913/05/25/100267539.pdf?pdf_redirect=true&ip=0; U.S. Post Off. Dep't., Annual Report of the Postmaster General for the Fiscal Year Ended June 30, 1911 6 (1912); U.S. Post Off. Dep't., Annual Report of the Postmaster General for the Fiscal Year Ended June 30, 1912 6–7 (1913); US Post Off. Dep't., Annual Report of the Postmaster General for the Fiscal Year Ended June 30, 1913 303 (1914).

in those countries while they were disbanded in the United States and the culture of savings they cultivated abroad.[71] During World War II, the United States Post Office sold postal savings bonds to schoolchildren and housewives who invested as a patriotic duty.[72] By the end of World War II, the government had raised about $8 billion in additional war funding through war bonds and Treasury bonds sold through the post office.[73]

Today, postal savings accounts have the potential to become a trustworthy receptacle for savings for the financially excluded. Just as our postal banks did successfully for half a century,[74] their rebirth can lead to increased saving by the broader public. By providing low barrier savings accounts, the post office can again offer a refuge for the countless small savers in the United States who have been shut out of the banking system because their too small savings accounts are no match for high bank fees. Increased access to low-cost savings accounts can greatly benefit a population living without any financial cushion. Even having a few hundred dollars stored away can make a significant difference to a moderate-income family who may face an emergency in their lives. It is difficult to measure how many people are not saving in banks because of financial and cultural barriers of entry, but it is possible that just as in the 1900s, hoarded money from across the country would pour into the postal banks from under mattresses, prepaid cards, or funds otherwise wired abroad.

Postal banking may seem radical to many in the United States who are convinced that banking should be a "private market" free from "government intervention," but it is a mundane part of life for the rest of the world.[75] Postal banking abroad is the norm, not an aberration.[76] "Posts in 87 countries hold some 2 billion current or savings accounts on behalf of around 1 billion customers."[77] Postal banking is the most successful means of financial inclusion worldwide with several countries, such as India and China, where postal banks are the main driver of financial inclusion in their countries.[78]

71 *See* Sheldon Garon, Beyond our Means: Why America Spends While the World Saves 374 (2011).

72 *Id.*

73 Nils Clotteau & Bsrat Measho, Universal Post Union, Global Panorama on Postal Financial Inclusion 2016 9 (2016), www.upu.int/uploads/tx_sbdownloader/globalPanoramaOnPostalFinancialInclusion2016En.pdf [https://perma.cc/EL4S-4EGJ]; US Post Off. Dep't., Annual Report of the Postmaster General for the Fiscal Year Ending June 30, 1942 18 (1943); US Post Off. Dep't., Annual Report of the Postmaster General for the Fiscal Year Ending June 30, 1945 13–14 (1946).

74 *See* Baradaran, *supra* note 42.

75 Clotteau & Measho, *supra* note 73, at 9.

76 *Id.*

77 *Id.*

78 The World Bank Group, Global Info. & Comm. Tech. Postal Policy, The Role of Postal Networks in Expanding Access to Financial Services: Worldwide Landscape of Postal Financial Services, Asia Region 5, http://documents.worldbank.org/curated/en/410191468337292692/704230ESW0P0850C0B0x370041B0000Asia.doc.

Postal banking has been operational in many Western countries since the 1800s, and currently, fifty-one countries have postal banking as their primary method of financial inclusion – only 6 percent of postal carriers worldwide do not offer banking services.[79] (It is estimated that postal banking has banked over 1 billion people worldwide.)[80] There are a variety of models worldwide – some focused on the poor and others that offer postal banking services to the entire population.[81] In fact, the United States is one of the only developed countries in the world without a postal banking network.[82] That said, we do not need to look abroad for a justification or even a model for postal banking when we can refer to our own rich history of postal banking.[83]

The transition to postal banking would not require substantial costs or changes to the post office's business. Financial transaction services are straightforward products that do not require a high level of sophistication. The post office can build on its existing network to offer these services. The post office already has the transactional capabilities to deal with cash as well as the back-end security systems in place to transport cash because it sells money orders. A simple ATM machine can be placed inside the post office and tellers can offer debit cards or other transactional services through USPS-contracted servicers or in partnership with a bank. Walmart, for example, came to dominate financial services to the poor, practically overnight, without causing a substantial ripple in its core business.[84] Walmart attempted to become its own bank in 2005, but when that route was blocked by regulators, they settled for a partnership with *Greendot* bank to offer low-cost checking accounts and transactional services.[85] The company has been able to use its size and existing infrastructure to offer financial products at a fraction of the price while making a healthy profit offering them. Amazon has announced that it will be accepting cash for payment for goods in partnership with brick and mortar stores in order to facilitate transactions for the underbanked. Amazon has claimed that it will not charge fees for these cash transactions.[86] These large companies are able to

79 Alexandre Berthaud & Gisela Davico, Universal Postal Union, Global Panorama on Postal Financial Inclusion: Business Models and Key Issues 9–10 (2013), www.uniglobalunion.org/sites/default/files/pictures/post/globalpanoramafinancial_inclusion_-upu_-en.pdf [https://perma.cc/43KU-FHB9].

80 *Id.* at 11.

81 *See id.* at 9, 19–20.

82 *See id.* at 81–82.

83 *Id.*

84 Zoë Miller, *13 Financial Services Walmart Offers That You Probably Didn't Know About*, Bankrate (April 18, 2019), www.bankrate.com/personal-finance/smart-money/walmart-financial-services/#slide=1 [https://perma.cc/SLQ9-6HPZ].

85 Ciara Linnane, *Green Dot, Wal-Mart Partnership is a Big Milestone: JP Morgan*, MarketWatch (September 25, 2014), www.marketwatch.com/story/green-dot-wal-mart-partnership-is-a-big-milestone-jp-morgan-2014-09-25 [https://perma.cc/BX3Q-49N5].

86 David Z. Morris, *You Can Now Pay Cash When Shopping on Amazon. Here's How*, Fortune (September 19, 2019), https://fortune.com/2019/09/19/you-can-now-pay-cash-when-shopping-on-amazon-heres-how.

underprice check-cashers and payday lenders due to their ability to cross-subsidize their products. Yet, these large companies do not have an egalitarian mandate. Insofar as offering financial transaction services can lead to greater market dominance through increased sales, they will offer such services, but we should be hesitant to outsource the essential right to participate in commerce to the profit/loss calculations of large corporations.

Estimates show that $89 billion is spent each year by the unbanked on financial fees and services, including payday lenders, check cashers, prepaid cards, and other services.[87] These are significant expenses for families. The average annual income for an unbanked family is $25,500, and about 10 percent of that income, or $2412, goes to the fees and interest paid to access credit or other financial services – services that those with bank accounts often get for free.[88] If these costs can be reduced through a public option, unbanked and underbanked families would be able to save more money, which would reduce the need for short-term borrowing. Providing these services at much lower costs has a triple advantage of reviving the beleaguered but too-important-to-fail postal service, putting the money back in the pockets of the poor, and providing an alternative to a harmful industry that has proved near impossible to regulate away.

The post office could offer small loans at lower interest rates than the payday lenders. Lending even small loans of less than $500 at a reasonable interest rate can help a significant portion of the American public withstand a short-term credit crunch.[89] Even with more just economic conditions, individuals may occasionally need to borrow small loans to cope with unexpected harms – so must have access to a low-cost loan so that they can survive their illiquidity before it turns into insolvency. In other words, if a person needs $500 to pay a bill for food or shelter, will they have to pay an additional $1000 in fees to extinguish the loan or something closer to $50 in interest? The difference can make the difference between sustainability and bankruptcy. A public option in lending can make a difference to many families struggling to make ends meet.

Consumer protection groups, credit unions, and religious organizations have in the meantime been piloting a number of alternatives to payday lending. In 2010 the National Credit Union Association (NCUA) relaxed its interest rate rules, which limit interest to 15 percent, to permit higher rates on short term, small dollar loans. The credit unions then created Payday Alternative Loans (PALs) provide an economically viable model to credit unions while offering a much cheaper option to consumers seeking short-term loans (with interest of up to 28 percent). Religious

87 *See* Mehrsa Baradaran, *Postal Banking's Public Benefits*, 3 AM. AFF. J. 18, 23 (2018).

88 OFF. OF THE INSPECTOR GEN., U.S. POSTAL SERV., PROVIDING NON-BANK FINANCIAL SERVICES FOR THE UNDERSERVED 2 (2014), www.uspsoig.gov/sites/default/files/document-library-files/2015/rarc-wp-14–007_0.pdf.

89 The Post Office White Paper suggests that they can offer loans with a 28 percent APR, a rate sustainable for the Post Office and its customers. *Id.* at 13.

organizations even set up their own credit unions: the Friendship-West Baptist Church and St. John Missionary Baptist Church in Dallas established the Faith Cooperative Federal Credit Union as a result of pastoral efforts to protect the churches' congregations from predatory lenders. Likewise, community groups and nonprofits have attempted to offer lower-cost alternatives. Thus far, these initiatives have not been scalable, but have demonstrated that low-interest lending can be a viable business model with limited underwriting.[90]

Since the 1990s, governments primarily in the Global South have experimented with conditional cash transfer (CCT) programs to alleviate poverty. These generally involve government payments to individuals or families based on specific behaviors or actions undertaken by the recipients of the funds: children's school attendance, doctor's visits, vaccinations, job training program attendance, and other similar activities. Studies have found that cash aid is more effective than any other form of charitable giving.[91]

9.5 OBJECTIONS AND DRAWBACKS

There are some pitfalls to be aware of in designing any public option or utility. Public institutions are just as prone to predation, mismanagement, and fraud as are private organizations.[92] In order to protect consumers against predatory products or fraud, the USPS would need to be monitored. The USPS has a system of fraud prevention in place through its own regulator and Inspector General. If it decides to lend, the CFPB should be empowered to provide oversight to ensure that consumers are protected. Moreover, the incentive structure of the USPS must be made coherent with its egalitarian mission. Thus far, any profits made by the USPS have been deposited into the US Treasury.[93] The USPS, unlike most banks and large corporations, is not under pressure by shareholders to maximize profits so it follows that it does not have an incentive to engage in predatory pricing. An example of how a public option can turn toward private profit-making can be found in the example of the GSE Fannie Mae. After Fannie Mae was privatized, its shareholders engaged in fraud and mismanagement. Ultimately, Fannie Mae took on so much risk (for the sake of profit) that it had to be rescued by the federal government. Even without a profit motive, public services can become predatory. An example is the student loan market. Here, the problem is that the Department of Education essentially has a monopoly in the provision of student loans. The Department of Education handles the majority of student loans through private servicers. These servicers have long

90 Susie Cagle, *Can a New Kind of Payday Lender Help the Poor?*, The Nation (July 9, 2018), www.thenation.com/article/can-new-kind-payday-lender-help-poor/.

91 Teresa Molina Millán et al., *Long-Term Impacts of Conditional Cash Transfers: Review of the Evidence*, 34 The World Bank Res. Observer 119, 151 (2019), https://academic.oup.com/wbro/article/34/1/119/5492445.

92 The World Bank Group, *supra* note 78.

93 *Id.*

been accused of fraud and below par service to students seeking information, loan modification, or other services. The Department of Education has been slow to respond to complaints and the private servicers have shielded themselves from all state AG lawsuits by claiming sovereign immunity.[94] The danger to be avoided here is a lack of sufficient oversight as well as the lack of any market competition. If the post office is the only provider of banking services, it would become a monopoly like the Department of Education and consumers would have no option but to use its products.[95]

The postal banking system would also need a system of strong and accurate underwriting procedures that can adequately separate the insolvent from the merely illiquid and only lend to the latter. Of course, this is easier said than done. There will always be loans that default as long as human beings are responsible for repaying them. Any individual or company, wealthy or poor, can take out too large a loan at too high a cost and be crushed by it. Still, formulas such as credit scores that track an individual's history of previous repayments can eliminate some of the guesswork. But when it comes to distinguishing creditworthy borrowers among the low income, credit scores are often too blunt a tool. Innovative private lenders have already realized this and are working to develop fine-tuned underwriting formulas based on publicly available borrower data to predict loan default with better results than credit scores.[96] Pioneering peer-to-peer Internet lenders have begun to boast of their success deploying these emerging mathematical models for small lending.[97] The post office can rely on this developed expertise in designing its own underwriting system. The bottom line is that doing any sort of underwriting, even simply using credit scores, would set the post office apart from the payday lending industry, which currently makes no attempt to distinguish between borrowers. The FDIC reports "the prevailing underwriting criteria of most payday lenders require that consumers need proof only of a documented regular income stream, a personal checking account, and valid personal identification to receive a payday loan."[98]

Distinguishing the merely illiquid from the insolvent is no easy task, but it is at the crux of any successful effort to provide credit to the poor. The credit unions and cooperative thrifts thrived because they succeeded in doing just that. They used the tools available to them at the time: they lent to neighbors and friends and people they already knew through a cooperative structure. Most banks used

94 *Id.*

95 *See* Julie Margetta Morgan, Roosevelt Inst., Who Pays? How Industry Insiders Rig the Student Loan System—And How to Stop It (2018), https://rooseveltinstitute.org/wp-content/uploads/2018/06/How-Industry-Insiders-Rig-the-Student-Loan-System.pdf [https://perma.cc/FEA6-ZALF].

96 Sarah Todd, *An Alternative Lender Whose Credit Reviews Are Academic*, Am. Banker (July 8, 2014), www.americanbanker.com/issues/179_130/an-alternative-lender-whose-credit-reviews-are-academic-1068506-1.html [https://perma.cc/9THJ-TC6F].

97 *Id.*

98 Fed. Deposit Ins. Corp., Payday Lending: An Update on Emerging Issues in Banking 4 (2003), www.fdic.gov/bank/analytical/fyi/012903fyi.pdf [https://perma.cc/LW4T-QAEP].

"character" or "relational lending" to make underwriting decisions.[99] Today, with wide-scale loan standardization, that is less common. Most lenders just plug in numbers to an underwriting formula or algorithm to make decisions.[100] Even credit unions no longer work the way they used to. Relational lending is difficult today and it would not be a practical way for the post office to lower costs – even though postal employees would probably be best suited for the task. After all, in many rural communities across the country, postal workers have more information about the town's population than any other citizen. However, this is not the case with every community, and it is not clear whether the knowledge acquired by postal workers can be parlayed into accurate loan underwriting without significant training.

And it turns out assessing that risk is surprisingly difficult, but more transparent data collection can be a solution to long-standing problems in this sector. One core barrier to research on the risk profile of payday lenders' clientele is that the payday loan industry uses an entirely different credit scoring system from FICO. It relies on Teletrack, a product of CoreLogic, an analytics and business intelligence company that had its roots in real estate. Teletrack captures data from categories of businesses that do not report to the major credit bureaus, such as "including payday loans, rent-to-own business, furniture stores, auto finance, subprime credit card issuers, and debt buyers" (The Balance). So, research reports that find, for example, "little to no effect of payday loans on credit scores, new delinquencies, or the likelihood of overdrawing credit lines" are probably flawed, because credit scores do not include data from these fringe banking businesses.[101]

This also means that in order to design an alternative to payday lending, questions about which data and metrics to use to score risk need fresh solutions. Some online lending services claim to use alternative sources of data to predict default, including those collected by TeleTrack. The three major credit-rating agencies are beginning to leverage alternative data, as well (with TransUnion having purchased the alternative data company FactorTrust, Experian touting its use of rental, utility, and other payment data, and Equifax partnering with data company Urjanet to leverage so-called consumer-permissioned data, or data a consumer shares with a business at the time of a transaction). Banks, credit unions, consumer protection groups, and financial justice advocates have been raising concerns about the potential for algorithmic risk scoring based on alternative data to result in a kind of digital redlining, replicating the problems of discrimination in lending that the original credit-rating agencies were meant to mitigate.

99 Caroline Banton, *Underwriting*, INVESTOPEDIA (May 13, 2019), www.investopedia.com/terms/u/underwriting.asp [https://perma.cc/KCW9-4NPN].

100 *Id.*

101 "Payday Loans and Consumer Financial Health," Bhutta, Neil. *Journal of Banking & Finance*, 2014. DOI: 10.1016/j.jbankfin.2014.04.024.

The Filene Research Institute's Reaching Minority Households Incubator has been testing a payday lending alternative driven by alternative credit scoring using LexisNexis Risk View. Risk View uses, among other things:

- Age and Predicted Income-related Attributes
- New Property Automated Valuation Model (AVM) attributes to reveal prospects' property values
- Education Attributes
- Characteristics of Input and Previous Address Attributes
- Most Recent Property Sale Attributes
- Transient Person Attributes
- Sub-prime Credit Service Solicitations Attributes
- Phone and Higher Risk Address Attributes[102]

The preliminary results of Filene's experiment are promising. It reports: "Kinecta Federal Credit Union and Nix Neighborhood Lending's program consolidates up to $2,500 of high-cost debt into an affordable installment loan. To date the program has issued over 11,700 loans with net charge-off rates of less than 6%."[103]

At the same time, the potential for algorithmic discrimination remains. Scholars and activists have repeatedly pointed out the ubiquity of race and gender discrimination in AI even when algorithms avoid using obvious race and gender categories (Race after AI, Algorithms of Oppression) Politico raised concerns, for example, about Risk View associating relatives and roommates of people who abuse opioids with opioid use (Politico 2019) – which may be a correct association, but problematic when used to assess health insurance premiums. Regardless of this specific example, there is growing awareness in the computer science and engineering community as well as in consumer protection that algorithmic decision-making will need to proceed in a fair, accountable, transparent, and ethical manner.

The post office or any public banking option must learn to adapt existing modern technology to offer fair, useful, and self-sustaining products to those neglected by mainstream banks.

9.6 THE CASE FOR POSTAL BANKING

There are several reasons to believe that the post office is uniquely capable of lending responsibly while reducing the costs of small loans. First, and most importantly, the post office is not primarily motivated by profitmaking, but rather is committed to a public service mission. Therefore, it can charge borrowers the actual

102 *LexisNexis RiskView Solutions is a Comprehensive Suite of Proven Credit Risk Management Data Analysis Tools and Non-tradeline Data*, LexisNexis, https://risk.lexisnexis.com/products/riskview (last visited May 5, 2020).

103 *Payday Payoff Installment Loans*, Filene Res. Inst., https://filene.org/do-something/programs/payday-payoff1 (last visited May 5, 2020).

cost of the loan. This was the necessary premise behind every successful movement to foster financial inclusion. The post office is not profit motivated because it is an independent agency connected to the federal government, meaning that all excess profits are forfeited to the Treasury.[104] The post office has no shareholders demanding a return on investment so it is unlikely that the organization will be motivated to take advantage of its customers for private gain.[105] All gains will be public, as will losses. A board of directors, public representatives chosen by a democratically elected president, should be tasked to oversee its activities with an Inspector General's office doing periodic audits as well as an independent regulatory agency that has rate-setting power.[106]

Second, the post office can naturally reduce the high costs of lending to the poor through "economies of scale" and "economies of scope."[107] It can use its already existing and large network of branches to sell new products without much additional startup, overhead, or marketing costs. Compared to payday lenders, the post office can reduce costs immediately by using its existing branches and staff thus saving money otherwise spent on advertising, personnel, and locations. This ability to offer more at a lower cost is the reason large banks now dominate the market. Likewise, the size and reach of the post office can lead to lower costs of credit. "Economies of scale," or control of a large market of a single product, could bring down the costs for financial services and even loans if the post office has many customers. "Economies of scope," costs saved when an institution can sell a variety of products, could mean, for example, lower costs on loans because the post office is attracting more deposits, cashing more checks, or wiring more funds.[108]

Finally, because the post office never left communities deserted by banks and other businesses, it is available in all the regions forsaken by banks and has also developed an ongoing relationship of trust within these communities.[109] Many unbanked individuals already buy their money orders at their local post office.[110] This means that the post office has access to a customer base that is not comfortable in banks.[111] Surveys of the unbanked show that minority groups are significantly

104 *See* Task Force on the U.S. Postal Sys., Dep't. of the Treasury, United States Postal Service: A Sustainable Path Forward 5, 33 (2018), https://home.treasury.gov/system/files/136/USPS_A_Sustainable_Path_Forward_report_12-04-2018.pdf [https://perma.cc/Q6AU-L4J8].

105 *Id.*

106 Off. of the Inspector Gen., U.S. Postal Serv., Governance of the U.S. Postal Service 1, 18 (2016), www.uspsoig.gov/sites/default/files/document-library-files/2016/RARC-WP-17-002.pdf.

107 Cathy M. Rogerson et al., *Economies of Scale and Scope and Competition in Postal Services*, *in* 12 Topics in Regulatory Economics and Policy Series: Regulation and the Nature of Postal and Delivery Services (1993).

108 Steven Nickolas, *How do Economies of Scope and Economies of Scale Differ?*, Investopedia (May 6, 2019), www.investopedia.com/ask/answers/042215/what-difference-between-economies-scope-and-economies-scale.asp [https://perma.cc/U9H5-QDMC].

109 *See* Baradaran, *supra* note 87, at 27.

110 *Id.*

111 *Id.*

more likely to be unbanked than other groups.[112] But the cultural and class barriers that keep many people away from the mainstream banks do not exist at the local post office. Americans rank the USPS highest among all federal agencies with more than 70 percent of those polled saying it does an excellent or good job.[113] With millennials, the rate is even higher at 81 percent.[114] About 70 percent of Americans trust the post office compared to 18 percent who trust payday lenders and 26 percent who trust banks.[115]

In both inner-city and rural communities, the post office can be crowded and bustling places where the neighborhood gathers to do its business, helped by clerks who are members of that same community. Even people who never go to the post office branch may be familiar with the mail carrier who visits their home daily. And following history's cue, the postal network can offer information in more languages than do banks and appeal to the large population of immigrants or even the undocumented who have money to save, but no access to banks. Many of these workers currently send their money abroad[116] – money that can be induced to stay within American borders. As it was in the 1900s, this can be a surprising source of revenue for the postal banks.

Trust, especially in banking, is more than just a nice feeling. It is a way to lower costs and reduce barriers of entry. This was the point of government deposit insurance. Banks cannot survive if their customers do not trust them to hold and lend their money. It is hard to predict whether the public will warm to postal banking, but in light of historical and international experience, and the significant modern distrust of fringe banks, the public may view the post office as a safer and more trustworthy place to store funds.

And this trust is not undeserved. The post office has a history of service to the American people, unrivaled by any other institution or any other government entity. In a way, the post office serves as a perfect foil for the banking industry. The latter receives hefty federal government support and rejects any public-serving functions and the former is currently receiving limited federal government support and yet sees public service as its primary mission. Even today, the stated mission of the US

[112] Fed. Deposit Ins. Corp., 2017 FDIC National Survey of Unbanked and Underbanked Households 10 (2018), www.fdic.gov/householdsurvey/2017/2017report.pdf.

[113] Steve Ander & Art Swift, *Americans Rate Postal Service Highest of 13 Major Agencies*, Gallup (November 21, 2014), https://news.gallup.com/poll/179519/americans-rate-postal-service-highest-major-agencies.aspx [https://perma.cc/J6CM-YR5C].

[114] *Id.*

[115] Dennis Jacobe, *Americans' Confidence in Banks Up for First Time in Years*, Gallup (June 13, 2013), https://news.gallup.com/poll/163073/americans-confidence-banks-first-time-years.aspx [https://perma.cc/WTZ4-MQPQ]; Peter Moore, *Poll Results: Post Office Bank*, YouGov (February 10, 2014), https://today.yougov.com/topics/finance/chapters-reports/2014/02/10/poll-results-post-office-bank [https://perma.cc/MPZ9-EAND].

[116] William Lacy Swing, *How Migrants Who Send Money Home Have Become a Global Economic Force*, World Econ. F. (June 14, 2018), www.weforum.org/agenda/2018/06/migrants-remittance-global-economic-force/ [https://perma.cc/B9RV-A2CY].

post office is: "to provide postal services to bind the Nation together through the personal, educational, literary, and business correspondence of the people. It shall provide prompt, reliable, and efficient services to patrons in all areas and shall render postal services to all communities."[117] This makes the post office an ideal means of providing a public option in banking.

Short-term credit is not a solution to inequality. The reason that most people need high-cost credit products is unstable work, inequality, and rising costs in health care and education – and the best solution is not credit, but addressing these structural problems. Full-scale reform of the economy is necessary to right the ship – employees must have a living wage, families must have affordable shelter, and health-care costs must not be so onerous. With these reforms in place, the need for payday loans will naturally be diminished. The industry, after all, has risen alongside trends in inequality.[118] Yet, credit can be a lifeline for many families and individuals who face unexpected circumstances.

A public option can take many forms and can offer an alternative for all banking services or it can be limited to small loans and bank accounts for the underbanked. Participation in commerce is essential for full civic engagement and today, many Americans are excluded from commerce or forced to pay fees for simple loans and transactions. A public option has the potential to resolve these inequalities. For a variety of historic and practical reasons, the US Postal System would be the best means of offering a public option to all communities.

117 The United States Postal Service is an independent establishment of the Executive Branch of the Government of the United States and operates in a business-like way. Its mission statement can be found in Section 101(a) of Title 39 of the U.S. Code, also known as the Postal Reorganization Act. Pub. L. 91–375, 84 Stat. 719 (1970) (codified as 39 U.S.C. § 101(a)).

118 Payday lending began to increase in the late 1980s and has risen since then, as has inequality. *See* John P. Caskey, Fringe Banking: Check-Cashing Outlets, Pawnshops, and the Poor 6 (1994); Gregory Elliehausen & Edward C. Lawrence, *A Comparative Analysis of Payday Loan Customers*, 26 Contemp. Econ. Pol'y 299 (2008).

CPSIA information can be obtained
at www.ICGtesting.com
Printed in the USA
LVHW081910220621
690867LV00002B/160

9 781108 487641